CREATING CAPABLE KIDS

CREATING CAPABLE KIDS

Twelve Skills That Will Help Kids Succeed in School and Life

Bruce Howlett and Caitlin Howlett

NEW HORIZON PRESS

Far Hills, New Jersey

Requests for permission should be addressed to:
New Horizon Press
P. O. Box 669
Far Hills, NJ 07931

Bruce Howlett and Caitlin Howlett
    Creating Capable Kids:
    Twelve Skills That Will Help Kids Succeed in School and Life

Cover design: Charley Nasta
Interior design: Scribe Inc.

Library of Congress Control Number: 2014950549

ISBN-13 (paperback): 978-0-88282-497-0
ISBN-13 (eBook): 978-0-88282-498-7

New Horizon Press

Manufactured in the U.S.A.

19   18   17   16   15   1   2   3   4   5

Author's Note

This book is based on the authors' research, personal experiences, interviews and real life experiences. In order to protect privacy, names have been changed and identifying characteristics have been altered except for contributing experts.

For purposes of simplifying usage, the pronouns his/her and s/he are sometimes used interchangeably. The information contained herein is not meant to be a substitute for professional evaluation and therapy with mental health professionals.

Acknowledgments

Tony, Dr. Gary Evans, Kay Inglin, Elise Feuer, Jen Wilkie, Denise Gelberg and Colleen Hill

Contents

Introduction

The most powerful gift that parents and teachers can give children isn't another toy, greater cognitive skills or academic superstardom. It's a set of twelve capabilities that allows children to excel in every aspect of their lives, from playing outside with friends to researching the inner workings of the human brain. Equally important at home and in school, these capabilities span the breadth of human experience. We see them in the natural curiosity of children exploring a park, pre-teens engaging in imaginative and creative activities and adolescents finding meaning in complex and confusing events.

The capabilities are found in their innate forms in all children. Children naturally learn from experience, listening, discussing and story-telling. They learn by assembling facts into systems of understanding and turning imagination into creativity. They have social and emotional capabilities, including empathy, mind reading and emotional insight, as well as an instinct to build friendships and other strong relationships.

Since the capabilities we've developed are primal in nature, they are relatively easy to nurture into their mature forms—far easier than trying to control children's behavior or doing most of their thinking and long-term planning for them. This is better than hoping they get into a good college decades down the road while depriving them of endless learning experiences in childhood.

Creating capable children is also rewarding for adults. Creating children and teens who are curious, inquisitive, knowledgeable and reasonable is an imperative goal. Parents and teachers need to focus on creating kind, helpful children who form strong friendships as much as they focus on homework. Adults need to be concerned with helping children understand how relationships and emotions work even more than teaching fractions or the names of fifteenth century explorers. The role of parents and teachers must include helping children understand how their minds work and creating curious and interested life-long learners. Most of all, we should be focused on creating capable children who can handle the problems life throws at them, while finding meaning and purpose. Childhood and the teen years are times of growth and learning, a period of wonder and enjoyment.

All children have a natural inclination to develop these capabilities. The capabilities approach is a fresh perspective and positive action plan that will renew parenting and teaching. It transfers all the misspent anxious energy surrounding children's long-term success into building relationships and interactions that create capable kids. All children are born with the twelve capabilities and many develop them with little conscious help from adults.

For countless generations, babies, children and teens have developed these capabilities largely through daily experiences, adult interactions, work and play. Today, the relationships that built capabilities have been supplanted by children learning in highly-controlled school environments that place little emphasis on developing experiential, perceptual and sensorial learning capabilities. Some teachers and parents operate under outdated ideas about behavior, doing much of the thinking, problem-solving and cognitive activities like planning, questioning and reasoning.

The capabilities have universal benefit, from high school dropouts to graduate students, enabling children to perform the three most important functions of life—to learn continuously, problem-solve fluidly and build meaning even around the simplest of events. They allow children and teens to gracefully handle the twists and turns of everyday life. Teaching kids how to read and write isn't enough. Parents who focus only on controlling behaviors and pushing for academic success are missing out on building a learning relationship with their children.

In this book we will present a Learning Capabilities Framework to parenting and education that incorporates two powerful lines of research that are reshaping child development. The first is primal, based on anthropology and evolutionary psychology, and it holds that hundreds of thousands of years of human evolution have shaped a child's mind to learn quickly and respond to life's challenges. Nature also selected for adults who instinctively know how to nurture these capabilities to fruition. The interaction between children's innate capabilities and adults' nurturing instincts has assured human survival for millennia.

The second force is based on major findings in the cognitive and neurosciences. We no longer live on farms or as hunter-gathers, so basic capabilities must be nurtured into advanced forms to learn, problem-solve and find meaning in our ridiculously complex world. We will show how primal capabilities can be developed into these advanced forms and we will give parents and teachers practical, actionable ideas to change bodies, behaviors, brains and minds.

As we present this format for learning, we will follow three students on their twisted paths to success: Zoe, an academic star who finds little meaning or joy in her school day; Mia, a solidly, dangerously average student with superior non-academic capabilities and Daniel, who ends up being categorized as learning disabled in school due to his "non-academic" brain that exhibits exceptional learning abilities in almost any other environment. All three are being defined in the narrowest of academic terms, as their parents and teachers are blind to the vital cognitive, perceptual, meaning-making and social-emotional capabilities they need to live a rich childhood and a satisfying life.

This book also presents the story of their parents, who see their children's potential but have succumbed to the common beliefs that restrain both parenting and education. For over a century, two influences sharing a common misconception about children and learning have obscured most of their innate capabilities and suppressed adults' natural capabilities-nurturing instincts and habits at home and in school. The shared belief is called *Instructionism*—a doctrine that falsely holds that children's minds are blank slates that require incessant adult instruction and control over every aspect of learning, behavior and thinking. In 1893, the Harvard-led Committee of Ten mandated Instructionism in schools, creating the framework still used to this day. At the same time, the parenting advice industry began, based on the nascent field of behavioral psychology. In school and at home, adults increasingly talk *at* (instead of *with*) kids, control their every behavior and do most of their thinking and problem-solving for them. The primal state, where adults and children explored, learned and problem-solved together, has faded.

A capabilities approach reverses the hidden pull of Instructionism by restoring the primal abilities of children and adults using an advanced understanding of their relationships. These capabilities span the full range of human experience, from sensory awareness, learning from experience and developing creative imagination to social, emotional and self-awareness. Each capability is personalized, such as the Action Character (embodied learner), the Caring Mind Reader (empathic) and the Knowledge Architect (systems thinking), and is told through the lives of the three children we will follow as they develop from infancy into adulthood.

To further combat Instructionism, each capability is developed using "Big L Learning," derived from our incredible, innate ways of learning refined over the course of evolution. "Big L Learning" involves multiple learning and problem-solving modules of our active, embodied minds, leading to meaningful long-term learning. It supplants "small L learning," so prevalent in schools today, which teaches isolated, irrelevant skills that engage only slivers of a child's memory, attention and thinking. Learning how to ride a bike is "Big L Learning." Learning multiplication facts is too often "small L learning."

We will provide action plans, called Small Moments, that transform the relationships that parents and teachers have with children. Small Moments are ways that adults can change their interactions with children, transforming everyday events into learning experiences. They shift the focus, open up a discussion, create curiosity, deepen experiences and turn ordinary events into extraordinary ones.

Part 1

· ·

Finding Children's Full Capabilities

1

. . . .
More Capable Lives

First we are going to focus on a talented, bright and promising child. If a committee of parents and teachers designed an ideal student, it would be Zoe. Bright, eager to learn and engaging, Zoe soaks up academic challenges with ease. Solving problems, thinking creatively and understanding concepts come naturally to her. While Zoe is currently in fourth grade, she performs more like a middle school student. More importantly, her success is not limited to school. Zoe has a diverse group of friends and participates in a range of community activities. She cares about herself as well as the wider world around her.

If every student had Zoe's capabilities, all teaching would be wondrous. Zoe is rewarding to teach because she embodies a set of abilities that makes learning easy. She has strong focus, solid listening abilities and a large store of easily-recalled facts. Zoe is a reasonable person who is not prone to rash or biased opinions. Her parents have encouraged her to confront problems, resolve conflicts and understand other people's points of view.

The Struggles of Successful Kids

Being a successful student today requires a specific set of skills and Zoe seems to possess them all. However, Zoe, our model child, dislikes school.

3

She feels that the education she is receiving is not meeting her needs. She often begs her mother to let her stay home. Why does such a promising child feel that school is the least likely place for her to learn?

Like many of her academically-successful classmates, Zoe excels at the subjects she is pressured by the system to succeed in but stifled by the inability to study the subjects she loves. Her school's mandated curriculum leaves little time to pursue personal interests or relevant content. No teacher has ever asked Zoe what she would like to learn, nor have parents or teachers been given a voice in the curriculum. It is often asked what Zoe needs to learn to be successful in college. But, apart from her parents, Jan and Jeff, rarely does anyone ask what Zoe needs to learn to succeed in life.

A sense of confusion, a lack of purpose, a feeling of doubt and a string of unanswered questions clog Jan and Jeff's minds. Zoe feels the confusion when instruction doesn't make sense or seems like a waste of time. She is torn between being the model student, satisfying the desires of her parents and teachers and pursuing her natural curiosity and inquisitiveness that has served children so well for millennia. It descends on parents and teachers alike in the form of vague uneasiness and enduring questions about raising and educating our children. Parents and teachers feel the fog when they see children who effortlessly and unceasingly learn from birth begin to lose that love of learning when confronted by formal schooling.

Jan and Jeff feel that something is lacking in Zoe's education. From their own educational struggles, they understand that success today requires much more than the traditional thinking skills and content knowledge at the core of standardized education. It pains them to see a child like Zoe, who is naturally curious and constantly exploring and experimenting, begin to dislike school. She has dozens of interests, from pet care to the martial arts. Jan and Jeff understand the need for a standardized curriculum, but wonder why it must be out of sync with Zoe's motivations, interests and natural learning ability.

Jan and Jeff also believe that there is little separation between parenting and teaching. The child who the teacher sees each day in class reflects the values and abilities that parents instill in their children. The child who is ready to learn is often the child who learns well at home. Parents and teachers both can do their best jobs when a child possesses cognitive skills such as focus and reasoning, emotional skills of self-regulation and concern for others and character skills like perseverance, frustration tolerance and the ability to work in groups. These critical abilities, developed during childhood, are exactly what children need to successfully participate in the classroom.

Jeff is not a helicopter parent nor is Jan a tiger mom (parents who are in control of most aspects of their children's lives). They are not the kind of parents who create imaginary outcomes for their children, planning their college and career decades in advance. They believe their roles are to guide Zoe through the maze of childhood without being too controlling or carefree. Jan and Jeff know that parenting is undergoing dramatic changes and presents a seemingly unending series of challenges. They have watched many of their childhood friends who were under pressure to excel academically turn into unsatisfied adults. Many were good at school but struggled to master the basic aspects of living a satisfying life. A surprising number ended up aimless, disgruntled and unmotivated. Others could never find enough money, possessions or status to feel secure and satisfied. They had all the trappings but none of the substance of good lives.

Jan and Jeff have witnessed many of Zoe's friends suffer from distant parenting styles largely devoid of the focused attention and relaxed interactions that are critical to a child's growth. Many are forced to study rather than play, as instruction that was once given in class is now "flipped" into the home. They see children, who need constant feedback to grow, starved of emotional support except when they are academically successful. They see many older students coerced into colleges and careers not of their choosing.

Most of all, Zoe's parents want her to fully experience the life of a nine-year-old. They see too many parents pushing their children to do better: to excel in the next grade, school or imagined career. The result is often stressed and anxious children. Children have an innate drive to learn and find meaning about themselves that adults often miss. We can see this in the ceaseless questioning of a three-year-old or the shifting identity of a teenager.

At Harvard University, like many elite institutions, the most popular major is business and the most popular concentration is finance. But one of the most popular courses is Ancient Chinese Philosophy, which provides a non-Western perspective on the meaning of life. We assume that many parents are steering their children toward material security rather than a life full of learning and meaning, but some of those children, when presented with the opportunity, follow a nontraditional path. Many of our academically-gifted children have their strongest traits squandered in jobs that aren't known for innovation, creativity or imagination. Their academic paths are steered away from the sciences and humanities that more naturally lend themselves to the development of critical and creative thinking and a strong sense of ethics. The only reward is monetary and they fall into ethical and emotional traps such as greed and narcissism. Clearly, that was not why their parents sent them to Harvard.

Luckily, Jan and Jeff understand the most important aspect of Zoe: how she learns and makes sense of the world. Zoe learns like children have for hundreds of thousands of years, through sensory-stimulating experiences and an almost experimental approach to life. She always asks "Why?" but demands the "Because..." as well. She learns by doing rather than merely through words and thoughts. Jan knows that the best path to a bright future is to allow Zoe to live and learn from her life now, complete with successes, failures and challenges.

Zoe, like most successful students, is an emotional learner who navigates social engagements well. Zoe's positive emotions motivate her and form a bridge to understanding her social connections. It is this profound insight into emotions and a deep understanding of how humans interact combined with a strong ability to focus on both internal and external phenomena that makes Zoe a wonder.

Jan and Jeff have considered homeschooling Zoe as they watch her excitement about learning wane and her moodiness and frustration grow. They cherish her independent streak and fear that it will be dulled by the constant drive toward conformity of one-size-fits-all schooling. They, like their daughter, are growing exhausted by endless curriculum changes that seem to produce only minimal gains.

Jan and Jeff feel too many kids are pushed toward individual achievements and then rewarded for being overly self-absorbed. Zoe's parents want her to engage in a world beyond her individual needs. They encourage Zoe to interact with a diverse group of friends and adults, allowing her to develop emotional and social problem-solving skills. Her life isn't an endless series of playdates, either; Zoe has a lot of time to be alone.

This creates a balance between outwardly-focused social engagement and quiet time for introversion. Zoe also enjoys her downtime, spending time with her quieter thoughts and daydreams that support insight and creativity.

Jeff and Jan balance intuitive parenting skills with an up-to-date understanding of child development. They give Zoe their undivided attention, possibly the deepest expression of love. They let Zoe concoct strange creations in the kitchen (with adult supervision, of course!) and let her try different tools in the garage. When she was younger, they let her pull the cat's tail, play in the mud and build forts out of chairs, all excellent learning situations. They kept the number of toys to a minimum, picking ones that maximized imaginative playfulness.

Jan and Jeff employed the most scientifically advanced ways of promoting language—talking and interactive play. Their focus was less on school readiness and more on some of the most difficult learning tasks: regulating emotions, learning to focus and building positive social interactions. They kept their anxiety to themselves and away from Zoe.

If we take the long view of anthropology and evolutionary psychology, the time between early childhood and the teen years is being squandered. What is now the elementary years was once a time of great cognitive, emotional and social growth. Learning took place in a contextually rich environment, where facts, skills and values had clear and immediate meaning. Kids learned by working and playing with other children, making mistakes and trying risky things. Children were given increasing responsibilities and engaged in ever-more-challenging tasks. Humans have generally lived in small tribes where children interacted with friends of different ages and adults who showed them the ways of their culture. Children were allowed the freedom to explore and learn on their own. As childhood progressed into adolescence, teens were permitted to experience the ways of the world with lessening adult interference.

Contrast this rich childhood with the constrained home life and restricted school life of many kids today. We can see why Zoe feels that her schooling goes against the grain of childhood. If we could transport her back a few hundred years to an ancestral farm in Scandinavia, she would be learning at a far more accelerated pace. She would be learning to regulate her own behavior instead of being told how to sit and walk, when to speak and how to think. Her daily life would provide a rich context and endless learning experiences. She would not be forced to learn material that is of little relevance or interest and that she will probably never use after the test. The Zoe that teachers love would be trusted with greater amounts of responsibility and independence.

All the questions, doubts and fears that surround Zoe, a "successful" student, create a mental fog that envelops her and the adults in her life. Some fog is expected around all children and teens as they struggle to make sense of themselves, their social relationships and the world. They spend endless hours worried and confused over their past, present and future selves. The fog extends to parents as they sort through conflicting parenting information. It grows thicker when confronted with inner doubts as they map the way to a secure and meaningful life in a time of unprecedented upheaval. Gone are the days when good grades, a solid degree and a well-paying job ensured success, let alone happiness and meaning. Many teachers experience a dense fog as they are battered by seemingly endless changes in the name of reform. The fog deepens when they confront conflicting standards and mandates, confusing assessment demands and goals that often do more to limit the education of their students than to enhance it.

The tension between a child's innate ability to learn and develop and an increasingly artificial learning structure in schools and digital existence at home limits a child's capabilities. However, there is no going back to the glories of an imagined earlier time. We should acknowledge the remarkable, innate learning skills provided by evolution. For all of human existence, children have developed a set of profound problem-solving and learning skills unmatched in the biological world.

The human brain hasn't changed much in the last hundred thousand years. If Zoe was born a hundred or a hundred thousand years ago she would still possess an amazing range of cognitive, emotional, social and perceptual abilities. These include learning from experience, trial and error experiments and attentive, self-motivated explorations. Some capabilities are grounded in our ability to turn perception into concepts, images and creative ideas. Others boost our capacity to absorb facts, translate them into systems of understanding and make hundreds of decisions and judgments each day. Some capabilities take longer to develop, such as our gift for conversation and storytelling. Others we continue to develop across our lifespans, such as emotional and social competencies.

Learning capabilities come so naturally that we often overlook them. We have historically discounted the profound verbal, social, emotional and physical learning that takes place during a child's first five years. Until recently, few have known about the burst of learning that begins at birth or that this burst doesn't slow down at age five but continues in different forms for twenty or so years. There has long been a feeling that learning actually begins in kindergarten and is qualitatively different from early learning. However, successful formal learning relies on adaptations and modifications of innate forms of learning.

We have much to learn about how children learn. Children aren't just born to learn, but from an early age are deeply inquisitive and make reasoned deductions and inferences—the heart of thinking. Teaching children to think or comprehend is like teaching a candle to shine. Toddlers make sense of complex perceptual information, have profound native intelligence and construct meaning in a myriad of ways. They learn to speak by learning the probability of sounds and word sequences using a complex form of statistics. All we can do is take these innate skills and coax them to greater brightness.

Zoe's teachers probably don't give much thought to her early learning abilities. In fact, Zoe's high test scores have her teachers and administrators feeling that she is reaching her full potential. But the system is not helping Zoe develop the habits of mind that she needs as a citizen or as a team member in the workplace. They praise Zoe for her classroom thinking skills but are not doing anything to deliberately develop social, emotional and cognitive abilities. They sense her creativity but have little time to develop it. They hope she develops refined reasoning skills to distinguish fact from opinion. She isn't learning to run open-ended experiments to solve problems nor how to arrive at reasonable opinions and make critical decisions. Zoe may be considered one of our best and brightest, but her formal schooling is doing little to bring her learning and problem-solving capabilities into full bloom.

Mia and the Dangers of Being Average

If we are overlooking the critical learning capabilities of proficient students, then what are we offering those who are less academically inclined? Our next student, Mia, is a member of one of the most at-risk groups of students—those who perform at grade level. They are the students who just meet standards and barely slide by in school. Mia ranks in the middle of the class and her teachers are generally happy with her grades. She sits in the back of the class, rarely calling attention to herself, as she falls into the largest crack in our educational system. Average students often occupy an academic limbo, not deemed "smart" enough to get the attention Zoe receives nor do they receive the extra help accorded to struggling students.

Teachers use some of the most damning terms in all of education to describe students like Mia: average, typical or decent. Often this is coded language for children who sit passively in the back of the class. This large group of students is at long-term risk of spectacular underperformance. The National Assessment of Educational Progress (NAEP), often called the nation's report card, shows students who read at grade level have more in common with struggling readers than they do with proficient readers. Proficient readers usually read two, three or more grade levels above their own, even in elementary school. For decades NAEP has shown that only about 30 percent of students are proficient readers. About 70 percent of our students, regardless of grade, are not strong readers.[1] And this subject consumes a large percentage of the school day and forms the core of standardized curricula.

Math is another subject Mia doesn't find interesting. For Mia, math is just boring memory exercises—all those facts and procedures that don't make sense. When Mia gets to high school she'll take the minimal math classes required to graduate. That is unfortunate, because the best predictor of success in college is the number and rigor of math classes taken in high school.[2] Students who struggle with math miss out on critical problem-solving, reasoning, planning and logic skills.

Most of Mia's academic difficulties are less obvious than her struggles with reading and math. Mandated assessments given in the name of accountability have turned Mia's school into a test prep academy. Yet no one has ever given Mia the one test that would diagnose the cause of her academic averageness. If Mia had received just thirty minutes of cognitive testing in first grade, then her teachers might have learned that her limited success in school is largely due to subtle weaknesses in listening and working memory. These minor deficits mean that after a few sentences of instruction or an extended conversation, Mia becomes lost in a sea of words. Her auditory issues extend into reading, which is a receptive, or listening, language task. They extend into key aspects of comprehension and thinking such as discussions and verbal reasoning. These abilities are arguably the most important in lecture, memorization and test-intensive schooling. Even sadder is that listening (auditory processing) and working memory are easily addressed during childhood. How can an education system ignore such critical capabilities?

Mia struggles with working memory, the ability to hold bits of information, like sentences, math facts or images in memory and actively think about them. As Susan Gathercole and Tracy Alloway illustrate in their book, *Working Memory and Learning*, very little goes on in school that isn't predicated on strong working memory. Students who can hold more information in this fragile form of memory are said to have large working memory capacity. This gives them a distinct advantage in almost all academic areas.[3] Differences in this capacity, as we will see, explain much of the difference in our three students' academic performance.

Cognitive scientist Daniel Willingham points out that working memory issues place a severe limit on learning and thinking: "Thinking occurs when you combine information (from the environment or long-term memory) in new ways. That combining happens in working memory."[4] We learn what we think about in working memory. Engaging working memory is a significant path to learning and it defines thinking.

Something as integral to learning and thinking as working memory should be a focus of assessment and intervention in schools. But, like auditory issues, working memory is rarely assessed or addressed. These two cognitive abilities are key components of most learning difficulties. However, unless Mia's mother pushes for her daughter to be assessed for a learning disability, Mia will most probably never be tested.

There is another type of testing, one that doesn't exist yet, that would greatly benefit students like Mia. This test wouldn't search for weaknesses but reveal her strengths and interests across a broad range of capabilities. Such an imaginary test would find that Mia has a powerful set of nascent abilities, from dance to design, that could easily flourish with the right adult guidance. This test would show that Mia has strong, even exceptional, visual skills and excellent ability to empathize, having great insight into other people's thoughts and feelings. It would reveal that Mia has excellent conversational and storytelling skills and a deep interest in how things, from animals to computer tablets, work.

Mia has the potential to be an exceptional artist, a teacher, social worker, psychologist or even a product designer. She could be a great writer if she wasn't forced into rigid, formulaic writing assignments. Mia is capable of many things, but right now she is labeled as "average" by teachers who have been told incorrectly that learning abilities are fixed.

Mia and Zoe, endowed with almost identical learning capabilities, may develop to different degrees as the two girls vary genetically, in life experiences and educational response. Despite these differences, they are limited in school by the same false belief—that they are performing at the upper range of their abilities. Zoe and Mia would be more successful if adults in their lives believed that learning abilities aren't fixed or confined to a few subjects.

The struggles of children trapped in the middle of their class don't end when they graduate from high school. Most will be accepted to two or four-year colleges. But their struggles with learning will continue to haunt them. Large numbers of community college students require remediation in basic reading, writing and math skills.[5] Those who attend four-year colleges also suffer. After six years, about half of four-year college students have dropped out or have failed to complete degrees.

This is a personal issue for the authors. Bruce Howlett experienced the low expectations and auditory issues that hold Mia back, while Caitlin, like Zoe, felt limited by an irrelevant curriculum that did little to help her find meaning and identity. In the days before special education, Bruce, though he excelled in math and science, struggled with reading and writing from kindergarten through graduate school. He only began to read in third grade and could still barely do so in fifth grade. When he was in his forties, a speech therapist gave him a test of specific auditory skills which revealed subtle issues. After a few months of weekly therapy, his reading skills moved from that of a thirteen-year-old into the adult range.

Caitlin intended to teach history, but she studied with professors teaching a wide range of subjects, from philosophy to nutrition. This led to graduate studies in philosophy programs covering topics including the history and philosophy of education, gender and ethnic studies and embodiment and cognitive philosophy. Along the way she worked with children struggling with cognitive and emotional issues. All the while,

Caitlin remained physically and socially active by swimming on her college's team and developing a taste for half-marathons. This provided a balance between academic life and social and physical pursuits.

A Mother's Concerns

Mia's mother, Melissa, a single black woman and teacher, wants to know what is causing her very promising daughter to be trapped in academic limbo. Like Mia, Melissa was an average student in math and reading and that wasn't easy. While almost half of white students are proficient readers in high school, only one in five black children reach that level.[6] To succeed in school, Melissa worked very hard to keep up with the reading load and to be seen as intelligent as her white friends. Homework took hours. Many of her friends could memorize facts for tests during class; Melissa stayed up late into the night in repetitive practice.

Melissa desires Mia to have an easier and more meaningful path through school. She worries that Mia's teachers wouldn't accept her average performance if she were white, male or rich. Melissa experienced this type of discrimination as she struggled through three secondary schools and four colleges. She heard more doubts than words of encouragement while experiencing subtle and blatant roadblocks thrown up by her race and gender. Melissa wants Mia to be seen not as a collection of categories and limitations but as a capable person. She sees Mia excelling at learning and living when she is taught through broader and more meaningful interactions, activities and conversations.

Where Zoe is held back by narrow and outdated beliefs about heavy thinking and academic success, Mia is constrained by equally limited ideas about intelligence. There is a tendency among educators to expect average academic results from children with average scores on intelligence tests. The advanced view is that intelligence isn't fixed but varies significantly, especially with those who score in the middle. High IQ doesn't guarantee success nor is it a measure of creativity. Children with high IQs often do well academically but sometimes at the cost of significant social and emotional growth. They aren't necessarily the most likely to come up with new inventions or creative ideas. High-IQ children may be weak at reasoning, as the two are not tightly linked.[7]

Even more so, we now understand that IQ is deeply imbedded in biased assumptions about intelligence and may remain there, which ties Mia to a deeper, more concerning history of American education in which what has been—and continues to count as—the marker of academic intelligence remains directly tied to middle to upper-class white notions of respectability and success. Mia is able to adhere to these notions enough to not cause problems, but her intelligence remains almost entirely unnoticed in the classroom. Despite the tedium Melissa experienced in school, she became a teacher, partly to better understand why she struggled and hoping to prevent her children from experiencing the same fate. Like almost every parent, she wanted her children to do better than she did.

Melissa quickly grew disillusioned with her teacher training. She learned the basics about child development, but little about the development of a child's mind. She received various opinions about how children learn math and reading but almost nothing about why some children read at age four and others are still struggling at fourteen. And, conscious of the role of race in her own educational experience, Melissa wanted information about the impact of race and class on educational inputs and outcomes. She wanted to have critical conversations about these issues. Yet, she received only statistics and the message that such questions weren't as important as adhering to standards. She wanted to find the purpose of teaching and big goals for which to aim but received methods to improve test scores instead.

Melissa began to ask more questions about education. What is the point of education? Is it only to prepare students for college and the elusive well-paying job? Is every child getting an equal education? Why are getting into college and getting a high-paying job the only measures of success? What is the importance of childhood? Should we downplay the value of a rich childhood for the distant and delayed satisfaction of college admissions?

Melissa longed for the strong foundation, tested methods and well-defined goals found in many professions. Medicine relies on anatomy and physiology and the legal profession on history and case law, while information technology is built on a framework of physics, cognition and well-established programming platforms. Education, she felt, should be based on how children learn and the ways their minds develop. Instead, she found a lack of consensus on basic principles and effective procedures, let alone a solid philosophy. Melissa felt like a technician learning the mechanisms that ensure testing success. She experienced nightmares of working in a factory, performing one fixed procedure as kids passed by on the assembly line. How was this going to contribute to a child's academic or personal success?

Melissa wondered why her students must learn prime factorization and order of operations in math class but no time is spent on areas critical to success, such as conflict resolution or emotional regulation. Why can't she teach kids how to plan and set goals, make decisions and balance personal needs against those of others? Why does she spend hours each day teaching reading comprehension while rarely developing critical oral language skills or cognitive skills such as reasoning, causality or making inferences and predictions?

When Melissa started teaching, she saw that her school was inundated by the constant wave of fads that substitute for learning and child development. As education historian Diane Ravitch points out in her book, *The Death and Life of the Great American School System*, education is constantly destabilized by every passing opinion, political whim, technological toy and self-serving economic fancy. Too often, Ravitch argues, classrooms become "a graveyard of fads." Untested ideas that do little to advance a child's cognitive, emotional, creative or personal growth are forced upon schools. Ravitch points to charter schools, laptops or tablets for every child, high-stakes assessments and pay for performance, to name a few.[8] As education focuses on passing trends, it loses sight of the larger issues that hold children back, including poverty, inequality, racism, family instability and emotional distress.

Melissa has little time to seek answers. She is consumed with mandated curricula and standardized testing and overwhelmed by the diversity of her students' academic, emotional and social needs. One minute she is performing the role of a social worker and the next a cognitive therapist, before morphing into a content expert. Melissa must contend with the toxic effects of malnutrition and income and housing insecurity that are no longer limited to the poor.

Paul Tough, in *How Children Succeed*, chronicles the plight of children who are discontent with both their schooling and upraising. Tough cites extensive research that shows that children from upper income households suffer from high rates of anxiety, depression and a lack of substantial meaning in their lives. He discusses Suniya Luthar's research that found higher rates of drug, alcohol and tobacco use and clinical depression in groups of affluent, urban tenth graders relative to a control group of low-income high school students.[9]

When Luthar looked more closely at this upsetting situation, she found that about 20 percent of the affluent group experienced persistent psychological and behavioral problems, including chronic academic difficulties. She found a common factor causing the difficulties of both low-income and affluent students—parenting styles. At both ends of the economic ladder, children are hindered by low levels of parental attachment. The lack of a strong relationship with a parent hinders social and emotional development. Another common trait is that low-income and affluent children experience higher levels of criticism. Children who receive overly negative feedback for their behavioral imperfections or academic shortcomings from parents are more likely to have diminished self-esteem. The final block to parent-child bonding is often minimal after-school adult supervision. Affluent kids have one more burden: "excessive achievement pressures and isolation from parents—both physical and emotional."[10]

Tough also discusses research showing that affluent parents try to compensate for these shortcomings by indulging their children materially. Wealth is used as a substitute for emotional involvement or as a distraction from a child's difficulties. Money helps us overcome many problems, from malnutrition to mechanical problems. When it is used to shelter children from all external struggles, it deprives them of chances to learn how to solve life's ongoing problems. Children need a manageable amount of problems, from handling an abusive text message to the loss of a loved one, to build character skills and develop critical problem-solving abilities.[11]

Dealing with this complex mix of issues requires constant improvising and split-second decisions. Melissa feels that one-size-fits-all standards are blind to these challenges. Methods that seem to draw in all students, such as explorations, experiments and storytelling, are put aside. Melissa worries that she is only adding to her students' anxiety with her curriculum and not lessening it with the way she'd like to teach if she could.

Daniel and the Dangers of Learning Differently

Melissa's concerns become more urgent when faced with children who think, learn and act in divergent ways. Daniel, our next student, is such a child. Most schools have many Daniels, complex students who present perplexing mixtures of strengths and weaknesses that shift from day to day. Daniel learns in a different manner from his classmates, Zoe and Mia. He doesn't learn in the way that schools teach. He is a very sturdy square peg being forced into the classic academic round hole.

For a moment, picture Daniel playing a math game on a computer tablet. He is solely focused on mastering the game, taking in every image and word. If we had a "think-o-meter" to measure the intensity of his thinking, it would be off the scale. He is figuring out how numbers, objects and concepts work together. He is mastering the game's complex strategies and the math behind it.

Daniel is utilizing the same learning skills that we admire in Zoe. But this will change as soon as his teacher goes into a ten-minute lecture on multiplication strategies. Daniel's issue with attention and auditory memory tasks has lead to a three-year struggle with multiplication facts. The kid who loves math strategy games dislikes classroom math, rating it between boredom and anxiety. Daniel's issues with academics don't end with math and attention. He has speech and language difficulties that include everything from listening to verbal expression.

Because he is in special education, Daniel has had extensive testing. Three psychological examinations, a visit to a neurologist, brain scans and endless academic and language tests have revealed a slew of weaknesses. The endless evaluations contain vague statements such as "Daniel has global processing issues that prevent him from performing at the level of a child with an above-average IQ." He may sound like a challenge to teach, but like Mia and Zoe, he has unexplored strengths. In fact, Daniel may be disabled in school but he transforms into a dynamic learner outside of it.

Humans have remarkably similar brains that develop in very predictable ways. Daniel's brain isn't that different from Zoe's or Mia's, but from conception its growth has been heavily influenced by his unique mixture of gene expression, experience, stimuli and learning. The finely-tuned interplay between nature and nurture, genes and the environment have worked together to produce Daniel's way of learning and development.

Daniel's psychologists believe that nothing is set in stone when it comes to Daniel and learning. His intelligence, imagination and creativity aren't unchangeable. All Daniel needs is a different form of learning, a teacher who understands how to grab his attention and parents who understand what motivates him—or something as simple as a supportive group of friends to play with in the woods behind his house.

The link between an innate and a learned capability grows more complex when children enter school. We have a natural capacity to count to ten that develops with little effort. The problem with humans is that we like to count higher, solve linear equations and figure out the trajectory of rockets. This requires a broad set of cognitive, perceptual and creative skills that we have long possessed that must operate at levels our ancestors could barely imagine.

Educators have long struggled to find the learning environments that develop and transform basic instinctual habits into exceptional learning abilities. Daniel's school has tried to instruct him by focusing on his brain, placing him in a classroom with a teacher who is a skilled instructor. It occasionally works, but requires great effort from Daniel, his parents and teachers. A more effective way of educating children would acknowledge that all learning resides in children's innate learning abilities. Upon this deep foundation of innate abilities, grow the complex and elaborate learning and knowledge needed by our exceedingly complicated social, emotional, cognitive, environmental and technological culture.

The combined innate and learned path to education requires an understanding of how children learn that isn't limited by our infatuation with intelligence, labeling, brain-based learning and heightened thinking skills. Neuroscientist David Eagleman sees the brain as a small but critical part of learning. Eagleman, like many researchers, no longer sees the brain as the master control center of life. The brain forms the "hub" of a mind embedded in the body that is connected into the environment. It is through this extended exchange of information that we learn, think and make sense of the world.[12] This perspective is often called the extended mind theory. It redefines what it means to educate the whole child as we no longer see children as separate from their biological, social, physical and psychological environment.

Daniel learns more through bodily and sensory experience than by passive thinking. This connection to the senses is a key to creative thinking and action. Daniel's strong bodily connection also provides him with a second, often overlooked learning factor: he is deeply aware of his bodily feelings, a critical factor in clear thinking and self-understanding.

Attention Deficit Hyperactivity Disorder (ADHD) haunts Daniel in school but attention isn't an issue when he is building models, exploring in the woods or playing strategy games with his friends. Intensely curious, Daniel is constantly moving, exploring and experiencing his world. He loves nature and is an expert on insects and birds. Daniel runs mini-experiments in his mind, asking "what if" and "why" questions and exploring cause and effect. Social studies lessons rarely stick, but Daniel remembers everything he hears about anything that flies. He struggles to listen even briefly at school but pays full attention for hours when helping his father build an addition onto their house.

Daniel's parents, Adrián and Lea, are concerned by their son's struggles in school, but enthralled by Daniel's marvelous capacity to learn when he is connected to body, emotions, friends and nature. They see that he is smart in many non-school ways and intelligent by any broader definition. Adrián and Lea want Daniel not just to be a good, compliant student, but a good learner who finds meaning in his experiences. They are more concerned with his human development and less with his brain development.

While Adrián and Lea both finished college, their hopes for Daniel extend far beyond academics. Lea and Adrián look at the percentage of Daniel's day away from school as a vital time for learning and building critical non-academic skills. He makes his own thought-out decisions, deals with reasonable problems and embraces the freedom to learn from all the little events of his life. While Daniel loves digital games as much as any ten-year-old, he balances his indoor time with life outside exploring his passion, living things. From insects and birds to human anatomy and behavior, Daniel is a passionate expert on life in all its forms. The child who has little to say about his school day can't stop talking about bugs. The labels assigned to his abilities in school become meaningless and inappropriate in his non-academic life.

Lea and Adrián's approach to parenting is a reflection of their distinct histories. Daniel's mother, Lea, comes from a family that has lived on the struggling edge of the middle class, with its share of successes and setbacks. Lea made it through college but saw that even a degree didn't inoculate her friends and siblings from struggles with alcohol, narcissism, conflict, confusion, depression and divorce. She wants nothing more than for her son to avoid these all-too-common fates. Lea hopes to shelter her children from this destiny by focusing on contentment, avoidance of conflicts, meaningfulness and enjoyment. She doesn't see her role as Daniel's manager but as a vital guide in promoting learning and growth. Lea engages with Daniel by expressing encouragement more than anxiety, support more than coaching for future success and praising effort over achievement.

Adrián's journey began in a farming village in Mexico. His trip from poverty to professorship was arduous. His parents brought him to an Arizona border town to give him access to a public education that was superior to out-of-reach private schooling in Mexico. They also wanted to avoid the most damaging effects of poverty; growing up poor isn't healthy for a child's brain. Adrián's parents knew this intuitively, long before neurological research proved it. Constant stress from income, food and shelter insecurity, combined with noisy, turbulent living conditions, has a profound effect on a child's brain. The development of emotional and cognitive abilities takes the biggest hit from poverty. Adrián worked twice as hard to counter the second-class status his educational and social condition afforded. He worked not just to master the complexities of English but to overcome his own learning difficulties, including stuttering and language issues that parallel his son's.

Adrián overcame prejudice and low expectations by relying on character traits that his parents nurtured during their long odyssey. They encouraged him to persevere and to keep clear goals in mind. They nourished Adrián's curiosity and helped him find a passion. He found it in history, exploring first the conflicts common to his people and then expanding this into an academic career focused on conflict resolution and human rights. Adrián sees similar positive traits in Daniel but worries that his son is picking up subtle negative messages from the labels he is given—and the treatment he receives—in school as a result of his supposed struggle to learn.

2

When Parenting and Teaching Lost Their Way

The three children we have focused upon have parents who are asking tough questions about educating and raising children in the face of potent social pressures affecting schooling and parenting. These pressures began to build with the advent of the Industrial Revolution, throwing parenting and teaching dramatically off track and changing the relationship between parent and child, worker and employment and individual and society. This disrupted the way that parents continuously supported their children's growth and learning, the patterns of learning that had proved so successful for humanity.

Since the start of formal education, the natural relationship between innate and learned capabilities has been largely supplanted by the limited set of skills and content that came to dominate education. This is apparent when children move from the incredible rate of learning that characterizes early childhood into formal schooling. A toddler may learn a song after a single hearing but struggles to count to thirty. A five-year-old who effortlessly adds thirty words a day to his speaking vocabulary may take a year or more to learn twenty-six alphabet letters at school. Speaking, an innate ability that requires massive amounts of informal schooling, comes naturally, but reading and writing, both educational extensions of speaking, can challenge students for years. This isn't all the fault of our schools. Rather, evolution had no need for spelling, mathematics, reading and writing, all very recent additions to our cognitive capabilities. As we will see, most school subjects hijack neural networks designed for other processes.

Toward the end of the nineteenth century, two events disrupted this balance and redefined schooling and parenting. These events were part of a historical movement to formalize education as a means of developing future working adults. This forced a separation between "learning" and "education," where education became largely detached from meaningful intuitive learning, reducing it to mean "doing well in school."

The first of the two events to forever change education was the meeting of the Committee of Ten. In 1893, a committee headed by Harvard University President Charles W. Eliot set the goal for secondary education as "training and disciplining the mind through academic studies." Schooling should prepare students for subjects taught at Harvard. The practical result was to align the subjects taught in high school with those taught in colleges, which at the time few attended.[1]

The Committee of Ten debated the merits of apprenticeships, experiential learning and the value of social and practical skills but rejected them. "Set the goal high" was their motto just as it is with today's educational system, but the goal was very narrow. They insisted that the number and scope of subjects taught in schools should be kept to a minimum.[2] The content of each subject was prescribed in mandated curricula. A series of tests became the sole measure of performance and success. The Committee's work is largely unchanged today. High school is still four years of reading, writing, math, science, history and a foreign language.

One of Charles Eliot's core beliefs was that instruction in college and high school should revolve around lectures and seminars. His committee rejected anything that looked like experiential ways of learning, such as apprenticeships and vocational training. Hands-on, practical ways of learning were for the weak-minded and those that toiled with their hands but had no place in schools. The system rewarded those who survived endless hours of lectures, memorized disembodied content and possessed test-taking skills and, beyond this, was only intended for a very small piece of the population: white males from financially-equipped families.[3]

The influence of the Committee of Ten has been periodically rein-forced by other committees and commissions. In 1895, the Committee of Fifteen was formed similarly to organize the elementary level curriculum. Almost every US president since Harry S. Truman has assembled a group to examine the perceived shortcomings of Eliot's style of education. Truman's report called for community colleges that emphasized Eliot's four subjects.[4] John F. Kennedy and George W. Bush's reports focused on devel-oping a competitive workforce, one of Eliot's central concerns.[5] The report of the commission held by President Ronald Reagan was *A Nation at Risk: The Imperative For Educational Reform*, which found a "rising tide of mediocrity." The report called for more time spent teaching the exact subjects Eliot had prescribed.[6] Commissions under Bill Clinton and George H.W. Bush focused more on K-12 education but extended Eliot's emphasis on testing to measure competency and the intensity of instruction sur-rounding the four subjects.[7] Each successive committee found the existing system of education insufficient and student progress lacking. Yet their prescription for improvement never varied far from the Committee of Ten's framework, nor did the population of students with which they were concerned.

The Committee of Ten took this extreme view by ignoring some of their most learned contemporaries. Charles Darwin famously stated that "A high degree of intelligence is certainly compatible with complex instincts."[8] For Darwin, survival of the fittest had little to do with great physical or social skills. Rather he felt that those who could learn quickly, adapt to changing situations easily and develop flexible problem-solving strategies would most likely prevail. The committee also ignored the father of psychology, William James, who believed that humans relied on instincts far more than animals. James felt that the primary purpose of education was to align our automatic reactions and habits with reason.[9] Both men felt that this was a better way to develop the human mind.

Finally, the committee paid little to no attention to the vast majority of American children, intending for education to be something accessible to a small part of the population. Their lofty goal for education worked only for a white, upper-class lifestyle, ignored contemporary research and perpetuated the issues of race, sex, class and ethnicity that already existed in society.

The second event which occurred in the late 1800s that radically changed how adults and children interacted was the rise of the parenting expert industry. This group of often self-declared authorities sometimes came from the emerging field of behavioral psychology but more often were family doctors with strong opinions grounded in stereotypes about intelligence that still affect our thinking today. They drafted child-rearing manuals telling parents how they could, but mostly should, raise children. They gravitated to two basic perspectives: a child-centered view that focused on warmly nurturing a child's development and a parent-centered focus that stressed discipline. The result, as shown in Ann Hulburt's book on the subject, *Raising America: Experts, Parents, and a Century of Advice About Children*, was the same as now—confusion and conflict. Hulburt sees our approach to parenting as bipolar, trapped between the stern, authoritative parent stressing discipline and the emotive and empathic parent who nurtures a child's growth. These two powerful emotional styles often exist side-by-side in most parents and are often carried into the classroom.[10]

The conflict surrounding parenting advice and style arises from its ungrounded nature. From one of the earliest authorities, L. Emmett Holt, who wrote *The Care and Feeding of Children* in 1894, parenting advice has been more influenced by the experts' own upbringing and personal opinions than research-based evidence. Fads and favorite methods that conflict with emotions have caused parents to express untold anxiety around their children and do little to address issues of race, class and gender that underpin such advice. Without a firm foundation or a practical, critical philosophy, parents, as well as teachers, drift from one child to the next, doing the best they can.

The Hidden Specter of Instructionism

The Committee of Ten's work dramatically changed the content of education while the parenting advice industry changed its style. The result is a way of training and disciplining children that is based on a set of assumptions that silently permeates teaching and parenting to this day and hurts all children. The assumptions hang over education, rarely discussed or even acknowledged, hiding out in our subconscious beliefs. The noted educational reformer and creativity expert Sir Kenneth Robinson believes that education is "hobbled by assumptions about intelligence and creativity that have squandered the talents and stifled the creative confidence of untold numbers of people."[11] All students, whether they're like Zoe, Mia or Daniel, are subjected to limited assumptions that form the hidden backbone of our educational system.

This backbone is Instructionism, which forms the framework that largely defines our core beliefs about how kids should learn and behave. The Committee of Ten and its more recent reincarnations, No Child Left Behind and Race to the Top, are based on a belief in Instructionism. Rarely discussed and deeply central to almost every lesson, Instructionism's core belief is that parents and teachers are the experts with knowledge and behavior plans that must be imparted to uneducated children. It is the adults' jobs to tell children everything they should know and how to act. As a result, parents and teachers end up doing much of the thinking, problem-solving, planning and goal setting, hindering children's learning and cognitive development. And, like the Committee of Ten, these new policies that promote Instructionism do little to address the social and economic issues that have deep influences on the kind of educational experiences children receive.

Instructionism has long been criticized as a major obstacle to educational progress. The great philosopher of education, John Dewey, starts *Experience and Education* with a critique of "traditional" education, stating that "the subject matter of education consists of bodies of information and skills that have been worked out in the past; therefore the chief business of the school is to transmit them to the next generation" through the establishment of standards and rules for instruction, "time schedules, schemes of classifications, of examinations and promotions." Dewey felt that this form of education leads to "docility, receptivity and obedience."[12] Paulo Freire called this idea "the banking concept of education," where students are "receptacles" for information that need to be filled with teacher or system-defined content. Students are to memorize, or bank, standardized information and regurgitate it "word for word" on tests. The main thesis of Freire's 1963 classic, *Pedagogy of the Oppressed*, is that a banking classroom led by a teacher/authority oppresses students: "The more students work at storing deposits entrusted to them, the less they develop the critical consciousness which would result from their intervention in the world as transformers of that world."[13]

Instructionism looks at children as "blank slates" waiting for adults to pour information into their empty heads. Few ideas have been so discredited as that of the "blank slate," the idea that children are born with blank minds that only grow when adults train and teach them. It is this view that keeps alive the idea that without this input children would remain little more than talking pets. But, as Dewey and Freire point out, children are far more than this.

There are students like Zoe who can flourish under almost any instructional framework, including Instructionism. They are good listeners who absorb information and are not easily bored. Learning content, facts and figures is critical, especially when students need to go deeper into subjects. Forming deeper opinions, becoming an expert and developing critical thinking skills all require contextual knowledge. But an Instructionism-influenced approach fails to meet these goals for students like Mia and Daniel.

Instructionism barely acknowledges a child's innate capacity to learn. It minimizes the vital role that experiences and relevant practice play in learning. Instructionism is also based on outdated understanding of the cognitive aspects of learning, such as how memory works, how attention is focused or that motivation heavily influences learning. Few researchers believe that children can absorb information passively told to them, then permanently memorize every word and adjust their behavior accordingly. If the information has little utility or interest to the child, then there is little chance that it will be permanently learned. Often children memorize information just long enough to be tested on it. Without repeated, well-spaced-out refreshment of the learning, retention of the instructed information is surprisingly low.

Instructionism lends itself to practices that force students into passive learning situations which turn embodied learners like Daniel into squirming blobs. He struggles with the lack of stimulation and movement combined with an abundance of distracting behaviors. The explosive growth in the prevalence of Attention Deficit Hyperactivity Disorder (ADHD) diagnoses may be tied to passive instructional educational practices like Instructionism.

Researchers Stephen Hinshaw and Richard Scheffler found, in their book, *The ADHD Explosion: Myths, Medication, Money and Today's Push for Performance*, that significantly more students are diagnosed with ADD or

ADHD in states where high levels of standardized tests, including exit exams, are common.[14]

In its rawest form, Instructionism looks on movement and conversations not as ways of reinforcing learning, but as behavioral shortcomings. From birth, children learn best in social situations, yet the current emphasis on content and assessment hinders group learning. While cooperative learning has been a buzz word in education for decades, it is often used to reinforce teacher-directed methods. Lesson plans are highly structured, rarely offering teachers and children the opportunity for open-ended learning. Signs of independent thinking, free discussion or creativity may be seen as off-task behaviors.

With the advent of standards, a teacher's job has been largely reduced to the transfer of information. Content is king. Teachers have less say in what to teach, less time to plan lessons and less freedom to use methods that have served them and their students well in the past. Engaging, hands-on lessons and successful but time-consuming projects, plays and experiments are put aside. Experiential and story-based learning, imagination and social/emotional explorations have been all but squeezed out of the school day.

Children are seen more like students than offspring, requiring constant instruction to keep in line. An idealized image of good behavior too often becomes the focus of parent-child interactions rather than building a deep relationship that fosters the development of creativity, inquisitiveness and exploration. This approach exhausts parents and turns off children.

Just as children are born to learn, adults have deep parenting instincts. These instincts often get lost in the current cacophony of parenting advice. The primal instincts of both parents and children develop through a relationship built on learning, playing, working, experiencing and relaxing together. These impulses have been favored by evolution, because they enhance the learning and survival skills of children and adults alike. Both children and adult instincts require constant refinement through endless learning and reflection.

The Assumed Curriculum

Another assumption unwittingly perpetrated by the Committee of Ten is the Assumed Curriculum. Simply put, the Assumed Curriculum holds that if students learn the content provided under Instructionism, then critical cognitive, perceptual, creative, social and emotional aspects of education will magically develop on their own. From an evolutionary perspective, our cognitive, perceptual and social-emotional skills developed to do one thing, to give humans a survival advantage by learning to solve problems in novel ways. This is still the most important ability that education should impart. To leave the advanced development of problem-solving and its associated abilities, such as decision making, planning, strategic thinking and reasoning, to chance is perhaps the greatest failing of global educational systems.

The Assumed Curriculum permeates parenting and schooling, resting on the idea that teaching facts and skills helps develop a broad range of capabilities even if children perceive them as abstract, irrelevant and decontextualized. There is little proof that teaching math reasoning helps students handle abstractions, understand symbols and improve their memories outside of math. We hope that reading comprehension instruction develops into general comprehension and strategic thinking. We hope classes in history and social studies will lead to an understanding of how society works and conflicts are resolved and expose the motivations and emotions that drive human events. We assume that biology and physics courses provide content knowledge that engender in students an experimental mindset and problem-solving skills.

Education at school and at home shouldn't rest on assumptions.

The Inverted Curriculum

Instructionism also inverts the curriculum: there is an inverse relationship between what schools feel is important to teach and what children need to learn to succeed. The more crucial a language, cognitive or social/emotional skill is to long-term success, the less time is spent on that activity in school. Conversely, the subjects that are commonly emphasized in school are secondary factors for success in our personal and public lives. Research supporting the idea of the Inverted Curriculum dates back to the mid-twentieth century where studies showed that we spend about 70 percent of our time communicating. About 45 percent of waking hours are spent listening and 30 percent speaking. Less than 15 percent of an adult's time was spent reading, while writing consumed less than 10 percent.[15] Remember that these studies were done during the radio age and at the dawn of television, long before the Internet, cell phones, e-readers and podcasts.

Building on this research, Madelyn Burley-Allen wrote *Listening: The Forgotten Skill* in 1982 and found similar numbers. She contrasted the percentage of time adults spent in different forms of communication with the time devoted to them in the average classroom. She found that students took twelve years of training in writing, six to eight years in reading, one or two years developing oral communication skills and almost no time learning to listen.[16] Students spend immense amounts of class time listening and in oral discourse, yet very little time is spent developing these skills.

The Inverted Curriculum also neglects our unique ability to communicate internally, our inner dialogue. The inner narrative is the strongest expression of our thoughts and feelings and is critical to reading and written expression. Yet schools are only beginning to recognize this inversion by heightening mindfulness, direct awareness of one's thoughts, feelings and body states and developing meta-cognition, the ability to think about one's thoughts.

Other parts of the school day are also inverted. Teachers spend much time on behavioral management but little direct time on social and emotional skills. Math provides a specific type of reasoning, problem-solving and logic instruction but these vital skills are rarely addressed in ways that would benefit children in their daily lives. Possibly the curriculum inversion with the greatest long-term ramifications is the secondary status given to physical education, the arts and second languages. These areas are critical to creativity and are proven to boost cognitive skills.[17]

When Content Overwhelms Context, Practice and Process

Instructionism requires more than the Assumed and Inverted curricula to rule the day. The idea that content should form the core of the school day is perhaps the most accepted aspect of schooling. The Committee of Ten felt that if content was the core of college instruction, then it must maintain the same place in K-12. The 1890s was a time when few students went to college. The committee believed that only a select few had the intelligence to graduate from high school. Still, content was king. Then, as now, the content tended to be abstract with little relevancy or utility to the student's life.

Anthropologists and evolutionary psychologists generally believe that for millennia learning was contextual and relevant. The context was most often the living environment and culture of the learner. Learning usually built directly on experiences, memories and knowledge that children had already sampled. The content, such as animal behavior, domestic and construction skills or career crafts, was imparted in a relevant setting. Learning was generally active and embodied with extended periods of lively practice. A broad range of abilities, from practical skills to behavioral development, was easily learned in this manner.[18]

Content instruction today generally relies more on memory than experience and more on passive understanding than on active engagement. Children and teens struggle with the dry content and the constant rush to teach to the test. Math instruction quickly moves from concrete representations of quantity to abstract operations. Algebra has moved from a high school subject to one that is mandated in elementary school. Reading rapidly proceeds from storybook reading to chapter books solely composed of written English, one of the most complex symbol systems. Science swiftly progresses from hands-on nature explorations to the unimaginable workings of cell replication, gene regulation and molecule interaction.

Daniel Willingham, a cognitive scientist with a deep interest in learning, believes that "the mind [of a child] does not care for abstractions. The mind prefers the concrete."[19] Not only are abstract ideas hard to grasp, but children struggle to transfer their learning to other situations. Children need concrete examples, metaphors and analogies to internalize the abstract. They need a firm grasp of the real world before confronting abstraction. In pre-industrial cultures, children learned abstract and symbolic knowledge in limited quantities and through culturally-enriched means, such as storytelling, song and ritual.

One of the greatest public voices of science today, Neil deGrasse Tyson, stated that, "I would teach how science works as much as what science knows."[20] The content of science provides knowledge about how bacteria grow, chemicals react and earthquakes move along faults. The process of science is the scientific method, a prime way that we learn and solve problems. The scientific method isn't just the step-by-step instructions used in many high school science laboratories, but an experimental approach to life. It starts with children's natural curiosity and grows into a problem-solving and experimental mindset. This process promotes asking what if, making predictions, inferring and determining cause and effect. It is equally useful for dealing with relationship issues and machine malfunctions. A practical and relevant understanding of the scientific method would serve students throughout their lives.

Tyson has pointed out another drawback of Instructionism: from the days of the Committee of Ten it has been inherently exclusive. He feels that an instructional approach to science and, in our opinion, math as well, too often limits those who are allowed to dive deeply into the subject. Tyson himself faced racist barriers as he pursued his deep interest in science. At nine, a teacher told the tall Tyson to pursue basketball rather than physics. He rarely saw a black or Hispanic child in his advanced courses and he's said that he personally knows every woman astrophysicist, because there are so few.[21] His point is that until we make science accessible across race, gender and class, we can't ask who is best suited for it. Sometimes it is not just the selection of content that restricts learning but the biased selection of students.

We are not arguing against the teaching of content. Knowledge is essential. Children should acquire a near-expert level of understanding in one or more areas of interest that can be generalized to help understand and solve problems in other areas. We are arguing that the way content is delivered in most educational settings hinders these goals. Children are intensely curious, absorbing information over a wide range of subject areas. Content and its delivery must tap into children's natural, broad interests.

Even the driest information can be reformulated into stories or expressed visually or metaphorically. Content should be presented so that students must engage with it on many levels. The best teachers are often mediocre lecturers, giving just enough information to begin the student's journey of understanding. Effective teachers and parents try to minimize their own mental effort, allowing children to do most of the thinking. They provide just enough background knowledge to engage students.

The Individual Assumption

The final hidden assumption that props up Instructionism is individualism. We live in a highly individualistic society, so the social forces that sustain Instructionism unwittingly promote individual achievement. Grades, wealth, personal status and the drive for self-satisfaction are entrenched in our parenting and educational system. There are few things as deeply ingrained into a parent's DNA as protecting and promoting a child's success.

Humans are caring, empathetic, cooperative and altruistic, with a deep drive to live harmoniously in small groups. Even in situations that demand individual survival, such as combat, natural disasters or accidents, society places the highest value on those who can override or even sacrifice the individual impulse to survive to help others. In contrast, greed and freeloading are frowned upon by most cultures.

Parenting and schooling are fine examples of learning taking place in social situations. Our intelligence grows when we put our minds together. Small, cooperative groups possess a collective intelligence that extends beyond the cognitive abilities of the individual. We see this synergistic intelligence in research laboratories and collaboratively-run businesses. Many famed individual inventors, from Alexander Graham Bell to Steve Jobs, worked in lab settings with many minds contributing to their success. Cooperative learning has long been a major theme in education. It provides a lessening of the competitive drive of individual instruction. Working in groups, if the instruction is truly open-ended, promotes creativity, communication skills and cognitive engagement. Most complaints about cooperative learning come from those who promote individual instructional goals.

Parents who stress individual achievement in school may favor individual happiness at home. This self-centered, temporary happiness may come at the cost of a greater sense of well-being. Children derive fulfillment through their connections to their bodies, nature or groups and by establishing broader identities based on gender, ethnicity, cultural heritage or citizenship.

An Advanced Primal Path to Capability

We have contrasted the very recent attempts to instruct our children with the immense and often-overlooked learning capabilities that have evolved over millions of years of human evolution. Our species, *Homo sapiens*, only arose from a long line of other human species a few hundred thousand years ago. Dozens of other human species preceded us, with the last species dying out as little as ten thousand years ago. In *The Last Ape Standing*, science journalist Chip Walter explores the reasons we survived while our evolutionary cousins perished. He believes that the prime reason was humans' long childhood that gave us time to learn and hone social, emotional and cognitive skills to a level not found in any other animal or human species.[22] We have so much to learn, so many survival and problem-solving abilities to develop, that it takes decades to reach independence. Our long childhood gives us an unprecedented survival edge.

This forms the foundation for a primal perspective on learning, which views a child's mind as the highly refined product of millions of years of natural selection. The emerging field of evolutionary psychology provides a fresh perspective on child development by looking at its deep roots in our evolutionary past, not just during the first two decades of a child's life. The ability to learn sets us apart from other human species and other animals. Language, abstract thought, imagination and other factors that make us unique are primal functions which promote learning.

Human children not only learn, but they do it at an amazing rate for an extended period of time. Human childhood is characterized by both a rapid rate of learning that starts before birth and an extended period of learning into adulthood. Human children are dependent on the adults in their world for far longer than any other species. The adaptive value of such a long childhood permits both the development of innate skills, such as language, as well as the acquired knowledge that is transmitted across generations. These forces give human children an unprecedented edge in the survival and problem-solving race that is evolution.

David Geary, a noted educational researcher, has studied how the primal mind functions in our modern system of education. He believes that most of the struggles children experience in school have their origins in our evolutionary past. There is a conflict between our primal capacity to learn and the artificial instruction in schools. In his article, "The Primal Brain in the Modern Classroom," Geary writes that we "...may not realize that the reasons children struggle with education lie deep in our evolutionary past. Charles Darwin's theory of natural selection provides a framework for organizing and understanding all living things. How we learn—and what we are interested in learning about—is also shaped by natural selection."[23]

Our children's extended period of learning also gives us another unique advantage, one that allows us to do truly marvelous things: the ability to create a knowledge-based civilization. Our extended and, hopefully, life-long learning enables children, teens and adults to adapt and thrive in the face of an incredibly complex society. We aren't primitive people nor are we a nation of farmers, as we were one hundred and fifty years ago. A primal perspective alone is no longer sufficient for survival or success. Letting children learn by playing together provides only a small piece of the learning needed in our massively complex world. For this reason the primal perspective must be balanced and enhanced with an advanced perspective, one that refines innate abilities into twenty-first century survival skills, one that pushes our amazing natural capacity to learn to neuroscience, philosophy, cognitive science, anthropology, etc.

While the challenges that children faced over the millennia were considerable, today's children need highly-refined and specialized skills to flourish in our incredibly complex social, emotional and technological world. The capabilities that we used to put people in space are built on those that allowed our ancestors to leave Africa tens of thousands of years ago and push all the way to Australia, Asia and the Americas. Most of the learning that children need relies on innate skills used in very sophisticated ways. Speech is innate but has been adapted to perform amazing feats of communication. Reading and writing are just innate speech reconfigured to help us learn and solve problems in an advanced manner. The basic ability to do math may be as limited as determining quantities as small as ten (fingers) or twenty (with toes). Counting using words is a human adaptation, a cognitive advancement.

Our learning needs are different, often relying on immense amounts of information in extremely specialized fields. However, our predecessors learned in other ways, since problem-solving, quick learning and arriving at creative solutions were a matter of life and death. The "higher-order" abilities of the human mind, from reasoning and planning to comprehension and creativity, are the product of thousands of generations where the more capable and responsive survived. Reading comprehension is child's play compared with the life challenges a typical twelve-year-old dealt with ten thousand or one hundred thousand years ago.

An advanced primal perspective acknowledges that the vast, innate capacities of a child's mind are best developed using insights derived from fields as diverse as anthropology and neuroscience. An advanced primal perspective on child guidance takes what nature provides to every newborn and nurtures it using an advanced understanding of how our minds work.

Big L Learning

The emphasis on learning embodied in an advanced primal perspective requires us to distinguish "Big L Learning" from simple learning. "Big L Learning" can be primal or advanced, but it pulls together many simple learning circuits into a massive network. The brain has hundreds of information-processing functions that solve most of the problems we have encountered for millennia. We have circuits that know how to read facial expressions, filter out extraneous noise and respond to threats. If all of these little programs operated independently we would be deeply enveloped in a constant state of confusion.

John Tooby, a leading voice in evolutionary psychology, believes that the mind pulls many of these individual programs together into "superordinate" networks. "Programs that are individually designed to solve specific adaptive problems could, if simultaneously activated, deliver outputs that conflict with one another, interfering with or nullifying each other's functional products."[24] This is why it is so difficult to go to sleep while your heart and mind are racing with fear.

"Big L Learning" functions like a superordinate network, pulling together smaller learning and problem-solving circuits. Conversation is a "Big L Learning" capability, pulling in many learning circuits and systems. Conversation engages critical emotional, attention and motivation learning pathways, as well as reasoned thinking, information retrieval and meaning capabilities.

"Small L learning," a vital part of "Big L Learning," is the simple education that takes place when we think about information in working memory, one of Mia's cognitive weaknesses, to the point that it links and consolidates with existing memories. Most schooling relies on "small L learning" based on memory and isolated thinking skills, rather than on the broad experience of "Big L Learning." "Big L Learning" is the most important capability that a child can develop, far surpassing mundane thinking and memorization skills.

Let's use piloting to explore the relationship between "Big L Learning" and "small L learning." A pilot may learn all there is to know about a plane's gauges which indicate altitude, airspeed, vertical speed and position relative to the horizon. It is absolutely necessary but extremely dangerous to fly a plane based solely on an understanding of the gauges. This is "small L learning." A pilot must physically practice flying, engaging a much wider system of learning. He must learn how to assimilate the individual gauge readings with how the plane responds to changing environmental conditions. He must engage many smaller programs, including intuition, habit formation, emotional response and social concerns. The "small L learning" is an important part—but only a part—of a "Big L Learning" situation.

Capable Children

Our children have enormous innate learning capabilities that the adults in their lives can nurture using advanced methods that engage "Big L Learning." These capabilities engage wide networks of children's minds and help them solve life's problems and find meaning. We believe that a dozen superordinate learning capabilities largely determine the moment-to-moment and long-term successes of our children. Each of these capabilities is rooted in primal ways of learning and can be nurtured into advanced, life-long skills. We have alluded to these learning capabilities as we discussed Zoe, Mia and Daniel's education and the concerns of their parents.

A Learning Capabilities Framework based on an advanced primal perspective gives children the abilities that have been the key to survival in the past and the path to flourish in a complex and challenging future. Children with the widest and most responsive set of learning capabilities have the best chance of creatively solving life's endless challenges.

The Learning Capabilities Framework offers children and the people who guide them one more vital advantage. It ends the confusion that so many children and adults feel by overcoming the fragmentation of and limited engagement with life. The Learning Capabilities Framework connects children to their bodies, minds and the natural world. It connects them to their emotions and their diverse and ever-changing social networks.

These capabilities develop embodied, experimental mindsets. They build on our perceptual abilities to make sense of the world. They address the flood of subconscious processes and refine our thoughts, emotions, information and, yes, content into higher-level systems of understanding. The capabilities bring social and emotional learning to the forefront of education, helping children, teens and adults solve some of our most vexing and persistent difficulties. And the capabilities are for all children, in all socioeconomic situations, across race and gender, in any home life situation and for all adults who play a parenting role in any child's life. Everyone has a broad range of life-sustaining skills and everyone can develop advanced capabilities.

We should also understand why kids need to go to school. A Learning Capabilities Framework proves a clear answer: to learn a broad range of embodied capabilities that all children need to succeed across their lifetimes and in almost every area of their lives. A Learning Capabilities Framework helps us move beyond the curriculum of the Committee of Ten to an education that fulfills the substantial needs of all of today's children.

Before we explore the capabilities in depth, we need some background knowledge including a clear, demystified definition of mind and a concrete understanding of how children's minds operate as they learn, reason and deal with life's unceasing difficulties. We should also understand what children need to learn in school and beyond so they flourish as both kids and adults. Maybe what our children need isn't to have smarter, better-functioning brains or more academic skills. Maybe they need to develop their full, "Big L Learning" capabilities.

3

Giving Learning Purpose and Meaning

The morning that Zoe asked her parents if fourth-graders could drop out of school was the morning that changed everything. Suddenly, college and career goals seemed like little more than fantasies. The subtle, subconscious doubts that Jan and Jeff had about Zoe's education and well-being rose to the surface. What should their goals be for Zoe, right now and in the long run? Is she learning the important things in life? Have they ceded too much of Zoe's education and development over to her school? Clearly, doing well in school is not going to satisfy Zoe or her parents.

Where did these strong emotions and thoughts come from? Zoe told her parents that her school time could be better used if it felt like the simple yet meaningful experiences that filled her free time outside of school. Why can't school offer more of the multisensory, moving, feeling, deeply engaging types of activities that define her afternoons and weekends? Why can't relevant and necessary content be taught in a livelier manner?

Children are quite aware that school life is different and harder than the enjoyable and meaningful experiences of everyday life. The rate of learning slows while the effort increases. Children who learn language and social, emotional and problem-solving skills rapidly before entering kindergarten may then take years to learn a few hundred reading words and how to add numbers bigger than ten.

Zoe made the academic transition into elementary school with greater ease than Mia and Daniel. However, well before she asked about dropping out of school, her parents saw that Zoe was growing resistant to formal instruction. They began to doubt the long-term value of years of compulsory education that didn't align with their larger goals for Zoe. Jeff and Jan saw little in Zoe's school day that sparked her inquisitiveness and curiosity or motivated her to explore her many interests more deeply. They saw Zoe becoming more passive—less physically energized to play and learn—and pulling back from engaging in the experiences of daily life. They worried that the enforced silence and behavior controls were stifling Zoe's love of conversation and storytelling. What were all the hours of schooling doing to expose her to the subconscious forces, images, impulses, dreams and ideas with which Zoe seemed so in touch? Was the mandated curriculum helping Zoe understand the bigger pictures, themes and take-home messages of science, history and literature? They worried that the empathic and ethical child they knew so well was growing less caring about others and less concerned about fairness. In short, Jan and Jeff worried that Zoe's formal education was neglecting the universal learning capabilities that give their daughter and all children a desire to learn. With so many questions and doubts, Jeff and Jan began to think again about the purpose and meaning of education—both formal and informal.

They also viewed Zoe's request as a challenge to the notion that the most meaningful education takes place in the classroom. The learning environment has a powerful effect on a child's body and mind. Gary Evans is an environmental and developmental psychologist whose major interest is in how the physical environment affects human health and well-being, especially in children who live under the stress of poverty, insecurity, anxiety or an unsettled social or environmental situation. His concern about the non-school environment and non-school activities arises from the finding that over 80 percent of the variation in student achievement is predicted by the non-school components of children's lives.[1]

Clearly, Zoe was satisfied with her away-from-school time. While the Industrial Revolution and the corporatization of work has taken time from family life, parents, peers and non-school adults still provide the bulk of children and teens' development. This extended group has been their primary educators since the dawn of our species. Nature has endowed humans with a complementary system where children are born to learn and older children and adults are full of natural and acquired teaching instincts, most of which are so natural that we hardly notice them. It is in a child's inborn nature to learn language, reasoning, creative thinking, skilled movement, social skills and hundreds of other abilities. For thousands of generations, adults have nurtured these nascent skills into their mature forms using a combination of instinct and cross-generational knowledge. Yet schools have created an artificial learning environment mostly devoid of these powerful forces.

Where Learning Takes Place

The ability to learn in a wide range of settings and from a vast assortment of individuals makes us a unique species. At times, children learn with such ease it is barely noticeable. Learning happens when adults act, not as classroom teachers, but as mentors and role models. This degree of learning requires that children remain under adult care and guidance longer than any other species. Most newborn animals are dependent for days to months. Human children are dependent for decades. There is so much to learn.

In contrast, classroom teachers have been children's primary instructors for only a century and are restricted to administering only a limited education. This is not the teachers' fault as they have had little say in the way schools operate. We believe teachers, policy makers and administrators need a clearer purpose, to rediscover the primal educational power that has been intuitive for generations of parents. Teachers could then deliver much-needed content more effectively with time left over to develop the broader range of capabilities that enrich children's lives. This would go a long way to motivating Zoe to stay interested in school and resolve her parents' doubts about the value of sending her to school six hours a day and forty weeks a year.

Why Is Parenting and Teaching So Hard?

Why is finding a meaningful way to parent and teach a child like Zoe so difficult? Why has raising children become so hard when adults have been doing it successfully for millennia? Why is guiding children so difficult during a revolution in neuroscience and cognitive and behavioral psychology? After all, helping children grow is deeply ingrained into the genes, thoughts and emotions of most teens and adults. The nature of babies, toddlers and children hasn't changed dramatically over the centuries, yet parenting and teaching has become a source of anxiety and insecurity.

The answer lies in the complexities of living in a rapidly changing time with dreams and goals for children that wildly surpass those held by typical parents in simpler times. We live in an age of incessant and unpredictable social, economic and technological change where our expectations of children include cognitive and academic superiority coupled with unparalleled material success. As Jennifer Senior, author of *All Joy and No Fun: The Paradox of Modern Parenthood*, says, "We believe we get to invent our future, our opportunities and who our children are going to be... which is wonderful, but also very troubling."[2] Senior finds this troubling, because today's adults have largely abandoned traditional child-raising methods without replacing them with solidly grounded strategies, sensible goals or a clear purpose. Adults are putting children on uncharted paths to the future.[3]

Senior believes that the most agreed-upon goal of American adults is that children should be happy and successful. But as she points out, these two goals are sometimes mutually exclusive, further complicating child development. Most forms of success require hard work, overcoming multiple obstacles and a positive response to failure. Overcoming problems isn't most people's definition of happiness but it offers meaning and a sense of accomplishment. Parents may value types of success, including wealth, fame and status, which fail to bring happiness to children and only temporary and superficial pleasure to adults.[4]

A transient emotional state like happiness isn't really something that parents can control. Senior believes that happiness is a very elusive goal: "Happiness and self-confidence can be the by-products of other things, but they cannot be goals unto themselves. A child's happiness is a very unfair burden to place on a parent. And happiness is an even more unfair burden to place on a kid."[5]

Inner, Other and Autonomous Focus

In the preceding chapters we offered a partial solution: children should develop innate capabilities to the degree that they can continuously learn, inventively problem-solve and build meaning. Before we get into the details of creating capabilities within this framework, we must first define the purpose of parenting and teaching.

This is a topic that Harry Brighouse, an educational philosopher, has long investigated, particularly the value of college and career for material success. Brighouse believes that one aspect, but not the primary aspect, of education should be to provide basic material security. He warns that "once income levels surpass [a] minimum absolute threshold, average satisfaction levels within a given country tend to be highly stable over time even in the face of significant economic growth."[6] Brighouse cites research that questions the connection between income and happiness. In the United States during the 1970s and 80s, economic inequality was less pronounced and the economy grew by about 40 percent, yet there was no improvement in the number of people reporting feelings of happiness. At the same time there was a marked increase in prescriptions for anxiety and depression. Material well-being is not a predictor of personal success nor should adult anxieties about it be transferred to children.[7]

If our current primary concern of economic and academic achievement is not allowing for success or happiness, what other concern might be more important? One solution is a shift from material concerns to enriching the inner life of children, from self-centered achievement to concern for others and from external control to living autonomous lives. This adds an "inner, other and autonomous" focus to parenting and education. In a world consumed with extroversion, the Learning Capabilities Framework focuses on developing the inner life of children. Purpose and meaning is found in concern for others, including people, animals and the environment. Yet we want children to develop independence in their decision-making and behavior.

By holding an "inner, other and autonomous" focus, we will be concerned not just about our children's achievement and happiness but their broader well-being. Brighouse believes that parents and educators should be deeply concerned with a child's well-being. In his book, *On Education*, he states that schools should place considerable emphasis on helping children flourish, promoting their well-being and helping them grow into independent adults. Education, whether it is derived from a parent or a teacher, should center on the interests of children and hold economic goals as secondary concerns.[8]

A Learning Capabilities Framework lends itself to such an "inner, other and autonomous" focus. All of the capabilities strengthen one or more of these focuses. They are natural outcomes of developing experiential, sense, meaning-making, interpersonal, emotional and social capabilities.

Inner

With tremendous social pressures for outward signs of success, Zoe's parents are focusing on her inner life—what Brighouse calls intrinsic education, "living life from the inside."[9] Much of what a child learns isn't the easily measurable material mandated by standards. It is the deeper learning that happens without the intense effort most "small L learning" requires. It is how children learn from experience and grow emotionally and cognitively. It is the social and emotional growth, the development of self-awareness, the way that children develop advanced capabilities mostly through processes that only vaguely rise into consciousness. These are inner abilities that children need to succeed that support their overall well-being, emotional resilience and social adaptability.

Other

Humans experience a dynamic tension between concerns for individual survival and that of the social group. We strive for individual success, yet are also deeply social beings. We are concerned about our emotional condition while able to express empathy, compassion and altruism toward others. Part of our primal makeup is that we are weary of freeloaders, individuals who take more than their share while neglecting the needs of others. As parents and teachers, we struggle to advance the individual while promoting the needs of groups.

American culture places an extreme emphasis on individual achievement, to the point of narcissism. Capable children are able to temper their singular success by maintaining concern for others. This is a central feature of many cultures where personal identity is second to group identity. The Japanese place strong emphasis on membership in family, locality and country to a degree that makes many individualistic Westerners uncomfortable.

While collective identity can lead to extremes, such as sectarianism and nationalism, an over-emphasis on individuality can lead to the self-absorption so apparent in social media selfies, narcissism and the second deadly sin, greed. As Jan and Jeff strive for their daughter's individual success, they also aim to raise a child who is concerned for others, growing into a caring and giving adult. Zoe cares about her friends, her pets and the well-being of her environment. She has a good balance between personal concerns and those of the social and natural world in which she lives.

Gaining Autonomy

If you ask Zoe why she is so frustrated in school, she will put a lack of independence high on the list. She bristles under the unceasing behavioral controls and rules that she isn't allowed to question. Zoe feels that she is ready for greater autonomy and desires a real voice in her schooling and free time. She is voicing another of Brighouse's key concepts, autonomy, the freedom to determine one's own direction in life. The natural purpose of childhood and adolescence, of all the nurturing and teaching, is to create independent children who develop into autonomous teens and adults. In many cultures around the world, children begin to act independently at the same age that our children are entering first or second grade. The controls and restrictions placed on teens today in America would be unheard of in these cultures and certainly also even a hundred years ago. Today's helicopter parenting and command-and-control teaching deprive children of the chance to exercise the autonomy that they have long been granted from an early age.

Independence isn't in conflict with an inner or other focus. It isn't about creating rugged individuals but rather group members who function as autonomous agents. An autonomous child has the freedom to think, explore emotions and relationships and act in an independent manner. This isn't freedom from rules and restrictions; rather, it is the freedom for children to find their own way in the world rather than to conform to one not of their making. It is the freedom to make autonomous choices and actions, to even question the values and lifestyle of one's parents and community. For Jeff and Jan it is raising a child who is free to question almost every value and belief they hold.

This autonomous drive is seen most strongly in so-called rebellious teens who seem to find so much of their parents' lives hypocritical and meaningless. The instinctual push for autonomy is felt by most adults when pre-teens begin to fight against adult control. It is felt when teens question teachings and rebel against authority, a tendency designed to accelerate learning and independence. This primal drive to rebel creates separation from parents as teens slowly and often painfully become autonomous agents with greater social responsibility. Autonomy is a natural remedy for the excessive protection that defines too much of parenting and schooling today.

Autonomy is not only lacking for students and children, but for teachers as well. Mia's mother, Melissa, feels the lack of autonomy as a teacher, sharing Zoe's frustration over the lack of control in her school day. Standardized instruction and testing have taken away much of a teacher's ability to teach freely and to use the intuitive teaching skills that make teaching an art. Melissa feels that the emphasis on individual student and teacher achievement, on measuring both students' and teachers' performances based on test scores, has dampened the collaborative and community feeling from schools. Melissa feels more like a technician reciting prescribed lessons than an educator delivering instruction in a creative and personalized manner. Melissa's supervisors make her feel like a child herself: she's told what to do, how to behave and increasingly how to think about teaching. Worst of all, children often share this feeling. They feel that school is about traditionalism rather than autonomy. Education has become a system where independent thinking, actions, creations and initiatives have been suppressed by standards that enforce conformity.

Zoe has developed many capabilities in an outwardly visible manner at a level that is appropriate for a ten-year-old. She is becoming a good learner and problem-solver even as she questions the meaning and purpose of her forced education. Yet her parents and, more importantly, Zoe realize that there is something missing in her development. As long as her teachers remain largely blind to her broader learning capabilities, she will also miss the deeper purpose of growing up: developing an inner perspective, a concern for others and independence in thinking and action.

Each of the twelve capabilities we will discuss in the next chapter has a decidedly inner side; inner experience, perception, perspective, imagination and creative impulse. The inner voice, internal conversations, personal meaning, emotional expression and sense of self are all capabilities upon which academic abilities like writing, reading and mental math are dependent.

The capabilities also promote autonomy, allowing children to become curious, independent adults who can creatively map their own path in life. They have a distinct "other" orientation, enabling children to take a more responsible role in social, physical and natural environments. As parents and teachers shift from focusing on outward signs of progress to creating inner capabilities, they can move from symbolic measures of progress to concentrating on the inner strengths that all children need.

Capabilities and Intelligence

Learning capabilities and an "inner, other and autonomous" focus don't develop in a vacuum; they require activities, experiences and interactions. There are numerous ways that a child's capabilities can be overlooked and a deeper purpose ignored. A primary way that adults blind themselves to a child's broader capabilities is by placing children in narrow categories by emphasizing only limited skills. Academic intelligence is a key example.

Why should a single measure of a child's ability (i.e. IQ) hold back a child with so much potential? Melissa sees that her daughter is constrained by an outdated perspective on intelligence, or, more precisely, the types of cognitive skills that promote a narrow range of academic talents valued by traditional schooling. How can any test give an accurate measure of a child's overall ability? Intelligence tests are a snapshot of a dynamically changing situation and a child's cognitive history.

Not only is IQ not fixed but it varies significantly, especially with students like Mia who score in the average range. High-IQ children also face significant drawbacks. Children with high IQs usually do well academically but often at the cost of significant social and emotional growth. High IQ doesn't guarantee success nor does it correlate with creativity.

Academically-gifted children aren't the most likely to come up with new inventions or creative ideas. Children possessing great academic intelligence may be weak at reasoning, since the two are not tightly linked. Intelligence doesn't inoculate us from motivated reasoning or making a lazy guess. In this way, there are two problems with grounding educational success in these notions of intelligence: such concepts are problematic and outdated themselves, demanding new notions of "intelligence," but discussions about intelligence also mislead us into thinking that it is at the heart of well-being and lifelong learning.

Challenging the first point, we now know that people with average IQs have a slew of abilities that can be developed into exceptional capabilities if we rewrite our understanding of intelligence. Howard Gardner challenged this view with his concept of multiple intelligences, currently centered on nine distinct types of intelligence.[10] Cognitive psychologist Scott Barry Kaufman proposed in his book, *Ungifted: Intelligence Redefined,* that children have an unlimited number of overlapping and interacting intelligences that can be developed with the right mindset, passion and practice.[11] We all have talents, intelligences and creative capacities that are largely overlooked by schools and parents who are overly-focused on academic success. We seek to redefine and expand the idea of intelligence to be more inclusive of the kinds of knowledge and skills that should be labeled as "intelligence" as well.

However, there are only a limited number of things we can do to make our children "smarter" or raise their IQ scores when we remain focused solely on traditional intelligence, as the improvement may barely affect their overall well-being or capacity to learn. Perhaps one of the best indications of the limits of attaching educational success to intelligence is in studies that show the effects of stress and anxiety on educational outcomes. Harvard economist Sendhil Mullainathan, who has extensively studied the role of poverty on intelligence, has proven that it's not that the poor are less intelligent than their middle-class peers. Intelligence is fragile, easily compromised by the constant stresses and insecurities of poverty that tax cognitive functions, from working memory and impulse control to attention. The fluid and experiential nature of intelligence can be most clearly seen in children raised in poverty, who suffer on average a ten point deficit in IQ compared to middle-class children.[12]

Further, intelligence tests have a long history of being used to separate students by class, race and gender and, in reality, were first established for purposes quite unrelated to education. In fact, the first intelligence tests were developed to sort soldiers during World War I: those with lower scores were sent to the trenches, while those with higher scores were given more substantial and safer desk jobs in the military.[13] Their early use in education, then, was for similar sorting purposes, as IQ tests were seen as a useful way to determine who should get what kind of education, especially during a time when education was growing in political and social importance. However, this sorting purpose quickly took on ethnic and racial overtones, problematically allowing for particular groups, historically white, rich and male, to be seen as "intelligent," with the rest being depicted as lacking intelligence and the ability to learn.[14] We see the continued impact of this today. Though arguments regarding intelligence, merit and ability remain strong in popular discourse, the sorting of students we see today perpetuates racist, classist and sexist prejudices. We therefore seek to distance the idea of education from such notions of intelligence and instead suggest that the focus of education should more rightly be on meaningful pursuits.

Meaningful Pursuits

Rather than trying to increase Mia's score on an intelligence test, Melissa is increasingly looking outside of school for activities and experiences that will expand Mia's capabilities. Harry Brighouse calls these learning activities "meaningful pursuits" and they play an important role in developing capabilities and creating an "inner, other and autonomous" focus.[15] These pursuits feed off Mia's broader range of abilities that cut across work, play, leisure and social time. Meaningful pursuits should promote the three most critical tools for survival and success: continuous learning, problem-solving and increased knowledge and meaning. They should be enjoyable, challenging, rewarding and demanding. Meaningful pursuits don't need to be big events, such as years of lessons or travel abroad. They can be simple experiences that promote learning.

Providing Opportunities

Brighouse believes that, "We owe a duty to children that their childhood be rich and enjoyable, but we also owe them a duty to prepare them so they can have a significant range of opportunities to lead a flourishing life in adulthood."[16] Mia has many such pursuits, ranging from dancing to cooking to playing with younger children to drawing pictures of flowers. She even has interests that seem old fashioned: she collects and dries flowers and loves to go fishing.

Melissa would like one of these or a future pursuit to blossom into a passion that could be transformed into an area of college study, but she has more immediate concerns. She helps Mia engage in a wide range of interests, talents and activities that are intrinsically rewarding and strengthen a broad range of capabilities. Melissa, as a single mother, isn't rich so she does what she can to offer Mia pursuits that are smaller in scale but large in value. In school, she feels that it is her job to offer all her students a rich and meaningful set of experiences, especially children of cash-strapped lower and middle class students.

One of the primary functions of schools should be to address the unequal distribution of opportunities that children experience. Children who might not finish high school or college or who struggle in the job market or find little value or meaning in their chosen career, need meaningful and rewarding interests and a solid set of capabilities to live a rich and meaningful life. Children of color who attend college are far more likely to drop out as compared to white, middle-class students with comparable academic achievement. Children of color who complete college often have similar opportunities to white high school graduates. Melissa struggles with race and gender issues herself, as well as the extra social burden of single motherhood. She wants to ensure that Mia maintains a love of learning apart from school and a raw fascination with so much of life. Melissa feels that if she focuses on these facets of Mia's life then she will be better prepared to face an unpredictable future.

Central to a Learning Capabilities Framework is the idea that all children have basic abilities that, given the opportunity, can develop into functional, meaningful capabilities. Families and schools should be able to work together to assure that all children have the opportunity to develop the full range of capabilities needed for a meaningful life. The opportunities don't have to be big or expensive. We will present *Small Moments* that any parent or teacher can offer a child to advance the twelve capabilities we will soon discuss. We have met many capable children from all walks of life, children who learned to overcome difficulties, to learn from and find meaning in every experience.

Brains—What Are They Good For?

Where Zoe's parents are focusing on inner, other and autonomy and Melissa's mother is focusing on creating meaningful pursuits, Daniel's parents have decided that the best path to success is to see Daniel as more than just a brain. While Daniel may not have the typical "school brain," he is able to learn, problem-solve and construct meaning better than most kids his age. This has prompted Lea and Adrián, who have consulted a long list of neurologists, psychologists and cognitive experts who have had Daniel's brain scanned and screened, to come to one conclusion—brains aren't all they are defined as being.

In an age that has produced explosive growth in the neurosciences, it is only natural that Daniel's brain has been the object of intense interest among his parents and teachers. He has had every imaginable type of examination of his brain, from neurological surveys to magnetic resonance imaging. This has led to a fascinating list of facts that his parents and teachers are constantly trying to interpret. He has weaknesses in the auditory circuits that support listening and reading. The communication between his prefrontal cortex and his eyes isn't filtered as much as neuro-typical students, so his attention floats around. He processes information—be it visual, auditory or tactile—slowly and more deliberately than most children. In school, where rapid and sustained attention is demanded, this is a deficit, but during his free time this becomes a benefit, allowing Daniel to be more reflective, deepening his inquisitiveness and curiosity.

As neuroscience evolves, there is a growing awareness that the fascinating discoveries regarding the brain's structure and function only partially explain how humans think, learn and develop. Knowing that the pre-frontal cortex is involved in self-regulation only tells us so much about this complex process and how to develop it in children. The list of functions and behaviors that the pre-frontal cortex is involved in is quite lengthy. Areas of the brain don't work in isolation, so this cortex is linked to scores of other brain areas. The level of complexity of the brain with its fluid patterns of connectivity means that for every academic weakness that Daniel experiences there are a dozen other patterns that can result in the same learning and thinking.

The current trend in brain research is moving away from looking at the brain as an isolated organ. Researchers are less interested in identifying particular areas of the brain responsible for specific functions. They're shifting their focus from looking at plasticity—how specific areas grow and shrink based on usage—to connectivity, which is how different areas of the brain and body are connected. Researchers are more excited about the *connectome*—the mapping of complex inter-connections in the brain and beyond. They now look not just at the grey matter, isolated groups of neurons, but also at the white matter—the connections between these areas. Areas that traditionally were seen as responsible for distinct functions, such as Broca's area for expressive language (the region of the brain that deals with speech production, discovered by Pierre Paul Broca), are now viewed as parts of complex, interconnected systems. The vast collections of neurons in Broca's area each have many thousands of synaptic connections. These in turn each reach out to distant regions of the brain. Broca's area, like expressive language itself, is deeply connected to emotions, images, concepts, perceptions and the body. This location of our verbal thoughts is interdependent on primitive parts of the brain found in many animals.

This shift, to use a simple mechanical analogy, is like moving from understanding how components of a computer work to tracking the billions of connections that define the Internet. The number of connections to, through and from the brain is staggering. We cannot possibly comprehend the hundreds of trillions of connections between these neurons. Mapping these connections even in a primitive way will take decades. But we know now that the brain is so much more than a physical thing. It functions, not surprisingly, like the mind. It is an information process that is grounded in the body. Neuroscientist Daniel Eagleman describes the brain as being a hub for information.[17] Looking at the brain as a process mirrors our best understanding of the mind: it is through profound interactions with the senses, movement, bodily functions and the body's connections to the environment that the brain gains value.

These connections are anything but static. The brain is constantly reconfiguring itself in response to the other aspects of the mind. The brain has trillions of different ways of configuring itself. It literally morphs every second. The child you are teaching one minute will change the next. We once looked at children's brains as vessels to fill with knowledge. We believed intelligence tests were great measures of ability. Children would be much better served if adults instead look at education as a way of connecting students with the almost unlimited processes of the mind.

From Individual Brains to Expanded Minds

As Bruce Hood points out in *The Self Illusion*, we may think that, "We are our brains, but the brain itself is surprisingly dependent on the world it processes and, when it comes to generating the self, the role of others is paramount in shaping us."[18] Our advanced cognitive functions adapted to the demands of the body, nature and social groups. David Eagleman similarly argues that our understanding of the brain will be quite limited until we understand the "greater nervous system" of the body and the physical and social environment.[19]

Adrián and Lea look at their son as much more than a collection of neurons. They see how Daniel interacts with his environment, both natural and man-made, how his senses work, the relationships he establishes with people, places and things and his growing awareness of himself. Just as Mia would benefit from an expanded understanding of intelligence, Daniel's school-based disability would greatly diminish in significance if we expanded our definition of the mind. The more we study the mind, the more we find that it may be equally influenced by the brain and the body.

Both the brain and the mind are embodied, inseparable from the activity of the body and affected by our tensions, feelings, sensations and movements. The brain constantly uses feedback from the body to shape its information processing. This is evident in children and teens, whose physicality and feelings seem to define their existence. Their bodies are the gateway to experience, the environment and social interactions. This is true of adults as well—when the brain begins to unravel, we turn to the body to calm us down, end confusion and regain focus. Yoga, meditation, breathing practices, physical exercise and stress reduction are all powerful ways the body provides positive feedback to the brain. These counteract the negative feedback loops between the brain and the body caused by stress, depression, anxiety and other bio-psychological disorders.

One of the clearest ways that the brain is controlled by the body is through feelings. Feelings are the bodily representations of emotions. They are the force behind most thoughts. We see this clearly in children and teens, whose emotions are often quick to rise to the surface. Yet even in "mature" teens and adults, thinking is heavily influenced by the feelings in our bodies. It is not just strong emotions like greed, anger and fear that influence our thinking but hopes, dreams, desires, motives and a confusing collection of positive and negative feelings that form the motive force for thoughts. Thinking, our most cherished higher-order brain activity, is in service to our bodies and our feelings. As famed neuroscientist Antonio Damasio states, "We are not thinking beings who feel; we are feeling beings who think. The mind is in the service of the body."[20] This shift in perspective from child development as a one-way path to rational thought to embodied brains driven by feelings (both positive and negative) opens up new windows to their development.

The prevailing view of philosophers and neuroscientists is that the brain is the "hub" of a mind very much embedded in the body and the social and physical environment. The brain depends on the flow of information to and from the body and the environment. It does more than manage the billions of neurons in the spinal cord and the sensory and motor neurons. There is a two-way system of communications with constant feedback and adjustments. The brain has immense innate capabilities but requires the "programming" that the extended mind provides. Children raised in conditions of extreme deprivation or even years of limited exposure to language may long suffer cognitively, emotionally and socially. It is through this extended exchange of information that we learn, think and make sense of the biological, social, physical and psychological worlds.

The words *mind* and *brain* are often used as general concepts rather than specific terms. Few parenting or education courses define brain and mind or map out their relationship. So let's start with a definition. Dr. Daniel Siegel, the author of *MindSight*, recruited forty scientists from many fields to define the concept of mind. It was no easy task. The computer scientists said it was the brain's operating system. The neurobiologists said that "the mind is just the activity of the brain." Psychologists thought it was just our thoughts and feelings. Philosophers debated whether the mind stands alone or is integrated into a larger system.[21]

Siegel and his associates agreed that "the human mind is a relational and embodied process that regulates the flow of energy and information."[22] All the members of the assembled group agreed that their diverse perspectives could converge on this definition. The definition took days to draft and far longer to explain. The gist of the definition is that the mind is not a static organ like the brain. The mind is activity, a constantly-changing event. There is an incessant flow of thoughts, emotions, sensations, perceptions, social interactions and behaviors. And they're all active—requiring energy—as we move, think and feel. It is a fluid process that changes more frequently than the weather. The mind is embodied, not trapped in the brain, locked in its cerebral cell. The mind takes neural activity places it can't go on its own, extending it into our movements, interactions, senses and emotions. It connects us with the physical, psychological and social realms.

Siegel believes that we need to do more than just define the mind. We need to develop *mindsight,* "the focused attention that allows us to see the internal workings of our own minds." This should be one of the primary functions of parenting and education. He argues that "the way that we are educating kids now is basically damaging their brains."[23] Instead of viewing children as brains or academic achievement or abstract measures of intelligence, we should take a broader view that is concerned with their greater well-being, has a clear purpose and is meaningful. We should help them develop diverse capabilities and fuller minds.

4

The Twelve Capabilities Children Need

The problems that are hindering parenting and education are leaving children with limited abilities and narrow paths to the future. They have not been solved by new standards or endless attempts to make our students better receivers of content. The central issue limiting academic progress and causing the economic, social and educational inequality experienced by impoverished children and the middle class remains unaddressed. Even those who excel academically are too often left adrift in life. Parents and teachers alike unthinkingly rely on traditions and decades-old habits or attempt to chart new futures for their children with little to guide them. Issues such as equality of opportunity or having a clear purpose for raising and teaching children are neglected.

Education includes some of the most innovative and creative forces in society, but it has been notoriously resistant to change. Many voices are calling for the development of individual capabilities, from making the school curriculum more creative to including computer programming. Reform efforts often suggest hazy goals and unclear purposes. Changes at home and school are frequently piecemeal or place greater instructional burdens on parents, making homework the primary focus of their interactions with their children.

We believe the solution to this crisis in parenting and education is to create a new framework, to see that learning is a critical part of all child development efforts. We call this approach a Learning Capabilities Framework, which puts the development of *twelve learning capabilities* at the center of parenting and teaching. We believe that the primary goal of everyone who contributes to the development of children should be to create capable kids: children and teens who have integrated minds, bodies and brains. Children who have developed the twelve learning capabilities are able to adapt to ever-changing physical, emotional and social environments.

Behind each capability is a "mini-mind" or mental module that brings the capability to life. Evolutionary psychology and the neurosciences both support the idea that the human mind that seems so singular in everyday life is really a fusion of about five hundred mini-minds, or modules, working together to learn, problem-solve and build meaning. They evolved to solve almost any problem, to develop almost every skill and to learn from almost any experience that humans have confronted. This is why Daniel so effortlessly derives knowledge from his environment when he is physically engaged, Zoe can solve all kinds of problems for which she has received little formal instruction and Mia is able to develop so many capabilities simply by having meaningful pursuits.

To cover the vast expanses of children's minds and how they learn and develop, we chose twelve capabilities, each with its own mini-mind. From the inquisitive mind of the *Curious Explorer* and the imaginative mind of the *Creative Dreamer* to the empathic mind of the *Caring Mind Reader*, each capability is dependent on multiple cognitive, emotional, perceptual and subconscious processes working together. The twelve capabilities each have an instinctual side, a natural learning aspect. The primal nature of the capabilities gives them deep roots in our subconscious minds. Abilities like exploring, building, imagining, conversing and socializing are among the deepest and most natural uses of a child's mind. Storytelling, daydreaming and building knowledge from facts are easy yet lasting ways of learning available to all children.

How We Chose the Twelve Capabilities

Choosing the twelve capabilities that form the Learning Capabilities Framework, we did two things that human beings like to do—making lists and placing things in categories. These innate tendencies of our minds force us to separate things that in reality are interconnected. The capabilities do not operate as isolated parts. A mini-mind may encompass dozens of mental processes. The capabilities themselves interconnect and intertwine to promote children's learning and development. Still, children learn better by dissecting their whole actions into parts.

We chose each Advanced Primal Capability using strict criteria. Each capability must:

1. Be primal, innate and universal in children

2. Mature into an Advanced Capability

3. Be based on a big idea in philosophy, the cognitive and/or neurosciences

4. Support "Big L Learning"

5. Develop the three critical processes for survival and thriving

6. Offer an alternative to Instructionism

1. Primal, Innate and Universal in Children

First, the capability must be at once primal and innate in children across the planet and throughout history. Rather than separating children into arbitrary categories, we looked for universals. We relied on two fields to identify primal capabilities that have benefited humans across time: anthropology and the emerging perspective of evolutionary psychology. Anthropology tells us that children and teens have learned great things and shouldered great responsibility for years. Evolutionary psychology tells us that the advanced functions of our minds are deeply rooted in primal survival abilities.

2. Mature into Advanced Capabilities

Primal capabilities may have helped us prosper in pre-industrial, agrarian and hunter-gatherer environments, but our children are growing up in times that present unique challenges. They must acquire knowledge unimaginable even a generation ago. We thus chose the capabilities from an advanced perspective, defined in two ways. One, the capability must mature into an advanced form that clearly benefits children's well-being now and as they mature into teens and adults. Two, the capability must be understood to be advanced based on research from fields that have a fresh perspective on child development and learning, such as the cognitive and neurosciences. The advanced primal nature of each capability means that it is at once deeply ingrained into our nature while capable of being nurtured into an advanced state required by our complex social, technological and physical environment.

3. Based on a Big Idea in Philosophy, the Cognitive and/or Neurosciences

Each of our suggested capabilities is based on a big idea created when advanced research met philosophy. Well-educated, caring parents and teachers have been flooded with research findings that are hard to put into a meaningful perspective. Conflicting information is becoming a major impediment to effective and secure parenting and teaching. Framing each capability on a big idea created when the cognitive or neurosciences confirm a relevant and powerful philosophical position creates a solid, meaningful platform from which to guide and nurture children. For example, the idea that children aren't blank slates has deep philosophical roots but has also been confirmed by recent cognitive studies of babies. This approach offers an alternative to the endless stream of brain minutia that is hard to put in context. By choosing capabilities that are supported by big ideas, we hope to present clear, meaningful, take-home messages.

4. Support "Big L Learning"

Each capability must support "Big L Learning," not just promote an isolated cognitive skill. Most books on parenting and education aim to promote "small L learning," such as memorizing a narrow set of facts, changing a challenging behavior or fostering one slice of child development. "Big L Learning" engages the multiple problem-solving, meaning-making and learning modules of the brain, body and mind. Each capability is expansive in nature but "Big L Learning" makes them even larger. This broad approach counteracts parents and teachers' tendency to focus on narrow skills.

5. Develop the Three Critical Processes for Survival and Thriving

We wanted our twelve capabilities to develop one or more of the three critical processes of survival and thriving:

- Flexible problem-solving
- Functional meaning-making
- Continuous learning

A Learning Capabilities Framework has a bigger goal than just creating individual capabilities—to create children who possess the three critical processes that have ensured our survival for thousands of generations and are the key to thriving in today's exceedingly complex world. Children who can continuously learn, solve problems in a flexible manner and find meaning to promote future learning and problem-solving are capable of facing almost any challenge, from primitive emotional conflicts to advanced technological complexities. Every capability serves this purpose. While parents and teachers may struggle to keep all twelve of the capabilities in mind, remembering these three "super capabilities" should come naturally.

6. Offer an Alternative to Instructionism

Finally, we chose the capabilities only if they offered an alternative to the dominant form of raising and teaching children—Instructionism. Parents and teachers are both operating from the same unnatural playbook, seeing children as blank slates in dire need of adult instruction and behavioral and thought control. Parents (children's primary teachers) and schoolteachers both spend too much time and effort telling children how to act, what to know and what to think. The capabilities shouldn't be just reactions to Instructionism that make a 180 degree turn, such as letting children become their own teachers. Rather they should offer children abilities that will benefit them in later stages of their lives.

A Learning Capabilities Framework for Parenting and Education

Let's return to the questions that Zoe, Mia and Daniel's experiences raised and see how they fit in our Learning Capabilities Framework. What do students need to learn to be successful in all areas of their lives? What can we teach children so that they can reason well, make informed decisions, live rich and imaginative lives and build strong bonds within themselves and with others? How can we create classroom experiences that promote thoughtful learning?

A number of educators have attempted to address these questions. Ellen Galinsky, President and Co-Founder of Families and Work Institute, has defined seven life skills that she thinks every child needs. "We all want the best for our children," she writes in *Mind in the Making*, "but how do we help them not only to survive but thrive, today and in the future? It is clear that there is information children need to learn—facts, figures, concepts, insights, and understanding. But we have neglected something that is equally essential—children need life skills."[1] Galinsky's seven life skills have a distinct cognitive flavor. They all involve "executive functions" that arise from one of the most evolved areas of the brain, the prefrontal cortex. Executive functions are more like a skilled manager than a boss: "We use them to manage our attention, our emotions, and our behavior in order to reach our goals. Nor are they just intellectual skills—they involve weaving together our social, emotional and intellectual capacities."[2]

Galinsky's primary skills are:

- Focus and self-control—pay attention, filter out diversions and control impulses
- Perspective taking—take another person's point of view and learn to reason together
- Communicating—observe the mind, self-reflect and avoid conflicts

- Making connections—see the big picture by sorting, categorizing and making representations
- Critical thinking—"the ongoing search for valid and reliable knowledge to guide the beliefs, decisions and actions...that parallels the reasoning used in the scientific method"[3]
- Taking on challenges—learn to overcome problems
- Self-directed, engaged learning—develop social, emotional and intellectual skills that are intrinsically motivating

Galinsky has developed methods to advance these skills, mostly with young children, and has met with varying levels of success. Her efforts take a somewhat instructional approach, often attempting to train isolated cognitive abilities.[4] While we applaud Galinsky's methods and her continuing research, we would rather not reduce child development to one area of the brain or to a few cognitive abilities. We prefer to utilize children's natural, embodied abilities, their imaginative and creative sides and their social and self-awareness.

We were also influenced by the work of Roger Schank, an innovative educator and activist. Schank is another researcher who has deeply questioned the value of our current approach to education, especially as it applies to high school and college. In his book, *Teaching Minds: How Cognitive Science Can Save Our Schools*, he states that little will change in our educational system—and with our children's minds—until we switch from a subject-based framework to one that develops cognitive processes: "A properly designed school system needs to focus on cognitive abilities, not scholarly subjects. Kids will recognize instantly that these activities are the ones they know how to do and that they need to get better in."[5]

Schank assembled twelve cognitive processes that underlie learning. His list is broader, reflecting the needs of teens and college students. He breaks these processes down into three categories: conceptual processes such as prediction, judgment, experimentation and evaluation; analytic processes such as diagnosis, planning, causation and judgment and social processes such as teamwork, negotiation and influencing. Schank believes, as we do, that these processes greatly contributed to the success of prehistoric and modern people.[6]

Schank stresses that these abilities should not be taught in isolation but rather in complex learning situations that suggest "Big L Learning."

He doubts that courses on prediction or negotiation would benefit students and notes that stand-alone courses on thinking or social skills have poor track records. Students need real-world context and connections to their experiences to learn. Schank brilliantly suggests that teens could best develop conceptual, analytic and social processes by learning how to date and drive. These two subjects cover most of the twelve cognitive skills and are highly relevant to teens.[7]

Schank and Galinsky have created a defined set of cognitive skills and abilities that form the core of children's and teens' academic abilities for success in school. We believe that parents and teachers have a bigger mission—to develop the capabilities that allow kids to learn, problem-solve and develop meaning in all aspects of their lives. To accomplish this goal, we looked for more comprehensive models for learning than are typically used at home and in school. We were inspired to take a capabilities approach after studying the work of Nobel Prize laureate Amartya Sen, who originally conceived of the Capabilities Approach.

Sen, an economist and philosopher, had a much broader purpose in mind, conceiving the approach to address economic development when traditional approaches had limited success or failed to address economic and social discrimination. He conceived of the Capabilities Approach as a way to look at poverty as much more than limited income or assets, but rather limited opportunities to develop social, political and economic capabilities.[8] Sen views poverty not just as a lack of money but as a deprivation of human capabilities. He is deeply invested in the democratic cultivation of opportunity for the development of capabilities at local levels. He therefore does not provide a list of capabilities but rather provides the fundamental principles upon which local communities might determine their own needs and standards.[9]

To use the term "capabilities" is different, then, from using "skills" or "abilities" like Schank and Galinsky. In Sen's approach, to name and address the cultivation of capabilities requires that one have the opportunity to act upon one's acquired skill or ability. In this sense, the problems of poverty and human flourishing Sen is concerned with cannot be solved by developing individual skills but by providing opportunities for improvement, too.

Philosopher Martha Nussbaum worked closely with Sen but has her own approach to capabilities and human development. Nussbaum forged a more targeted line of attack, clearly listing ten capabilities that ideally ensure that adults, regardless of their circumstances, have substantial opportunities to develop social, economic and political capabilities that allow them to live meaningful lives with dignity.[10] Nussbaum stresses that the Capabilities Approach should be applied universally, supporting all people regardless of their class, gender, ethnicity, ability or other characteristics that usually divide people.

While most of Nussbaum's capabilities center on humans living in a dignified manner, capable of enjoying mental, emotional and bodily health, she included capabilities that we also see as important and relevant to thinking about children and learning. These include the opportunity to develop cognitive, creative and imaginative capabilities, including developing reasoning and decision-making abilities from an ethical perspective.[11] She included educational capabilities, including the development of literacy and numeracy and the freedom to have pleasurable and meaningful experiences, which forms the foundation for our first capability.

We diverged from Nussbaum's expansive work in a few important ways. First, we took a more narrow approach, exclusively concerning ourselves with learning capabilities. Further, Nussbaum was wholly concerned with developing adult capabilities, even speaking critically about the possibility of children being able to develop such capabilities.[12] However, we argue that the idea of capabilities, as well as her ideas regarding educational capabilities, can and should be extended to children and teens. Finally, Nussbaum is primarily interested in attaining freedom through changes at the national level. We wish to expand children's freedom at home and school.

Elaine Unterhalter, Rosie Vaughan and Melanie Walker, in their paper, "The Capability Approach and Education," have opened up the possibility of this expansion and believe that if any area of society would benefit from an expanded perspective on human capabilities it is education. Walker and her colleagues believe, generally speaking, that a Capabilities Approach allows us to look at a richer set of outcomes than what is currently acceptable. Cognitive, emotional and social capabilities become planned outcomes rather than assumed conditions.[13] Most of all, educational capabilities should be functional, benefiting children not in some distant and imagined future but in their everyday lives.

Their approach, which they call the Capabilities Approach to Education, addresses one issue that has long haunted education—equality. Walker and her colleagues are concerned that standardized curricula, where everybody receives the same instruction, falls short of ensuring equality: "It is evident that there are considerable inequalities that standard evaluation method-ologies tend to overlook."[14] Academic success, or more precisely, success on tests of subject matter and basic skills, ceases to be the only measure of benefit. A more grounded measure would be a child's ability to function experientially, cognitively, emotionally and socially. They use the example of disadvantaged students, whose first language isn't English, attending an overcrowded urban school. These children's homes lives are compromised by food insecurity and limited access to physical and mental health care. Does such a child have the same opportunities, let alone the same capabilities, as a child who attends a small private school?

We propose an even more targeted approach, the Learning Capa-bilities Framework. The capabilities chosen here are specifically focused on learning in a broader sense than what is currently happening in schools. They all have primal roots and require extensive development to support the needs of teens and adults.

Our Learning Capabilities Framework retains Sen, Nussbaum and Walker's concern for inequality in a way we think is best for addressing the education problems with which we are concerned. Education has a long history of gender, race and class inequality, largely determining aca-demic and life outcomes. Inequality is not just an issue for children of poverty, as there is also a growing gap in academic abilities and outcomes between middle-class and affluent children. In his article, "No Rich Child Left Behind," Sean F. Reardon states, "Family income is now a better pre-dictor of children's success in school than race."[15] In the 1980s there was little measurable difference in academic outcomes between middle-class and affluent children. By 2010, wealthier students were outperforming middle class kids on test scores, graduation rates, college acceptances and graduate school admissions. Surprisingly, little of this is due to schooling, as the gap between the classes shrinks during the school year but reap-pears over the summer.[16]

Reardon believes the gap starts early: "The academic gap is widening because rich students are increasingly entering kindergarten much better prepared to succeed in school than middle-class students. This difference in preparation persists through elementary and high school."[17] The rich are focusing their financial power on education. Money buys pre-school tutors, more enriching experiences and access to higher quality childcare and better schools. Yet Reardon points to a hopeful sign: "If the relationship between family income and educational success can change this rapidly, then it is not an immutable, inevitable pattern. What changed once can change again."[18]

A Learning Capabilities Framework to parenting and education offers a solution to lessen educational inequality by developing a broad range of abilities in all children, alongside a call to provide the opportunities for such abilities to be utilized in everyday life. The experiences and education that enrich the academic skills of wealthy children can be modified to nurture a wide range of capabilities in all children. A major focus of schools should be to offer all children an equal opportunity to develop functional capabilities and provide the experiences, interests, activities, knowledge and skills all children need to thrive.

Zoe, Mia and Daniel are told to work hard and get good grades with the promise that, in a decade or so, they will be rewarded with college admission. The benefits of education are often placed far into the future. Each level of schooling prepares the child for the next level. Kindergarten prepares a child for first grade. Elementary school is a stepping stone for middle school. High school is preparation for college and college is practice for the workplace. The constant anxiety produces endless stress and very little sense of positive presence. Individuals rarely have the opportunity to enjoy immediate experiences and activities as they are always striving for distant goals and delayed satisfaction. With a Learning Capabilities Framework, growth in children's emotional, social and cognitive capabilities benefits them in their daily life.

The downside of delayed benefits is that students get the message that there is only one way to succeed—go to college and get a high-paying job. Children are rarely motivated when the reward is not directly visible. Worrying about meeting nebulous distant goals places undue stress on children and on their parents and teachers. Too many adults feel cheated after attaining a college degree and a job, yet experiencing little personal fulfillment. By developing capabilities that benefit children in their daily lives, we can avoid students experiencing the dissatisfaction of a career that is far from being a satisfying livelihood. A Learning Capabilities Framework also expands what it means to learn and be educated, allowing for a diversity of outcomes.

Delayed benefit also enforces a limited view of education, one that says that to be educated is to get a degree and a job. This Framework instead envisions the purpose of education as enabling a much broader version of success than we currently promote in our educational policies and allows children more diverse and consistent opportunities to understand themselves as being educated and successful.

Children, by nature, struggle with putting off rewards for a few hours and cannot do so for decades. Learning capabilities are immediately and intrinsically rewarding, because they are based on traits such as curiosity, inquisitiveness and creativity that are gratifying by nature. A Learning Capabilities Framework to parenting and education will help Zoe feel that school is worthwhile. It will ensure that her parents feel that Zoe is engaged in purposeful and meaningful activities that are helping her grow into an independent yet socially connected teen and adult. This approach will address Melissa's concerns about inequality and the subtle discrimination embedded in academic testing and mandated content while giving Mia new opportunities to learn and grow. A Learning Capabilities Framework will enable Daniel to move from the narrow classification of learning disabled to that of fully capable. For parents, seeing that their children are enjoying learning and benefiting from experience is far more rewarding than anxiously pushing for distant and nebulous goals.

Twelve Learning Capabilities

We believe that the following twelve learning capabilities we have developed offer universal benefit to children while answering many of the questions and doubts that parents and teachers have about child development. We have divided the twelve capabilities into four groups, starting with the experiential capabilities that are most evident in young children. The second set of capabilities is grounded in the perceptual world of sense-making, including imagination, listening and storytelling. The third set involves meaning-making capabilities including reasoning, ethical decision-making and the subconscious processes behind learning. The final capabilities are social and emotional, including the ability to make sense and find meaning in our inner lives.

Embodied, Engaged, Exploratory and Experimental Capabilities

Neuroscience, evolution and modern philosophy tell us that the body and physical experience are central to the development of the mind. Movement, sensory perception, feelings and emotions connect the brain to the environment. The brain's primary job is to identify and interpret bodily experiences. The state of the body is an essential ingredient in learning, including motivation, attentiveness and engagement. Compulsory education often supplants experience and bodily involvement with lectures on abstract content. Learning that includes nature, the body and experience is critical to the development of a child's mind.

The Curious Explorer's Experimental Mind

This capability builds on children's innate inquisitiveness by connecting them to the wealth of learning developed through experience and to the physical environment and nature. Children should be able to use experience, exploration and experimentation (the three Ex's) as primary paths to thoughtful learning and action. Children should have the functional capability to apply the scientific method, ask questions, test hypotheses and develop trial-and-error learning. The big idea is that children don't just thrive on experience and exploration; they are instead naturally curious experimentalists. The Three Ex's connect us to the natural world, one of Nussbaum's central capabilities.

The Action Character's Embodied and Extended Mind

This capability is based on children's profound ability to learn and express understanding through bodily action. The Action Character connects the environment to the body and the body to the brain, creating the essential partnership that is the mind. Reasoned physical action has long been our central way of expressing our intelligence. Action is more important than words—words are a recent addition to our evolutionary toolkit. We are very skilled in embodied action. Children should know how to take reasoned action, build models and structures and create maps and diagrams. They should have a connection with their bodies that provides a tether to the brain's tendency to run wild.

The Fascinated Learner's Attentive Mind

This capability helps children find their interests or what gains their attention and motivation. Fascinated Learners should be capable of directing their cognitive and motivational resources to develop an engaging interest in the world, promoting life-long learning. The big idea is that attention, memory and learning aren't separate from motivation and reward. This is an ancient system involved with some of our most basic drives. We normally don't put eating, sex and playing in the same category as learning. But the nature of learning puts it too into a basic survival drive. And learning is the ultimate survival skill.

Sense-Making Capabilities

One critical learning process of an active, engaged body is an enriched ability to process sensory information. Our perceptual powers allow us to create vivid images and imaginative ideas. Our ability to listen has led to speech as well as reasoning. Traditional schooling diminishes the importance of the senses, imagination and creativity. Even with the high value placed on language arts, very little time is devoted to building listening skills, conversational abilities or the narratives that fill our thoughts and literature.

The Creative Dreamer's Imaginative Mind

The Creative Dreamer connects children to their senses, stimulates imagination, sparks creativity and offers the opportunity for children to develop rich perceptual and conceptual powers that arouse imagination and creativity. A child's mind contains a learning path that starts with the senses and flows into concepts as words, images or feelings. When the concepts become rich, they spark our imagination. Finely-tuned perceptual skills enrich our conceptual power and promote imaginative insights that lead to creative problem-solving.

The Storyteller's Narrative Mind

By developing the Storyteller in each of our children, we connect them to the rich world of narratives that are a prime method for explaining almost everything. Storytellers sense narratives in their internal dialogue, daily conversations and deepest explanations. This capability enables children, teens and adults to construct engaging stories as a major way of understanding themselves and their place in the world. Storytelling is central to learning and understanding and is deeply involved with problem-solving and building meaning. The narrative structures of stories stick in our minds. The generational transmission of knowledge before the advent of writing was largely through storytelling. The well-developed Storyteller builds a fluid, coherent story about himself, his relationship to his listener's mind, his society and the biophysical world. The development of the Storyteller should take precedence over the development of writing skills.

The Careful Communicator's Thoughtful Mind

This capability helps children transform random mental chatter into meaningful inner and outer dialogues. The Careful Communicator is more than a talker, excelling at listening, dialogue and reasoning. When this capability develops into its mature form, children, teens and adults are able to engage in meaningful discussions as a primary way of learning and developing cognitive skills. The development of speech and verbal reasoning is through our innate ability to listen. Reading and written expression skills reflect a child's listening and conversational skills. Auditory reasoning, attentive listening and conversational skills are critical human capacities. The Careful Communicator should be developed with the same vigor that we use to teach reading and writing.

Meaning-Making Capabilities

Children must move beyond active, embodied learning and sense-making. They must learn to translate endless streams of information into meaningful structures. Luckily, our minds are well adapted to this task. The subconscious mind handles most of the heavier tasks, which frees our conscious mind to work on processes that require rethinking and novel responses.

The Backstage Director/Time Traveler's Subconscious Mind

This capability, which takes many forms, connects children to the subconscious processes behind all learning. The Backstage Director and Time Traveler help children become aware of feelings, memories, intuitions, emotions, sensations, images and body states that influence our thoughts and actions. A capable Backstage Director who is a skilled Time Traveler is capable of excelling at academic pursuits, from reading comprehension to written expression.

The Knowledge Architect's Meaningful Mind

This capability takes a child's natural ability and fascination with factual information and transforms the child into a Knowledge Architect who constructs systems of meaning. The Knowledge Architect is a systems thinker—structuring big pictures, arriving at take-home messages and sensing themes. We have an innate need to gain factual knowledge that, especially with the advent of the Internet, can rival our need for food. Education should nurture this hunger by shaping it into big pictures. Instruction evolves from simply the delivery of content to developing systems of understanding.

The Reasonable Judge's Ethical Mind

Children constantly make judgments about themselves, others and their environment. This primal ability helped us make quick decisions about friend or foe, safe or dangerous, good or bad. This response can be transformed into the Reasonable Judge, helping children make fair, reasoned and ethical decisions. Reasoning is fragile, especially in children, often detached from intuition and knowledge. It is prone to errors, biases and distortions that cloud our minds. Fair and ethical children are able to make healthy decisions that benefit themselves as well as society.

Emotional, Social and Self-Awareness Capabilities

Nothing consumes as much brain power or is as important to learn as understanding and regulating one's emotions and social relationships. Humans are uniquely social beings with many ingrained capabilities, from empathy to self-awareness. Learning social and emotional skills isn't an easy task. Many homes are emotional battlegrounds and many schools behavioral control facilities. Parents and educators alike are realizing that developing happy, well-adjusted children who can regulate and learn from their emotions will grow individuals who have positive interactions and will be self-aware.

The Caring Mind Reader's Insightful Mind

This capability relies on our innate ability to express empathy, develop emotional insight and understand the thoughts and feelings of others. The Caring Mind Reader is a person who cares, takes multiple perspectives, assesses intentions and anticipates actions. The Caring Mind Reader is capable of understanding herself and her role in social interactions.

The Inclusive Friend's Social Mind

Human beings are intensely social beings but we struggle with balancing individual beliefs, ideas, emotions and needs with those of groups and society. The Inclusive Friend is capable of positively participating in groups while balancing individual and social needs. One of the most important ideas from recent neurological research is that the human brain is a social brain. Much of our enhanced cognitive capacity is devoted to navigating the emotional and social complexities that arise from living in large groups. We need large brains to perform complex cognitive, emotional and social activities such as building trust and cooperation, negotiating, solving conflicts and putting group needs before individual needs. The social bonding that is so critical for infants must be guided so children can participate in groups productively.

The Balanced Mindful Juggler's Mind

This capability is based on an innate sense of self, the desire to understand who we are and live a balanced life in an unbalanced time. Balanced Mindful Jugglers are aware of their thoughts and emotions and are aware of themselves. They are able to learn from disappointments and confusing situations, avoid disordered thoughts and unproductive emotions and gain a sense of purpose and direction.

Creating Capabilities

We will spell out each capability in a separate chapter where we explore its Advanced Primal nature, the big idea behind the capability and, most importantly, how to develop it. The methods we suggest to develop the capabilities all arise from the Advanced Primal capabilities that exist in most caring adults. We are not starting from scratch; we are working with both the child and the adult's innate abilities. The capabilities are developed not by specialized instruction but by changing the relationship and the nature of adult interaction with children. We are not forcing change on children but creating subtle changes in adults' behaviors that can profoundly influence a child's growth and development.

To combat our instructional urges to modify children's behavior, the source of incredible friction with children and teens, we will focus on changing the parents and teachers' behaviors first. This is as simple as changing how adults talk to children, approach their experiences and engage their attention. It will require a reexamination of the adult-child relationship. When we do try to change children's behavior it will be subtle, aiming only to redirect cognition, promote positive emotions or encourage questioning. When content, facts and knowledge need to be transmitted we will offer methods equally as gentle, but ones that are powerful forces for shaping learning in school and during free time.

All this is done with minimal stress and anxiety, as capabilities are best developed slowly over long periods of time. There are no tests to prep, no homework to complete or distant goals to achieve. The learning capabilities are meant to be accessible to all children and their parents and teachers as they don't require ample resources. They are not grounded on the premise that a white, upper-class lifestyle is the only way of gaining ability in life. Creating capabilities mimics how parents help a child discover a passion or a teen develops an internal strength. We want all the adults in all children's lives to rediscover the simple joy of nurturing child development, free from the worries of reaching some fantasized milestone a decade down the road.

Most capabilities are hard to teach but easy to develop over an extended period of time. Taking a class on embodying thought or subconscious learning strategies would be counter-productive. Instead, the capabilities are developed using a distributed learning approach. Distributed learning, providing small bursts of practice or activities over an extended period of time, is one of the most proven and effective paths to learning. It is a great remedy for Instructionism's reliance on massed instruction, where a unit of study is presented intensely over the course of a week or so—often leading to a "learn and forget" cycle. Distributed instruction promotes long-term retention and diminishes learning and test anxiety, making it an ideal way to create capabilities.

Beyond Child-Centered Play and Adult-Dominated Instructionism

For decades, education and parenting have been consumed by a number of wars, most prominently reading and math wars. Another source of conflict has been the tension between child-centered and adult-dominated approaches to schooling and parenting. The adult-dominated approach is embodied in Instructionism. Child-centered approaches rest on the belief that children can figure out what they need to learn with little adult help. In its extreme form, children are left to play with few rules or adult interactions. Child-centered approaches are known for excesses, including over-reliance on individual needs and innate capacities for children to motivate and self-direct learning.

The Learning Capabilities Framework takes a different view of learning and success. It takes the middle ground between adult-dominated and child-centered parenting and instruction. It creates a new model for the relationship between the child and adult, one that helps both parties learn and find meaning together. The most positive, nurturing of relationships that promote learning, problem-solving and the creation of meaning are when older children and adults act as loving mentors, tutors, demonstrators and guides, working, playing and learning together.

Simple actions, called *Small Moments*, are used to develop the twelve capabilities. Small Moments are changes in a parent or teacher's behavior that strengthen the interaction between adult and child. Small Moments help adults shift their concern from how children behave to how children learn. They are ways of caring for children by working side-by-side as co-learners, mentors, coaches and guides. They provide gentle nudges that have a purpose, such as heightening curiosity and creativity, focusing attention and motivation or changing perspective. They rely on both parents and teachers' innate ability to nurture and their desire to advance a child's capabilities.

Small Moments don't have to be large, expensive or special, nor should they dominate a child's life. They can be as simple as changing the rules of a game, breaking a household routine, pointing out a relationship or discussing a topic from a unique perspective. They take but a moment, as long as it takes to ask a question, point out a problem or look freshly at a situation.

Capable Children

A Learning Capabilities Framework does more than instill twelve individual capabilities. It does more than develop the three critical abilities of continuous learning, problem-solving and constructing meaning. It does more than support an "inner, other and autonomous" framework. It creates capable kids who are flexible, adapting to ever-changing situations. Children, teens and adults need broad capabilities that they can apply in malleable ways, responding to changes and challenges and thus growing into children, teens and adults who flourish. Our children will need to learn and respond to life's challenges in a flexible and creative manner.

A Learning Capabilities Framework requires that all children have the opportunity to develop capabilities in a fair and equal manner. All children should have the same access to experiences, situations, interactions, activities and other learning opportunities that nurture the capable kid in every child. These opportunities are not restricted only to children of wealth, material and social privilege. They don't require special classrooms, expensive toys or private tutors. Zoe, Mia and Daniel differ based on outdated ideas of academic achievement but are on equal footing when it comes to developing capabilities that enrich them as children and, in the future, as teens and adults.

Part 2

. . . .

Engaged, Embodied and Experimental Capabilities

5

....

Children as Curious Explorers

If there is one thing that allows us to learn, problem-solve and find meaning, it is exploration. Learning through exploration is clearly one of children's greatest assets. From a baby's incessant gazing, touching, tasting and examining of everything with which he or she comes into contact, to our exploration of inner and outer space, we are a species that is immensely inquisitive, with near-limitless interests. The natural-born Curious Explorer in each child propels much learning, helping to gain knowledge about our world, adapt to change and understand the complexities of our fragile existence. Our inquisitive nature is behind most of our great discoveries about the natural world and allows us to explore our inner life. Parents, teachers and other caregivers should put a high priority on helping children develop the Curious Explorer through childhood, the teen years and into adulthood. We should guard against practices that dampen children's exploratory nature.

Humanity's primal capability to explore is special in many ways. We have minds that are not only curious and inquisitive but hold unique learning capabilities. Science writer David Dobbs tells of the meeting of Captain James Cook and the Tahitian chief Tupaia in 1769. In Tupaia, Cook found the answer to the question that had troubled him on his journeys: how could humans without European technology settle the distant islands of the Pacific in scattered settlements with no outside contact?[1] Tupaia carried a map in his mind of the locations of all the major island groups of the South Pacific. Tupaia's culture developed this map during their two thousand year exploration of the Southern Ocean. This was more than static knowledge that Tupaia possessed as he was able to navigate to distant islands, which Cook quickly exploited, while returning easily to Tahiti even on cloudy days with the accuracy of a compass.[2]

We find this impressive ability to explore in almost every child at birth. Nowhere will you find greater inquisitiveness, a desire for experience and the urge to make fresh discoveries than in babies. They don't go on long journeys to distant lands or contemplate trips to Mars but their toddling, crawling, clawing and suckling allows them to make wonderful discoveries about their environment, body, emotions and relationships. From birth, or possibly before, exploring and learning are the same for young children.

The Curious Explorer's abilities start early, with the development of the brain, body and senses. The baby's physical experience in the womb, as well as the mother's physical and emotional experiences, dramatically influences the brain. Science writer Annie Paul Murphy's book, *Origins,* explores the amazing learning capabilities of unborn children. Even before birth, experience profoundly shapes the brain, with the nervous system developing at an incredible rate.[3] The numbers alone are staggering. A baby is born with about one hundred billion neurons, with an average of about a quarter million neurons created every minute from conception to birth. A newborn baby's brain has almost the same number of neurons as an adult brain but, unlike almost all other mammals, the human brain isn't fully developed at birth. The British educator John Abbott states, "If pregnancy was to go to its natural term it would last 27 months, and the baby would never get down the birth canal."[4]

A fully-formed brain isn't receptive to learning. Abbott notes that a baby's brain is only 40 percent developed at birth. A full 60 percent of a human's brain development is dependent on experience—the emotional, social and environmental situations that they are exposed to during life. If we had a fully-formed brain at birth we would be limited to simple conditioned learning, relying almost solely on instincts. The flexible response of our nervous system to the environment and experience is the neurological key to our immense and adaptable learning abilities.

A baby's brain may have the same number of neurons as an adult brain, but it hasn't developed the interconnections between neurons, or synapses, that form as a result of experience. It is these trillions of connections that give us our unending and flexible ability to learn. These trillions of synapses are an amazing feature of a child's mind, comparable in number to all of the sand grains on every beach. Far more amazing is the ability of the brain to reconfigure these connections based on experience and changes in the environment, enabling all the primal abilities and advanced learning capabilities of our children's minds. Psychologist Gary Marcus, author of *The Birth of the Mind*, says that while it is significant that children are born to learn, we should look at how nature, nurture, brain structure and experience work together: "Nature provides a first draft which experience then revises."[5]

The expansion of children's brains and mental capabilities is driven by an instinctual hunger for information, explanation and understanding that is propelled by a child's immense inquisitiveness. Our mind's five hundred learning and problem-solving modules allow us to learn from almost every conceivable experience. This is the foundation for our first capability, the Curious Explorer, the most fundamental learning capability. The Curious Explorer, be it a baby at play or a teenager pushing the boundaries of her environment, arises from children's natural desires to know, learn, wonder and investigate. Curious Explorers crave meaningful experiences that come from examining the many worlds we inhabit.

Educational psychologist David Geary believes that both adults and children possess folk knowledge, an innate capability to learn, about four worlds: the physical world, the living world, the world of psychology/emotions and the world of social interactions.[6] This is why children love to interact with toys and animals and respond so readily to smiles and scolding. Childhood curiosity and experiences propel children to learn about these worlds and learning naturally aids their acquisition of folk knowledge. With further learning and sophisticated experiences, this primal curiosity grows into advanced learning in fields as diverse as physics, history, psychology and philosophy.

The Capable Curious Explorer

Our goal for creating capable Curious Explorers is to provide all children with rich and meaningful experiences, both positive and challenging, that engender learning and nurture their curiosity and inquisitiveness into an experimental mindset. The capable Curious Explorer continually learns and derives meaning from life's problematic, mundane and amazing experiences. In its mature form, the Curious Explorer holds a continuous fascination with experiences and engages in a lifelong learning journey while maintaining a child-like curiosity with ever-changing psychological, physical, emotional and social situations.

Born to Explore and Experiment

To develop the Curious Explorer we need to look beyond neurons and synapses, which only record and process experiences. The Curious Explorer is embodied in children such as Mia, the child who is academically average. What age was Mia when Melissa told her daughter's teachers that she had developed a fundamental grasp of physics? How old was Mia when she learned two languages and mastered many comprehension strategies, including cause and effect, predictions and inferences? How many birthdays had Mia experienced by the time she developed a core philosophy based on a range of basic existential experiments using statistical analysis that resulted in testable theories? How mature was Mia before she began to investigate the role of emotions in human relations and predict the outcome of social interactions? Would you be surprised if we told you that Mia did all of this before she turned three? Can we put away the notion that children are blank slates now?

These are just the capabilities that almost every child is able to develop from an early age from experiences and experiments with the four worlds. Kids may be dependent physically on adults for decades but that is so that their minds are free to learn, problem-solve and discover meaning. Alison Gopnik has deeply researched the amazing capabilities of babies for decades. In her book, *The Philosophical Baby*, she shatters many of the myths about how young children learn, problem-solve and derive meaning from their experiences and interactions.[7] Gopnik challenges the work of pioneering child psychologist, Jean Piaget, who believed that the minds of young children were consumed by irrational, simplistic and egocentric thoughts. In Piaget's view, adults have to fill this void. Gopnik shows how Piaget's blank slate, Instructionism, was built on dozens of adult biases about cognition based on misconceptions about young children's limited language ability and childlike ways of thinking.[8]

Gopnik and many others have found that kids in diapers have cognitive, perceptual, emotional and social capabilities that parallel those that Melissa found in her three-year-old. Children don't just experience their world but derive meaning from almost every exploration and interaction. They aren't just explorers but experimenters. They constantly ask "why" questions. Their minds are able to extract large amounts of information from often small events, making inferences and establishing not just associations but causality. In fact, babies are really scientists in diapers. Gopnik explains, "Children learn about the world in much the same way that scientists do—by conducting experiments, analyzing data, and forming intuitive theories of the physical, biological, and psychological realms."[9]

Psychologist Kristy vanMarle has shown that babies have an innate understanding of Newtonian physics. Far from being born without any knowledge of the world, children are born with very specific and sophisticated knowledge that is drawn out by experience. They don't just link the motion of their hand with the movement of a ball but that it moves with a defined direction and speed based on the applied force. They then use this most fundamental concept of physics to understand the properties of physical objects and gravity. Their innate knowledge is readily drawn out from routine experiences that adults hardly notice.[10]

Like Gopnik, vanMarle uses "looking time" techniques. Similarly to children with ADHD, newborns and infants tend to look longer at novel and unexpected events; Babies will look at a purple apple more intently than a red one. vanMarle has found that babies can classify objects based on their physical characteristics, a sophisticated cognitive function.[11] Not only can babies distinguish solids from liquids but they classify objects based on their cohesiveness. They are fascinated by objects that are not quite liquids and not quite solids. If a substance is gelatinous, they will explore it more intensely, possibly making an experimental mess in the process. They understand that solids are solid and are surprised when apparently solid objects allow things to pass through them. vanMarle finds that salt shakers and sieves fascinate children, because they seem to violate physical laws.[12]

VanMarle believes that gravity holds a special place in every young heart. At first, babies understand that objects like tables can block the effects of gravity. Then they start dropping things. The high chair becomes an essential laboratory tool for experimenting with gravity. To parents these activities look like child's play. But to evolutionary psychologists these activities form the framework for our most advanced scientific and philosophic forms of inquiry.[13]

Babies also have the ability to learn about the much more unpredictable and constantly changing world of emotions and social interactions. Babies are born with innate knowledge of how facial expressions and emotions are linked. Shortly after birth their eyes quickly learn to focus on eyes and faces to read expressions. Our natural response is to smile and respond empathetically. These small experiences teach babies and young children the emotional communication that is at the heart of social interaction.

Babies use both positive and negative emotional interactions as experiments to learn social cause and effect. You may think they are just throwing peas on the floor under their high chair but they are inferring cause and effect and making and revising hypotheses about how the social and emotional worlds work. They collect data on word frequency, facial reactions and emotions and, when they see a familiar pattern of interaction, will respond in a similar way.

Young children's experimental approaches to learning are supported by another primal component—their caregiver's evolved ability to nurture learning. Our ability to guide, teach and encourage our children's growth and learning has given our species an evolutionary edge. The social nature of humans adds to this advantage by placing great importance on child-rearing and education. Even with an extended period of growth and guidance, our children have so much to learn that it must be accelerated by skilled and capable caregivers. Our long investment in children to protect, guide and nurture them is one of the defining features of our species.

Without these universal learning interactions, our children wouldn't learn language, which is dependent on a rich and varied exposure to "Motherese," the distinct way that adults talk to children. They wouldn't learn emotional or social skills if adults didn't have a deep attachment to young children and have the innate and learned capability to express empathy and compassion. Our children wouldn't develop incredible control over movement, including tool use, without universal patterns of play and support that adults provide. We will further explore the child-adult learning interactions as we define other capabilities.

Enriching the Middle Years of Childhood

The nature of learning and experience undergoes a number of transitions as young children enter the middle years between early childhood and adolescence. The middle years, now dominated by elementary school, have often been viewed as a period of slow and uninteresting growth, lacking the fascinating growth of the first five years or the dynamic changes of the teen years. Researchers and educators now believe that this is as biased a view as the blank slate fallacy regarding young children.[14] If we examine the middle years with open eyes, they are actually a special period of social, emotional and cognitive growth.

As science writer Natalie Angier states, the middle years are "a time of great cognitive creativity and ambition, when the brain has pretty much reached its adult size and can focus on threading together its private intranet service — on forging, organizing, amplifying and annotating the tens of billions of synaptic connections that allow brain cells and brain domains to communicate."[15] Angier points out that the middle years are the period when children refine their attention, discover new interests and motivations and learn the positive aspects of emotional regulation. The middle years have long been the time when children develop basic autonomy with advanced cognitive skills, including the ability to plan, solve problems, reason clearly and think creatively.

The power of the middle years has been obscured in recent decades as compulsory traditional schooling has grown in importance. The switch of learning environments from home to school places new demands on children's minds. The nearly effortless learning of early childhood, dominated by play and intimate interactions, gives way to effortful learning of abstract material. Learning through living experience gives way to learning largely dependent on memory. Young Zoe learned through play, side-by-side work, storytelling, conversation and social interactions. Zoe in her middle years relies increasingly on making and recalling memories—memories that are often detached from experience. Learning experiences that only required a combination of perception and imagination are supplanted by more abstract learning laden with concepts, symbols and ideas. If Zoe was born in most places a few generations ago, the idea that she would spend much of her middle years learning to read, write and learn pre-algebra would have seemed absurd.

The middle years have also traditionally been times of great responsibility and growth, forged from new experiences and deepening inquisitiveness. Anthropologist David Lancy, author of *The Anthropology of Childhood*, has studied the middle years in many cultures and believes that middle-class, elementary-aged children live in a very constrained and limited world, deprived of a multitude of meaningful and challenging interactions and situations.[16] While Zoe, Daniel and Mia are walking in a single file line down halls with their social interactions, conversations and interests heavily controlled by school culture, in earlier times they would be subjected to more engaging experiences and responsibilities. All three would be constantly interacting with older children and adults, learning, problem-solving and becoming more knowledgeable about the ways of their cultures.

If we want children to develop critical capabilities and an "inner, other and autonomous" framework, we need to question our constricted, culture-bound conceptions of childhood. The American way of parenting, as Lancy points out, where adults heavily invest emotional and physical resources in children without the support of an extended family, is rare. While we rightfully reject child labor and other exploitation of children, we fail to see "the extraordinarily diverse forms that children's development has taken" in other countries.[17] Steven Mintz of Columbia University, a colleague of Lancy, says, "our increasingly narrow notions of what constitutes a normal childhood...[prevents us] from envisioning alternatives to the over-pressured, over-organized, over-commercialized world that today's middle-class children inhabit."[18]

The Teenage Curious Explorer

We know that babies have wonderful minds and second graders are capable of impressive feats of cognitive, social and emotional development. But what about the teen years? Do the innate capabilities to learn, plan and act smartly really disappear in the fog of hormones, emotions and impulses? The prevailing view among child psychologists and educators during the last century was that adolescence was simply a problematic stage of life. However, as we saw with babies and kids in the middle years, these are outdated adult perspectives.

Here again researchers have discovered that the teenage behaviors adults find so challenging are really just more powerful expressions of the human capability to learn by experimenting. Nature provides teens with a late surge of primal learning that is designed to complete the "inner, other and autonomous" plan. They are learning how to use their minds and bodies in mature ways, experimenting with emotional, sexual and social interactions. Rather than passing judgments about teen behavior, parents and educators need to understand that teen experimentation, even risk taking, is critical to the development of advanced capabilities and mature minds.

As with young children and those in the middle years, the current, culturally-prescribed way of raising and educating teens too often ignores both their primal and advanced capabilities. Again, it blinds us to the diversity of shapes that teen lives can take. While state and national educational administrators are concerned with how math and reading scores fare on the international economic stage, they are ignoring the overwhelming needs and capabilities of teens. This creates significant problems for teens today. Currently, American teenagers have suicide rates that are triple those of a generation ago.[19] Our rates of teen pregnancy are three times greater than those of German and French teens.[20] Rates of depression and substance abuse are also exceptionally high. These cold facts alone should cause us to rethink how we see the teenage years.

Robert Epstein, psychologist and author of *The Case Against Adolescence: Rediscovering the Adult in Every Teen*, believes that adolescence is an artificial period that has little value in its current form. It causes unnaturally high rates of conflict with adults, compromises academic progress and forces emotional stress on teens and adults alike:

• •

In more than 100 cultures around the world, teen turmoil is entirely absent; the serious problems of American teens are the creation of a culture that infantilizes young people and isolates them from adults…Teen problems in the United States are caused by a host of factors related to the artificial extension of childhood: poor role models (peers and media icons), peer pressure, isolation from adults and conflict with parents, mandatory schooling, a lack of control over their lives, and so on.[21]

. . . .

Epstein believes that we should not treat teens as immature adults but should instead acknowledge their abilities, including their drive to learn and achieve. They have leadership abilities and develop talents and knowledge from the practical to the theoretical. Adults should run their own experiments to gauge a teenager's ability to engage in new experiences and handle greater responsibilities and challenges. Adults should examine their protective instincts that may have served their younger children well, but are over-cautious and controlling toward teens. To take advantage of the unique learning, problem-solving and meaning-making experiences that define the teen years, mature peers and adults should gently guide teens through learning experiences, not just mark behavioral limits. We should judge teens on their individual ability and understand that teens across time and cultures have demonstrated far greater capabilities than they are allowed to demonstrate at home, in school or on athletic fields in the United States.

Most teens are ready to make complex decisions and solve difficult problems. Yes, they need guidance with "risky" behaviors, relationships and sexuality. While adults feel pushed away by increasingly independent teens, teens are concerned about being controlled. While they naturally gravitate toward their peers, they need help becoming role models who can question the toxic aspects of media-fueled teen culture. Epstein and his colleagues have developed a test of "adultness," the Epstein-Dumas Test of Adultness (EDTA), which identifies areas in which teenagers are ready for mature activities. It measures skills, knowledge and abilities that indicate a teen's readiness to enjoy greater freedom. These range from knowledge about road and sexual safety to relationships and self-care.[22]

Let's look forward and see how Daniel will use his innate and learned abilities to be an experimental Curious Explorer in his teens. He will be testing his parents, conventions and rules and solidifying newly-learned knowledge with personal experience. He will be testing himself physically, socially and emotionally, trying to develop theories of how David Geary's four worlds work. He will seem more unpredictable as he pushes further, revising and generalizing basic principles into hypotheses which will undergo more testing and refinement.

Daniel's parents embrace the questioning, rethinking and challenges to their beliefs and solutions as a sign that Daniel is developing the more advanced strengths of the Curious Explorer. These strengths are curiosity, inquisitiveness and a growing desire to find out on a deeper level if what he has been taught is true. Questioning, testing, hypothesizing and revising one's beliefs make up the heartbeat of the Curious Explorer. Teens repeat this cycle of inquisitiveness until the Curious Explorer makes the most critical of discoveries—general theories about how the worlds work. This may be the most powerful path to learning—one that works for babies as well as graduate students.

Do we promote this path to learning at home and in schools? Do we support teens in their quest to be Curious Explorers or do we pour on more Instructionism, telling them how to act, filling their heads with information pulled from the past and asking them to accept it without questioning? Are teens' academic and free-time experiences helping them develop independent learning skills and reflect on their own beliefs and behaviors?

There are few areas of a child's life that are not transformed during the teen years. Primal abilities that have lain dormant suddenly arise. Daniel's sleep cycle will shift, allowing him to be active later into the night. Anthropologists assume that this allowed earlier generations of teens to take greater adult-like responsibilities, possibly including working later on domestic chores, night travel or guarding against predators and invaders. Staying up late at night traditionally involved greater risks and responsibilities, exposing teens to more challenging experiences and experimental learning situations. Could this be the adaptive value of the more competitive, aggressive and risk-taking behavior we see in teens?

Even at age ten, Daniel has taken interest in video and physical games that involve greater imagination, heightened challenges and physicality. They provide simulations and small experiments that help him define his rapidly-changing physical, mental and social limits. Many of the experiments will end in failure or embarrassment, which will hopefully fuel more informed tests in the future. Other experiments will occur in social settings as teens seek approval and positive feedback from peers.

Experiences That Lead to Learning

While children learn from an incredible range of experiences, not all experiences lead to learning. The idea that experience and education are not always linked is central to the thinking of the great education philosopher and psychologist John Dewey. In *Experience and Education*, Dewey argues that not all situations and activities lead to learning. Dewey saw the disconnection of experience and education both in traditional schools with instructional mindsets and in "progressive" schools that were fueled only by playful activities.[23] Dewey faulted traditional schools not because they didn't provide learning experiences but because the content, subjects and methods "reduce the material of education so largely to a diet of predigested materials."[24] The experiences that students have in traditional schools are of a "defective and wrong character—wrong and defective from the standpoint of connection with further experience."[25] The experiences of traditional education relies heavily on other people's past experiences and not on the present or future experiences of students.

Dewey felt that progressive schools, which promoted independent exploration, were simply a reaction and not a solution to the Instructionism of traditional schools. To truly make learning through experience meaningful, progressive schools, like many of the constructivist, discovery and play-oriented schools of today, should incorporate Dewey's two critical components of learning experiences: continuity and purposeful interaction. Dewey felt that "educative experiences" should embrace continuity, a connection to the past and future. They should "prepare a person for later experiences of a deeper and more expansive quality. That is the very meaning of growth, continuity, reconstruction of experience."[26] Experiences shouldn't be just isolated incidents, but spark interest and "arouse curiosity, strengthen initiatives and set up desires and purposes" to expand understanding and knowledge.[27] He felt that continuity in traditional education was tied too much to the past, largely ignoring children's interests, motivations and curiosities. Progressive schools erred in the other direction, placing full weight on immediate desires and the situation that the child was engaged with, ignoring past findings and insights and/or deeper explorations in the future.

Dewey's second critical component that links learning to experience is purposeful interaction. Ideally, meaningful experiences include interactions with the child's inner world, other people and the environment. The inner state of the Curious Explorer, including motivations and interests, is full of critical educational experiences. Learning interactions have a social component, either with fellow Curious Explorers or adults. Dewey felt that both traditional and progressive schools failed to provide experiential situations that were true interactions.[28] Traditional schools neglected the social and motivational nature of learning experiences, while progressive schools often left them to chance, with no thoughtful purpose in view. Dewey felt that progressive schools needed more planning than traditional schools to ensure that experiences were both interactive and continuous. Where traditional schools could get along by relying only on "customs, institutional habits and established routines," progressive schools needed a clear philosophy of experience and purpose to transform experiences into learning.[29]

The Place for Adults in Educational Experiences

The final tension between traditional and progressive parenting and schooling involves the role of adults in developing the Curious Explorer. The social nature of learning experiences requires interaction, communication and collective explorations. Dewey also felt that both progressive and traditional schools limit the role of adults in learning experiences. Traditional schools, deeply rooted in Instructionism, take an adult-dominated, blank slate approach. Progressive schools put their full faith in children's abilities to create their own learning experiences, viewing adults as intruders who limit children's freedom to learn. Dewey felt that unrestricted and unguided activities don't equate to freedom. Sidelining adults and teachers deprives children of connections to the past.[30]

In Dewey's era, the most famous of progressive schools was Summerhill, founded in 1921 by A.S. Neill. Neill believed that traditional schools force children to fit their model, molding the diverse shapes that children come in into round holes. Family and school structures are often so rigid that children must conform to narrow behavioral and academic expectations that deny their capabilities and interests. Neill's response was to allow children to control schools freely in a democratic manner.[31]

Neill felt that adults were coercive forces in children's upbringings: "The function of a child is to live his own life—not the life desired by anxious parents...not a life according to the purpose of an educator who thinks he knows best."[32] Free discovery, constructivist and play-centered schools have adopted a similar view of adult involvement over the intervening decades. Perhaps the best expression of Neill's views today is found in developmental psychologist Peter Gray's book, *Free to Learn*. Gray takes an evolutionary view of play, showing that it has been a critical component of childhood learning in many times and places.[33] He promotes play as a cure for children who have grown depressed, anxious and bored by restrictive school and home environments. Gray strongly believes that the antidote to over-scheduled, over-taught and over-controlled children is to limit adult interactions with children during play except when they request it.[34]

Gray and Neill's schools, as well as most alternative forms of schooling, including progressive, discovery, inquiry, problem-based and experiential schools of the last century, are based on Constructivism. The basic tenet of Constructivism is that learning is an active process where children construct and organize their own understanding. This well-supported idea forms a natural alternative to Instructionism. However, the second tenet of Constructivism is more problematic; children best construct meaning with minimal interference from adults. This tenet is as much a reaction as a solution; the cure to adult-centered Instructionism isn't child-centered instruction free from adult guidance. Rather, it is building a new relationship between children and adults that nurtures learning in all its forms.

Psychologist Richard Mayer has reviewed the role of adults in the many forms that constructivist schools have taken over the last century. Mayer and others have found that minimal adult intervention, or minimal guidance, is most successful in cognitively-engaging situations, but of limited value in experiential situations—minds-on situations like group discussions rather than hands-on activity like free play and discovery learning.[35] Constructivist and discovery approaches have repeatedly been shown to be significantly strengthened when children receive adult guidance and mentoring that includes feedback and suggestions and promotes questioning and redirection.

Paul Kirschner, John Sweller and Richard Clark have also examined the role of adults in constructivist education, providing extensive support that adult guidance provides marked cognitive and learning benefits.[36] Limiting adult guidance compromises a key aspect of learning; children need background knowledge, memory prompts and framing to learn from experience, which are best provided by more experienced children and adults. Fundamentally, learning takes place when experience connects to past experiences and background knowledge stored in long-term memory. This process takes place in working memory, where we do much of our active thinking. Children often need mentors to provide background information and the relevant contexts to trigger a learning experience. When an experience is largely composed of physical and sensory activity there is no guarantee that cognitive and memory activity will rise. Learning from experience becomes more difficult during the middle and teen years as learning becomes more conceptual in nature, centered on ideas, images, concepts and opinions. This increases the need for more knowledgeable and experienced help.

Creating the Curious Explorer

Clearly the Curious Explorer is an important capability for learning, problem-solving and making sense of the many worlds that we inhabit. Inquisitiveness, curiosity, a sense of wonder and an experimental mindset are critical to creating the Curious Explorer. We have seen that experience translates into learning when it connects to the past and promotes interactions with children's inner and physical worlds. It arises from social interactions, benefiting from mentors, coaches and guides who can help children construct learning. The Curious Explorer extracts much from the immediate experience by integrating it with background knowledge and the urge to search deeper. If we nurture these primal factors then our children should maintain a life-long love of learning. Too often the Curious Explorer in all of us is forgotten in the quest for achievement or when the urge to learn more becomes secondary to the urge to earn more. Boredom, distraction and avoidance limit the Curious Explorer's capability. Experience is reduced to repetitive activities that do little to ignite passions and interests.

. . . .

SMALL MOMENTS THAT CREATE THE CURIOUS EXPLORER

As with all capabilities, the Curious Explorer is best developed neither by the extremes of Instructionism or Constructivism, nor by heavy-handed, anxious or controlling parenting or hands-off detachment.

Transform activities into experiments. Daniel's parents often ask him, "What would happen if…?" questions. "What would happen to birds if we killed all the insects?" "What would happen if you grew up in an apartment complex in a city?" Parents and teachers can set up true, open-ended experiments where the results may be unexpected or without a fixed answer. Most school laboratories aren't experiments as much as they are reports on activities with known outcomes and black-and-white answers.

Promote inquiry. Inquiry draws out the experimental side of learning. Help children ask questions, create hypotheses, investigate more deeply and construct knowledge by combining immediate information with existing knowledge. The advanced form of inquiry involves investigating and proposing solutions to real-world problems, issues and controversies. It involves questioning and rethinking habitual ideas and actions.

Nurture Curiosity. Regardless of the activity or the subject, promote the urge to know more, see in a different way and dig deeper. Curious children have a hard time being bored. They desire more experience, knowledge and learning in both general and specific ways. Help general interests to become specialized interests. Children have a natural tendency to develop expert-like abilities in specific areas, from types of toys or animals to genres of music and scientific specialties.

Embrace Trial-and-Error Learning. Overcoming mistakes, errors and manageable problems are essential ways of learning from experience. Sheltering children from problems or valuing detached happiness is harmful to learning and deprives children of essential life lessons.

Prompt Inferences. Inferring, making educated guesses and drawing conclusions are critical to developing the experimental mindset. Humans are very good at taking small amounts of information and using our imaginative powers to find patterns and meaning. Provide or point out small bits of information, clues or hints that the child can use to make inferences.

Value Experiential Play. While we have stressed that only certain types of experience are beneficial, there is great benefit in playful experiences. Peter Gray believes that play has either been removed from many children's lives or it is structured by adults, hindering the development of critical cognitive and social skills.[37] Some children who have had little play experience or haven't embraced their curious and inquisitive side may need guidance with play.

Take it Outside. There is also great benefit in being outdoors, a city park, an open field or deep woods. Children need to be reconnected not just with experience but with nature, as our ability to learn was largely forged through our interaction with and connection to the natural world. As Richard Louv, author of *Last Child in the Woods: Saving Our Children from Nature-Deficit Disorder*, so clearly points out, being outside is critical to our mental and physical health and provides a vital connection for children.[38]

6

The Action Character

If you watch children explore, for instance Mia as a baby crawling around her apartment, middle-years Zoe engaging in an animated discussion with her friends or a teenage Daniel on his daily expeditions around his neighborhood, you would most likely overlook one very important aspect of their learning experience—the vital role their bodies play in learning. The body and physical action are an integral part of our brains and minds. Nowhere is this truer than with children. They are Action Characters who learn through embodied experiences built on sensory perception, movement, feelings and constantly shifting body states. While children can passively absorb information, learning comes easily when they are mentally and physically engaged. Mia may sit idly during lessons but during her free time she becomes active and art, dance and song spring to life. Zoe shows good cognitive skills in the confines of school but when she moves, builds and explores she is transformed into an amateur architect, inventor and scientist. When Daniel is physically active his senses come alive, his attention and memory sharpen and he enters a deeper level of understanding. He ceases to be a brain with academic issues; instead, he becomes an embodied mind that is learning, problem-solving and making connections with ease.

If we want our children to develop vital learning capabilities, then we need to embrace the body's role in learning. It is through the body that we actively learn, stimulating the unique two-way communication system between the brain and the psychological world within and the social, physical and natural worlds in which we are embedded. Sensation, perception, movement, feelings, muscle tension and a host of bodily bio-chemical signals are the language the body uses to communicate with the brain. Even the amount of sun exposure, the weather and the feeling of clothes on our skin influence our state of mind. As Sharon Begley and Richard Davidson wrote in their book, *The Emotional Life of Your Brain,* "communication between the mind and the body is bidirectional, and not only at the simplistic level of feeling upset if you stub your toe or blissful when you get a massage. The brain, it turns out, uses feedback from the body in basic information processing."[1]

Children who are connected to their bodies and senses experience greater cognitive, emotional and physical well-being. Many of the surest ways of focusing the mind, softening emotions and calming excessive and repetitive thinking are through the body. Most anti-anxiety medicines are muscle relaxants. Exercise is a proven anti-depressant. Yoga and massage release stress and tension, while the cognitive benefits of body awareness and meditation have been documented by many fields of research.

This isn't surprising as the brain is largely devoted to processing and controlling the muscles and movement, physiological activity and sensory perception. Three of the four regions of the cerebral cortex are largely devoted to communicating with the body; the occipital lobe is devoted to vision and imaging, the auditory cortex to sounds and speech and the parietal lobe to sensory integration and skilled movement. Even the fourth region, our specialized frontal cortex, devotes much of its anatomy and processing power to sensory-motor processing and planning and controlling physical activity.

The body and brain are inseparable, each a vital part of our embodied mind. The body and brain work together to construct meaning and give life to our thoughts. The concepts, ideas and abstractions themselves are deeply linked to bodily experience. Embodied learning enhances memory and attention and, as we will shortly see, is critical even to reading comprehension.

The Action Character is possibly our most misunderstood and underappreciated learning capability. In a world consumed with cognitive skills, brain development and language, it is easy to exclude the body from discussions of learning and cognition. While many non-Western cultures have long embraced the wisdom of the body through practices such as yoga, meditation, dance and martial arts, the West is biased toward thinking and brain-based cognitive skills over embodied actions. To turn the inborn ability to learn through action into a capable Action Character, children need greater connections to the wordless worlds of engaged activity, experiential learning, perceptual awareness, imagination and embodied cognition.

For the Action Character, the limited cognitive skills that we gather together under the term "thinking" are deeply embedded in the body, for abstract thinking arose from brain-body interactions. Annie Murphy Paul, a fellow at the New America Foundation, believes that advanced cognitive processes evolved from existing sensory, motor and simple cognitive systems and not as new, separate modules: "From an evolutionary perspective, our brains developed to help us solve problems in the real world, moving through space and manipulating actual objects. More abstract forms of thought, such as mathematics and written language, came later and they repurposed older regions of the brain originally dedicated to processing input from the senses and from the motor system."[2] The idea that thinking is separate and superior to perception and action does as much to inform our understanding of children as the blank slate theory.

The Capable Action Character

The well-developed Action Character is able to engage life in an active, involved manner, utilizing the body as a vital part of the mind and as a source of learning, problem-solving and meaning. The Action Character has the ability to turn abstract ideas and concepts into movement and action through the body and in the environment. The Action Character is physically aware of his body, physical health and movement.

Daniel is an example of a Capable Action Character. At an early age, Daniel's embodied mind was handling messages from his body and senses, transforming basic information into the rich reality we experience in the world. Daniel's brain and his body engage in a back-and-forth game between receptive and expressive capabilities. Experience and sensation elicit active responses. His eyes take in light as 2D images on his retina and his brain creates a 3D simulation of the visual world. His ears pick up simple sound vibrations and turn them into language. His body transmits internal sensations including balance, position and motion and they become skilled movements.

The play between receptive and expressive messages allows us to take in tactile sensations and respond with art or feelings of joy. We can observe and envision, listen and sing, taste and bake. Daniel's parents can sense his thoughts, ideas and feelings from his gestures, facial expressions and bodily postures and movement. From these physical cues they can instantly infer his emotional state and respond with words, feelings and action.

Of Body and Thought

If we want to create capable Action Characters, we first must question why children often look more like sculptor Auguste Rodin's famous *The Thinker*, immobile and consumed, than active, engaged and physically-aware learners. We should value action as much as thought and understand that the development of movement and motor skills, from crawling and walking to painting, drawing and building with blocks, is as important as learning to speak. Bodies aren't passive transportation machines for brains that are too often lost in thought. The body, including physiological functions, muscle movement, feeling and sensory perception, is a critical element of a child's learning mind.

The brain isn't just a passive receptor of bodily sensation. As a child in the age of black-and-white movies, co-author Bruce loved to watch sci-fi "B" movies. The plot sometimes revolved around an evil scientist who desires to understand what humans would be like if we were only brains. To answer this question the scientist excised a poor victim's brain and, to aid in communication, its ears and mouth; he confined the diminished being in a large beaker. The brain was then connected by wires and electrodes to a computer that simulated the body and environmental sensations. The madman used the computer to trick the bodiless brain into believing anything his evil heart desired. Deprived of a body and sensory and motor links to the greater world, the brain was easily deceived, reduced to powerless anger.

These movies exploited a deep philosophical question: does the brain merely create simulations based on sensory and bodily input or is thinking by itself a higher force? The brain is easily swayed by bodily and sensory experience; think of the effect of the color, shape and feeling of clothes on children's emotional states. Researchers pull off embodied tricks on the brain by having subjects force a smile by holding pencils between their teeth or sitting up straight as if excited. Just these simple bodily postures trick the brain into happiness.

We want children to be good thinkers and possess great knowledge but we should be aware of the interplay between body and brain. We should be equally concerned with thinking, action, ideas and activities. We should be concerned not just with what children learn but also how they apply it through meaningful and purposeful action. It's equally as important to assess our children's understanding as it is to assess their ability to transform thoughts into behaviors, actions and constructions.

Perceptual-Action Learning

The ability to learn from action is the birthright of every child. It will take decades of active experience to create a capable Action Character who is far more interesting than any cartoon action figure or superhero. This is clearly visible in infant Daniel's physical engagement with his environment. Almost every time he touches, grabs, throws, chews and kicks, he is feeling and sensing his way to learning. From the moment he first grasped his mother's hand and their eyes met, Lea could have shouted out, "Look! Daniel's first embodied learning experience." Of course, this would be true for most moments of a baby's life that involve interactions with people, places and things.

Young children's lives are uniquely embodied. With limited language and abstract cognitive skills, they rely almost totally on movement, sensory perception, bodily feelings, emotional responses and active experiences to learn. While their learning largely takes place at the subconscious level, little children are hardly passive consumers of information. They plan, execute and test one action after another, all the while building very important parts of the body, brain and mind, including coordinated muscle action, sensory pattern recognition and speech. Throw baby Daniel a ball and, at first, he will observe its basic properties while poking, biting and pushing his way to understanding. Then he will actively investigate the nature of the ball and experiment with its properties. As a result, learning will occur.

The basis of Daniel's embodied learning abilities is perceptual-action learning. This innate ability relies on sensory perception, bodily movements and young children's simple way of paying attention, remembering and learning. Perceptual-action learning is critical to the development of the Curious Explorer and the Action Character. It immerses them in a rich sensory world of internal and external stimuli, physically extracting information from the environment and deriving critical lessons from every stimulus and action. Daniel moves, sees, feels, hears and then investigates, testing through sensation and physical interaction, learning basic facts, predicable patterns and responses. He expands his perceptual-action learning repertoire every time he investigates a toy or grabs a kitten's tail.

Daniel will rely on perceptual-action learning throughout his developmental years. It will be a critical factor when he observes demonstrations in class, watches his mother model the proper use of a vacuum cleaner or participates in social and biological interactions at the neighborhood park. This isn't surprising as children easily learn when they are fully attentive and physically engaged.

The nature of perceptual-action learning does change over time, especially when children develop abstract thinking. Slowly, concrete reality experienced by the body, unfiltered perception and attention acquire new dimensions as thoughts, images, concepts and ideas are imagined to have a life of their own. The solid sense of grasping a stick gives way to the imaginary world of thoughts. This abstract world is deeply embedded in the embodied mind, arising from a foundation of perceptual-action learning and the sensory-motor network.

Evolution rarely starts from scratch when it selects new functions; instead it continually adapts existing structures and functions rather than selecting untested creations. Our newer abstract thinking abilities are founded on our older sensory-motor, brain-body system. We use the same network to visualize a painting as to physically view it and the same auditory circuits to replay a song in our minds as to listen to it. These imagined events don't just reside in our brain; our eyes may shine brightly as we think about a picture and our body may sway to the music.

Embodied thinking is easy to see when we deal with emotionally-laden thoughts. All thoughts are intertwined with emotions and emotions play out in our bodies. We can sense this in the physical fatigue of a stressful day or the buoyant feeling of an enjoyable discussion. Reading fictional descriptions of touch, smell, movement and emotion trigger the same sensory-motor areas aroused by the parallel physical experience. Our shoulders tense up, our skin crawls and we experience physical disgust in our stomachs when we read about disturbing situations. Reading about positive events may cause a smile or send a tingling sensation up our spines.

Language the Body Speaks

Perhaps we can see the nature of embodied thought best when we engage our most abstract ability, language. Language provides a rich example of how thought isn't confined to our minds and, though abstract, is grounded in our concrete connections to the world. Sentences are constructed using objects, places and living things (nouns) and actions (verbs), giving language a physical backbone. Nouns have physical properties and spatial relationships while verbs reflect motion, situations, activities and experiences—all the domain of the body. Prepositions begin life as bodily relationships. Above, below, in front of and behind are relationships between the body and space. Adjectives and adverbs enhance our ability to describe the physical and sensorial properties of objects and people.

Metaphors are the spice of language, exploiting almost every aspect of the physical world. We turn "up" into "more," as in "the price is high" and into control, as in "I'm on top of it" and even to mean hard to comprehend, as in "over my head" and "out there." Physical relationships are a source of rich metaphors, such as "out of reach," "on one hand," "over the edge," a "close relationship" or "grasping" an idea. Love, metaphorically, is a temperature, hot or cold or a warm glow. Motion can define time, as in the saying "time flies," or craziness, as in "rushing around with our heads cut off" or being on track—"moving in the right direction." Listen for metaphors in simple conversations or complex lectures and you will certainly find embodied language.

Like thought and language, emotions use "the body as their theater," according to neuroscientist Antonio Damasio.[3] In children and adults, emotions are a rich source of information and are critical to learning, problem-solving and understanding. Emotions live in the interactions between body, brain and environment, fine-tuned by evolution to aid learning and problem-solving. We tend to notice children's negative emotions more forcefully than their positive affect as they signal problems that demand our attention. While emotions often cause social and psychological distress, children's lives are enriched when they become aware of all colors of emotions as ways of learning. This requires a sensitivity to how emotions are expressed in the body, since every emotion has a corresponding feeling in the body. We feel the lightness of a joyful discussion, the tightness of a tense confrontation and the pain of rejection. Children are particularly sensitive to their feelings, showing them physically for all to see.

Bringing Words and Ideas to Life

Mia, because of her average academic ability, struggles with symbols and abstractions, but has a decided bodily advantage. She is well aware of her body, its movement and emotional states. Mia is healthy, fit and very comfortable with her physical presence and image. Melissa helps her daughter manage emotional upsets, anxiety and stress on a physical level by making sure that each day contains enough small moments of relaxation, tension release and body awareness.

Mia, like many children, has always been a natural-born performer. She loves to turn little situations into mini-plays, acting out thoughts, feelings and interactions. Melissa has removed much of the furniture from their small apartment to give Mia a larger stage. Mia uses this stage not only to act but also to sing and dance. If she has something heavy on her mind, the thought or feeling will grow into a complete play with an evolved storyline. Melissa prompts Mia to act out short stories, poems and even events from history books.

This may seem like child's play, but expressing ideas and emotions through bodily action can offer a deeper level of comprehension than discussions, including reading comprehension. Reading is near and dear to most parents' and teachers' hearts and has been the focus of intense efforts at home, in schools and in the halls of Congress for decades. Despite the time and effort put into literacy, there has been very little improvement in reading comprehension scores in the last thirty years, as measured by the National Assessment of Educational Progress, often called the nation's report card. In recent years, reading comprehension scores for high school students have been falling.[4]

It's not surprising that many children struggle with reading in English, as this language has an unusually difficult sound structure or *phonology* and is difficult to understand in both written and spoken form. English is the hardest written major alphabetic language to translate into speech. While speech arises with sufficient exposure and practice, reading is an artificial skill; until recently, most languages lacked written scripts. Only in the last hundred years has literacy been afforded to more than an elite few. Our nervous system lacks a distinct neural network for reading. We are only able to read because areas devoted to understanding spoken language have been hijacked to understand written language. As a result, English-speaking nations around the world have significant numbers of children who struggle with reading.

We should look to the body to address the difficulties that English literacy (and second language acquisition) presents and the minimal progress in reading scores. Psychologist Arthur Glenberg, a leader in the field of embodied cognition, has a special interest in how the body and movement promote learning, especially reading comprehension. Glenberg's research shows the value of integrating the senses and movement to simulate the action embodied in print. Glenberg has shown that, much like the way we understand situations, experiences, interactions and language, reading comprehension is embodied, enhanced by bringing mental simulations to life.[5] He has exploited these abilities to produce marked improvements in reading comprehension by turning words into action.

Glenberg grouped some historically resistant readers—Native American children raised in poverty under the difficult conditions of the reservation—and permanently raised comprehension scores. These gains generally surpassed those derived from traditional methods, such as oral discussions. Glenberg raises comprehension scores by using a method that mimics Mia's living room acting: children read short stories and then, using toys, paper cut-outs or digital illustrations, simulate the action.[6] This helps readers imagine and physically interact with language, a perfect "Big

L Learning" experience. Glenberg believes that active, embodied learning works, because language comprehension, which encompasses most of reading comprehension, requires the projection of meaning onto the perceptual, emotional and movement systems of the mind. This brings words built of abstract symbols to life. Glenberg has also produced sizable gains in reading comprehension by having children mentally manipulate images to simulate the action in stories.[7]

Memory Isn't for Memorization

For Mia, with slight but limiting memory problems, learning to simulate ideas alleviates the problem. As she moves and imagines, learning becomes solidified and the memory problems disappear. Glenberg suggests that we have the wrong idea about memory, one that has hindered Mia's academic performance. He argues that memory is not for memorization, but is an aid to perception and action, helping us interact with our environment.[8] The misuse of memory is easily seen in the concerted effort that children must use to store math facts, historical dates, spelling lists and reading strategies disembodied from action or experience.

The Teenage Body of Knowledge

As Mia matures into a teen, she will enter into a time of expanded physical activity that will further transform her active learning abilities into those of a capable Action Character. For teens, the relationship between physical exercise and learning grows even stronger. In addition to being critical to a teen's mental and physical health, exercise provides another way of activating the brain-body mind.

Exercise by itself has a pronounced effect on mental well-being and academics and counters the effects of the long hours children spend inactive and inside. Physically active and fit kids outperform unfit children academically, as do active overweight children. They pay greater attention and have sharper memories then their inactive peers.[9]

Perhaps in the past, in more challenging environments, we responded to challenges through increased physical and cognitive output, by boosting the brain and the body in tandem. Our primitive fight-or-flight responses produce hormones that enhance physical and cognitive readiness.

Researchers have discovered a number of growth-promoting proteins that have the dual role of increasing both the growth of neurons and physical endurance. The separation of the mental and the physical may be a comforting abstract concept but has little meaning in the real lives of children.

Mia's mother Melissa is exploiting this dual approach to cognitive and physical readiness by encouraging Mia to participate in physical activities and sports. Melissa goes one step further by helping Mia develop body sense, an awareness of movement, feeling, body position and internal state. Body sense connects the physical and cognitive, the brain and the body, and transforms exercise into an activity that enhances her mind. Psychologist Alan Fogel believes that "noticing your muscle exertion, movement, coordination, breathing, weight shifting and any emotions that come up (good or bad) improves fitness, well-being, cognitive function and social relationships over and above those conferred by exercise alone."[10]

Melissa uses body sense as one way of helping Mia understand the wonderful and powerful central physical changes of the teenage years, including awareness and comfort with a sexually-maturing body. She helps Mia navigate changing physical and social relationships and helps her understand the role that stress and anxiety play in the body.

Speaking with Our Body

Melissa also employs movement to aid in learning by consciously gesturing as she talks, thinks and moves. These small hand movements provide a critical communication aid for babies, who learn the meaning of many words by watching the way that language and gestures work together. Children have been shown to better understand instruction from parents and teachers when the adults use hand gestures and body motions.[11] Gestures form a silent, subconscious form of language for children and adults. Even apes use specific hand gestures to communicate; researchers have deciphered thirty-six communicative gestures in chimpanzees.[12] Our gesturing is not random either but plays a vital role in the expression of emotions and helps us work out complex thoughts. We often use gestures when we lack the words to express our thoughts and emotions.

One of the most profound examples of the power of gestures in learning and communications is sign language. It uses hand and body movement and facial expressions as communication for the hearing or speech impaired. Throughout history, sign language has arisen as naturally as speech in communities of deaf people, with over a hundred distinct forms of sign language in existence today.

One example of the primal nature of sign language and embodied communication occurred in Nicaragua around 1980 when groups of deaf children were brought together in a single school, having been displaced from their individual communities due to war. Their school attempted to teach them Spanish by finger spelling and lip reading, which turned into another failure for Instructionism. The children developed sign language outside of the classroom, as they socialized on the playground, during meals and on bus rides. The resulting language has a street-wise grammatical structure with a complex use of verbs and nouns.[13]

Having the Thought in Hand

Our hands can aid in communication in other ways, especially through drawing and handwriting. Children have often learned these skills as domestic activities, but over the last few decades they have migrated to the classroom. Unfortunately, drawing and handwriting are slowly being squeezed out of the school day by other activities that appear to be more academic in nature. Print handwriting is still part of the primary grades, but cursive and artistic drawing are falling by the wayside. The use of keyboards and tablets is also limiting the time spent at home and school on these critical embodied skills. This hinders the development of the Action Character, as most children can learn cursive and drawing with enough deliberate practice.

These fine motor skills have a profound effect on the development of other academic skills, including reading, as well as critical body-brain circuits. Here again, the development of sensory-motor skills grows in tandem with communication skills; handwriting and written expression are tightly linked, as are drawing and creative arts. Psychologist Virginia Berninger has found that children who wrote by hand consistently produced longer writing samples that were conceptually richer than those who typed. Students who wrote by hand were also better at idea generation and showed greater use of working memory, a sign of active thinking and intelligence. Berninger also found that students who were trained in cursive showed greater self-control—that learning to control the fine movements in the hand led to greater ability to control other aspects of one's behavior.[14]

Hands On, Minds On

Another way that child and teen learning can be enhanced by movement is through hands-on learning. This type of learning should follow the same principles we discussed in the last chapter for experiential learning: hands-on learning should center on purposeful interactions that stimulate children to pursue further learning. Adults should allow students the freedom to experiment while providing hints and feedback.

Hands-on learning that follows these principles is a staple of Montessori schools. When co-authors Bruce and Caitlin wanted to see embodied, active learning in action, they spent time in Bruce's wife's (Caitlin's mother's) Montessori classroom watching her guide students in the discovery process that has proven its power for almost a century. Arthur Glenberg's reading comprehension manipulatives are one of dozens of such materials in the classroom. She prepares the materials and shows her students how to interact with them. When they understand the basics, she steps back and lets the students practice and learn with only occasional adult guidance. The hands-on activities present a surprisingly large amount of factual information and content knowledge, especially in science and math.

Building Action

A new slant to hands-on learning is the Maker Movement, which is an updated version of the building and breaking activities that were part of an idealized childhood a half a century ago. Then, in garages, basements, kitchens, shop classes, home economics classes, backyards and playgrounds, the Action Character spent a good chunk of time taking stuff apart, making arts and crafts and building things out of materials that normally go into recycling and garbage cans. The work and play involved in building things, of working together and being mentored in crafts and skills, are some of the most rewarding learning experiences. Children have a natural inclination to build and create things, using their physical abilities and tools. The mature representation of this primal drive is visible in our architectural and artistic creations, as well as in the thousands of items in a department store.

Bruce has been building since he can remember. Starting with log cabins and building blocks and endless experiments in his parents' kitchen, then progressing to a few forts in the woods, three boats, a house and a barn and finally arriving at a dozen educational software programs, his life has been one building adventure after another. The process of planning, gathering materials, organizing groups of workers, solving endless problems and physically working has been challenging and rewarding for him.

The Maker Movement is an attempt to reinvigorate the joys of making, creating, disassembling and analyzing objects. Maker communities meet in universities or basements. Some have 3D printers and laser cutters, while others rely on material scavenged from construction and industrial sites. Regardless of their source, the purpose is the same; younger children and teens learn how things work and engage in experimental crafting and problem-solving. The method relies on curiosity coupled to an experimental mindset. It also relies on children's creative spirit, imagining and conceptualizing grand things from simple objects. The creations are tested and redesigned, problems are addressed and even the successes are modified and improved.[15]

Kids still love to build things, even in the digital realm, from cities and mines to medieval villages and futuristic fortresses. Technology offers an outlet for children's creative and constructive abilities but will often come up short as far as true physical, social, mind and body engagement. At home and in school digital activity is being used to compensate for physical activity that is an ingrained way of developing the capable Action Character.

The Power of Practice

Another learning process that develops the Action Character is practice, especially deliberate practice that engages body, mind, movement and perception. This type of practice improves performance on a wide range of physical and mental tasks, from wrestling to writing.

Deliberate practice is not like the practice of multiplication facts or spelling words. Deliberate practice is distinguished from play and repetitive activities since it is designed to improve performance. Here again a child benefits from the guiding hand of a more experienced child or adult who corrects, guides and provides feedback without dominating the situation.

Practice should not only be deliberate but should continue beyond the point of the basic skill being learned or the exam being passed. This process, called over-learning, is the reason students who learn to read, write and calculate at an early age have an advantage over students who struggle. Almost every important skill or ability a child needs to learn should be practiced beyond the point of proficiency. Proficient students are over-learning their skills to the point that they become effortless, while the strugglers have limited chances to practice, limiting their achievement.

Scott Barry Kaufman, in his book *Ungifted: Intelligence Redefined*, reviews the research on superior performance and finds that, in many areas, it is not a result of great intelligence or inborn talent. Rather, extended deliberate practice is a critical element in the development of exceptional ability. Chess masters are not born nor do they usually exhibit exceptional memory skills. Rather, they develop the ability to visualize fifty thousand chess patterns through years of active practice that follows a trial-and-error, experiential learning format.[16]

For students like Mia and Daniel with academic memory issues, deliberate practice and over-learning level the playing field cognitively. They practice until their skills are automatic, freeing up their thoughts and memories for deeper tasks.

. . . .

SMALL MOMENTS THAT CREATE THE ACTION CHARACTER

A few Small Moments that help create the Capable Action Character can be integrated into every child's day at home or school. While we discourage adults from demanding that children become more active and embodied, we encourage them to participate, model or engage in parallel activities. Spending fifteen minutes walking, de-stressing, drawing or any of the following Small Moments with children and even reluctant teens will, over time, create the Action Character. Small

Moments are easily added to any school-based or free-time activity.

Parents and teachers should take the long view in developing capabilities. There is no rush and no schedule, but rather years to encourage embodied action, especially action that children have an interest or desire in.

Use the body to respond to stress and anxiety via simple exercises, movement breaks, stress reduction techniques or massages. As time passes, children will become aware of tension and automatically respond without adult prompting.

Promote exercise and movement to counteract the hazards of long periods of inactivity. Adult-organized team sports, especially those that promote high levels of competition, may not be the most productive ways of promoting exercise and movement. Again, children should be allowed the freedom to develop physical pursuits that are interesting and self-motivating.

Act and demonstrate for understanding. Ask children to show you what they mean and recreate situations to explore their meaning.

Ask them how their bodies feel as they express feelings or ideas.

Promote small motor skills like gesturing, drawing and handwriting through deliberate practice.

Develop body sense and awareness to add a cognitive dimension to exercise and movement.

Build, make and create small and large things. Once children graduate from building with blocks and playing with dollhouses during their elementary and secondary years, they often have a deeper desire to build, take apart or create.

. . . .

7

The Fascinated Learner

The Pleasure of Learning

What words do you most associate with education and learning? Probably your answer revolves around concepts such as cognitive abilities, knowledge acquisition or studying. Now, ask your child or student what comes to mind when they hear the word *education*. We are sure that neither you nor the child included "rewarding" or "pleasurable" on the list. If we were to ask Zoe, Mia or Daniel if learning is pleasurable and rewarding, they might respond with a puzzled look, at best. However, these two emotions are arguably among the most important ingredients in learning.

It is easy to see that a baby's playful primal learning or a teenager's passionate pursuit of an interest evokes positive feelings. They will engage in these without the need for external motivation. Yet even the most sophisticated types of learning are deeply intertwined with instinctual emotions and drives, including motivation, desire, pleasure and reward. These emotions are essential ingredients in creating Fascinated Learners and their closely related friends, the Action Character and the Curious Explorer. If we wish to move from primal abilities to advanced capabilities, we must factor motivation and enjoyment into learning. We must consider what grabs children's—especially teenagers'—attention and sparks their interests. At home or school, learning that factors in motivation and interest will be more effective and meaningful.

Engaged learning, even when it involves hard work and extended practice, starts with a child's basic ability to develop interests and pursue pleasurable activities. Fascinated Learners are self-motivated, effortlessly attentive and enthusiastic about learning. When we help children discover the enjoyment of becoming Fascinated Learners, we give them something more substantial than happiness and success—we help them find life-long interests.

Children have an immense capacity to engage cognitive and motivational resources to learn. This reward system is the motivating force behind our greatest and most satisfying capabilities, including interests, passions, talents and practices. It proves the inspiration for creativity, transforming boredom into fascination, distractions into undivided attention and restlessness into focused practice. It helps older children and teens retain their child-like fascination with so many things, big and small. Self-motivated learning engrosses them so completely that they become hard to distract, with fully focused attention.

Like most of the activities that are essential to our survival, engaged learning involves primitive reward and motivation networks in our brains. We can sense how important learning is to survival and well-being by the length of the list of pleasurable learning activities. Children experience positive feelings by learning new information and skills and by exploring abstract ideas. Knowledge gained through deep conversations and social interactions has the potential to be both informative and pleasurable. Capabilities that we will explore in future chapters include storytelling, subconscious learning processes, knowledge construction and self-awareness. They are sources of pleasurable learning. In fact, all twelve learning capabilities we present are intrinsically motivating, interesting and rewarding.

The capabilities of the Fascinated Learner stand in sharp contrast to Instructionism, which has contributed mightily to the wave of inattention, distraction, boredom and depression consuming students and children. The last hundred years of Instructionism have generally ignored motivational factors in learning, hindered children's desire to find interests and passions and done little to inspire a childlike fascination with life. By placing academic and career goals first, we have suppressed our children's natural drive to understand the many worlds they inhabit. Despite these trends, the natural drive to learn and develop interests burns strongly in children and teens. With a little understanding, adults find that reigniting the learning drive is quite simple.

The Capable Fascinated Learner

Fascinated Learners find life enchanting and have the opportunity to engage in intrinsically motivating activities that grab their attention. They are able to develop interests and passions that lead to life-long growth and learning. They are free to pursue interests that are personally meaningful and may contribute to a greater good. They are fascinated by the endless array of problems and opportunities in life, engaging in mundane activities and special explorations with effortless attention.

Kids Aren't Neurotransmitters

We must violate one of our cardinal rules by mentioning specific areas of the brain and neuro-chemicals. It is almost impossible to talk about reward and pleasure without bringing up certain brain networks, specifically the ventral tegmental area, and neurotransmitters, specifically dopamine, which is often misunderstood as the "reward hormone." Neuroscience is a young and evolving field, full of wonderful discoveries and vast simplifications. Our understanding of the reward system is also advancing, as researchers are discovering that it plays a far more complex role than simply linking survival behaviors and pleasurable feelings.

While dopamine is involved in motivation and reward, it also plays a role in a wide range of activities from muscle control to regulating attention. Researchers believe that dopamine is stimulated equally by the anticipation of a reward, such as an upcoming meal, and by novelty, as a post-behavior reinforcement.

The reward system of the brain is complicated, not yielding to simple explanations. We have a tendency to reduce complex behaviors, especially those as complex as learning, to simple, easily-imagined concepts. Reducing motivation, attention and engagement to a single molecule is worse than looking at children largely as brains. The Fascinated Learner has passions, is motivated by goals and will work for years to understand complex information. Reward for hard work or creative efforts may be delayed for years. Someday we will understand these drives but for now we need to take a wider perspective. Children derive a deep pleasure from learning, which should evoke our deep fascination and curiosity.

Dangerous Rewards and Counterproductive Punishment

Pleasure is often viewed not as a motivator but as a danger in need of control. People who care about children, who have an instinctual desire to protect them, struggle to balance their enjoyment with risks. As a result, we attempt to regulate their behavior. Sex, food consumption, clothing, social interactions and drug and alcohol use are high on the long list of pleasurable activities that parents, teachers, societies and religions have traditionally sought to control. It's hardly surprising that a social institution as massive and conformist as formal education tries to regulate pleasure, even at the expense of learning. Endless rules, regulations and punishments are formulated to regulate casual behaviors, including learning activities such as play, physical interactions and conversation. Too often, the motivational needs of learners are subsumed to the maintenance of order. Excessive behavioral controls do little to motivate children or help them to independently find interests.

Children need rules to feel safe and to promote positive relationships. They need guidance as they search for the boundaries between positive and harmful behaviors. They need structures that balance personal needs and desires with those of a group. However, many schools utilize thick conduct manuals that have little to do with education. Too often the controls are based on simplistic and outdated ideas from behavioral psychology. Rules are reinforced by reward and punishment schemes that are of limited effectiveness, especially with teens. Parents and teachers continue to rely on long lists of immediate punishments usually coupled with limited and distant rewards. Often the effect is short-term compliance at the expense of long-term self-regulation.

Parents and teachers may become primarily concerned with children's behavior and succumb to perceived social pressures to control children, rather than promoting their growth and development. Children need to learn to set their own course in life, to regulate their own behaviors. This doesn't happen when they are subjected to endless rules stipulating how they should walk, talk, sit and think. Children will follow rules that make sense and they have the opportunity to freely question the meaning and purpose of regulations.

Educational critic and divergent thinker Alfie Kohn has long been an advocate for ending reward and punishment schemes in schools. His books, including *Punished by Rewards: The Trouble with Gold Stars, Incentive Plans, A's, Praise, and Other Bribes*, and *Unconditional Parenting: Moving from Rewards and Punishments to Love and Reason*, have a simple but profound message: reward and punishment plans rarely benefit children cognitively or psychologically. He says, "Our basic strategy for raising children, teaching students, and managing workers can be summarized in six words: Do this and you'll get that. We dangle goodies (from candy bars to sales commissions) in front of people in much the same way that we train the family pet."[1] Manipulating children with incentives works in the short run but contributes to long-term behavior issues, including declining interest in academics and personal pursuits.

A more pleasurable and rewarding experience for children and adults results when, together, they focus on building learning relationships and search for interests that can grow into meaningful pursuits and passions. The primary goal of parenting and education should be to help children develop meaningful, intrinsically-motivating interests. In school and during free time, children should have the opportunity to develop and pursue these interests. This creates a powerful learning environment and has a secondary benefit—when children are self-motivated and pursuing personal interests, behavioral issues are greatly diminished.

We are not suggesting that teaching and parenting should become the equivalent of eating ice cream, offering children the learning equivalent of empty, but delicious, calories. We are not promoting open-ended liberties embraced by programs that equate play with freedom and learning. Children and teens should be challenged with complex assignments and difficult problems. Teens, especially, need manageable challenges and the chance to test and prove themselves through risky behaviors. The adults in their life should help teens sort out activities that are dangerous without depriving them of a powerful way of learning.

Interests and Motivation

What will happen when adults shift from looking at pleasure and reward from a behavioral standpoint to seeing them as integral to the learning process? Zoe exhibits capabilities accessible to almost every child. Like most children, Zoe finds many activities interesting. As she has grown up, Zoe has retained a child-like fascination with the many worlds she occupies. She is equally intrigued by the changing colors of leaves in the fall as understanding why her brother detests spiders and loves rap music. Rarely do her parents have to motivate her, since she naturally seeks out pleasurable and meaningful experiences. They also don't offer her rewards or subtle bribes, preferring that Zoe discover the intrinsic value in activities. Jan and Jeff put their energy into creating situations for Zoe to explore potential interests.

In school, Zoe enjoys the small bursts of positive feelings that come from giving a correct answer or completing a long-term assignment. Like most children and teens, she seeks acknowledgement and recognition for her efforts, not just her achievements. She values the hard work more than the letter grade. However, it is her deep desire to find out more and to discover how everything from nature to relationships works that is her real motivation.

Another trait that Zoe has retained from her pre-school days is a near-universal fascination with almost everything she encounters. Her parents don't take her on expensive trips or pay for specialized lessons, but Zoe is interested in a seemingly endless list of common events, ideas and activities. She is fascinated by objects (leaves and book covers), nature (waterfalls and fish), ideas (irrational fears and the possibility of life on other planets) and creative endeavors (drawing and origami). She is intrigued by relevant social issues (homelessness and children's rights), entertainment (rap music and jazz dance) and activities (running and kayaking). Zoe is never bored.

When Zoe isn't pursuing her simple interests, she is engaged in her current all-consuming passion, film and video production. When she was eight, Zoe's uncle gave her a hand-me-down video camera and hands-on lessons with free editing software. Zoe doesn't seem to care how much time, effort or hardships the videos involve, often doing tedious editing for hours. It is normal for children to have a slew of general interests as well as a more specialized area of expertise. For Zoe, right now, it is videography.

Meaning, Purpose and Autonomy

Interests that most deeply engage children are usually both rewarding and meaningful. Studies by Paul O'Keefe and Lisa Linnenbrink-Garcia have researched interests and found that we are most engaged when activities are both emotionally fulfilling and deeply meaningful.[2] Film-making is emotionally rewarding but, more importantly, Zoe finds it meaningful. She enjoys creating videos of sporting events, family gatherings or of any of her other interests.

Daniel Pink, in his popular book *Drive*, postulates that motivation has three critical elements: autonomy, mastery and purpose. Paralleling Brighouse's ideas on autonomy, which we discussed in chapter three, Pink says that humans have a deep need to manage their own lives.[3] Controlling people, whether they are seven or seventy, robs them of motivation and meaning, stifling their work intensity and creativity. He proposes that managers, including parents and teachers, put their efforts into creating "conditions for people to do their best work."[4] This gives children the opportunity to find their own interests and the motivation to pursue them deeply. It feeds their drive to learn, be creative and develop mastery.

Parents and teachers are often concerned about the amount of effort that children expend on tasks. This can become a non-issue when children have the opportunity to work independently on activities of their own choosing. Pink quotes Carol Dweck, whose research shows that, "Effort is one of the things that gives meaning to life. Effort means you care about something, that something is important to you and you are willing to work for it. It would be an impoverished existence if you were not willing to value things and commit yourself to working towards them."[5]

Pink's third element is purpose. Echoing Brighouse, O'Keefe and Linnenbrink-Garcia's insistence on the importance of meaning, Pink states that it "is in our nature to seek purpose." While autonomy and mastery are often enough to motive people, "those who do so in the service of some greater objective [are]...the most deeply motivated people... hitching their desires to a cause larger than themselves."[6] Mastery of an interest, skill or concept is a great problem-solving tool, as we can transfer our understanding from one domain to tackle challenges in other areas.

Psychologist David Yeager has investigated the relationship between high school students' hopes, dreams and goals and their desire to contribute positively to society. He has repeatedly found that, initially, teens express self-interested desires, such as getting rich, becoming famous and powerful. Yet, these desires eventually give way to deeper goals, including helping others, benefitting their community or making a difference to society. Yeager finds that self-interest quickly fades, replaced by searching for meaning and a sense of purpose, a significant inspiration for further education. He believes that cultivating a "purposeful learning mindset" results in students who are driven to study, not just for grades, but to obtain long-term significant goals.[7]

We often impose purposes and meanings on children that are superficial, relevant only to adults. We may tell children to study hard so they can get into college, instead of inspiring them to pursue studies that align with their bigger dreams. What children really need is a sense of purpose that includes positive social goals. This is particularly important for children in the middle years and teens. While they may seem detached and self-absorbed, below the surface most desire to gain positive social recognition by making a difference and contributing meaningfully. For example, instead of pushing a college or career goal, adults could start a discussion that explores how teens could benefit society. Do they want to help the sick, solve urban issues, overcome environmental concerns or help people build businesses that solve social problems? Discussions about long-term goals are much simpler when children and teens envision themselves in socially productive roles.

Relevancy

Purpose and meaning offer children a path to relevancy, which answers many of the more troubling questions children have about learning. For many younger children a pursuit simply needs to be fun. As children grow into the middle and teen years they often require that activities be relevant. As they seek a greater sense of identity and meaning in life, simple pleasures need to be fortified with something deeper. This may appear as a rebellious streak, coupled to endless *why* questions that delve into the perceived absurdity and pointlessness of life. Simple requests from parents or teachers seem neither purposeful nor meaningful. There is a period in most teens' lives when they are constantly asking, "What difference does it make?" and "Why do I have to do this?"

Adults may attempt to make topics and activities relevant, but they sometimes fail since children and teens often see relevancy in a very different light. Our attempts to link lessons or activities to children's perceived interests or popular culture often backfire, as we lack the expertise and nuanced understanding of a well-versed teen. In her book, *The Power of Mindful Learning*, Harvard researcher Ellen Langer states that relevancy lightens the burden that teaching places on two critical learning abilities, memory and attention: "Memorization is a way of taking in material when it is personally irrelevant."[8] When information has some connection to the child, then it will be easily absorbed. The intense level of memorization that children are subjected to in schools reflects the general lack of relevancy of the content.

Langer believes that children should be engaged in the search to find relevancy. They should be challenged to find personal ways to make material meaningful. Children do this by using Langer's mindful learning techniques, such as drawing distinctions, finding relationships and establishing different perspectives between their interests, ideas or life and the material.[9] Mindful learning helps students find relevancy by exploring the topic or activity's meaning, both to themselves and from the perspective of others.

Langer has done studies comparing retention of material between students who were actively engaged in building relevancy and those who relied on traditional memorization strategies. The relevancy-building students outperformed the memorizers on a wide range of tasks, including information recall, depth of understanding and creativity.[10]

The Benefits of Engaged Learning

Thinker and writer Annie Murphy Paul has chronicled the benefits that interests have for children and adults. In her article, *The Power of Interests*, Paul discusses John Dewey, a constant source of educational wisdom, to explain why interests are so alluring and educational. Dewey felt that, unlike much of school-based learning, interests make learning effortless, drawing in attention willingly instead of by "forced effort." This drives active, engaged learning: "If we can secure interest in a given set of facts or ideas we may be perfectly sure that the pupil will direct his energies toward mastering them."[11]

When children are engaged in meaningful pursuits, they rarely need encouragement or rewards and behavioral issues fade. The chronic concerns about effort and persistence dissipate as children pursue their passions with amazing levels of determination. The ever-present issue of digital distraction fades as children often become deeply absorbed in their self-chosen pursuits.

Attention and Its Distracters

Motivated, engaged learning offers parents and teachers another advantage: they rarely have to be concerned with one of the biggest challenges at home and in the classroom—attention. Nothing is more critical to learning than attention. When attention is diffused, all other aspects of learning—memory, language, perception, etc.—operate on partial power. Learning experiences that effortlessly draw in deep focus and concentration are key factors in creating the Fascinated Learner.

Children are paradoxical beings, especially when it comes to attention. They swing from effortless attention to total distraction. Their focus is fragile, shifting and easily ensnared by the sight of an animal or the sound of a song. One minute a child can be so deeply engaged in an activity that we struggle to break her attention. The next minute we can become frustrated by her inability to follow a simple directive. Children with no apparent attention issues may be selectively attentive and only able to maintain focus under certain conditions, such as when engaged in interests.

The paradoxical, shifting nature of children's and teens' attention can lead the adults in their lives to hold mistaken ideas about their cognitive abilities. Our first experience with children may reinforce our false blank-slate beliefs, including that babies have very little ability to focus. Psychologists used to believe that babies had very limited capacity to focus, spending most of their time in a type of infant attention deficit disorder, chasing every passing stimulus. Alison Gopnik calls this "the brain deficient baby, the idea that newborn babies are crying carrots, vegetables with a few reflexes."[12]

Researchers and observant parents often learn that babies are more attentive than the adults who care for them. Their attention is a narrowly-focused spotlight as well as eyes-wide-open global attentiveness, finding almost everything in their environment fascinating. They take in experiences in an open, inquisitive manner that is not encumbered by the internal distractions and dialogue that dominate adult consciousness.

Adults who guide children should become aware of how some of their habits hinder attention. Motivations, interests, drives and attention are all inner, primal abilities which children only have a limited ability to control outwardly. When we demand children's and teens' attention, it will soon fade, not because they are disobedient but because we only have their attention because we demanded it. The children in the quietest classroom or the most controlled home are often the ones who are the wildest when released.

As with language development, adults have a profound effect on how attention develops. One of the greatest gifts an adult can give a child is undivided attention. By engaging in activities together without distraction, children develop the emotional and cognitive underpinnings of focus. Outwardly, children learn to focus when they learn to control impulses, resist distractions and refocus effort. Inwardly, we should help older children and teens learn to concentrate, become aware and attentive and become conscious of their thoughts and actions.

Engaging Attention

The contrast between Daniel's inattention in school and fascination when engaged during his free time is both striking and informative. If we understand attention and how it shifts and focuses, then we see that Daniel's attention disability in school and full capability outside is perfectly normal. From Daniel's perspective, schools are a sea of inattention, distraction and confusion while the outside world provides endless and riveting fascination. His classroom is filled with kids to talk to, objects to play with and activities to explore. However, most of the time, they are distractions, not sources of fascination. In his free time, Daniel can explore every interest and actively interact and play with whoever and whatever he wants.

It's not that school isn't engaging or is devoid of interesting activities. Daniel clearly finds parts of each intriguing. The problem is that attention is an afterthought of instruction, not a primary factor in designing daily lessons or national curricula. Lacking a motivational and attentional foundation, Daniel's school day oscillates between engaging and distracting, pleasurable and boring. He is barely able to stay alert one minute and yet can be energetically engaged the next.

Daniel's parents aren't simply observers of their son's attentional strengths and weaknesses. They understand that attention isn't fixed by genetics, like eye color, but continues to develop as children age. Look at the change in attention and concentration from kindergarten to fourth grade or in ten-year-olds to older teens. Researchers and practitioners understand that children can learn to strengthen their attention through specific practices, strategies and activities. Specially-designed computer games improve selective attention and vigilance. Stress reduction practices have been showed to markedly improve attention caused by heavy workloads, weighty decisions, personal conflicts or living in poverty. Mindfulness-based stress reduction programs have consistently been shown to relieve children's tensions and worries and produce marked improvements in their ability to sustain attention.

Mindfulness training for children focuses on general awareness, concentration and attention. Children learn to develop listening and visual attention, sensitivity to the embodied nature of focus and awareness of inner sources of distraction, especially the conversational nature of thoughts and emotions. They may practice focusing on a single image, like the fading sound of a bell or the moment of breathing in.

There is a substantial body of research supporting mindfulness training, as it improves academic and behavioral abilities and, more importantly, a child's well-being. Mindfulness practices help children see that, when thoughts and emotions wander, so does attention. Children who become aware of waves of thought and emotions and the unceasing bodily feeling and sensations begin to develop the inner ability to attend and engage.

Daniel's parents have made mindfulness and other types of attention training an integral part of their son's daily life. However, they don't feel that these practices must be separated from his normal interests and activities. Daniel's interest in nature provides a natural ground for developing attention. For countless generations, nature has provided the perfect environment for attentive minds to develop. Children's eyes and ears become animated when they venture outside, be it into deep woods, an urban park or a backyard garden.

Daniel, with support from his parents, has become aware of the sounds of the woods and has learned to identify the calls of over twenty common birds. This in turn has prompted Daniel to learn the names of ten tree species and observe the different ways insects move. One of his teacher's favorite mindfulness lessons is the "two-minute observation," which builds visual attentiveness. For this brief period, Daniel pours all his attention into watching a candle burn, a fish swim or a cloud move across the sky. He does this with his parents when they walk in the woods, make bread or watch movies. Once, Adrián asked his son to sort eating utensils with his eyes closed, based on their shape. Lea challenged him to learn to identify the taste of seven green spices.

Through these formal and spontaneous activities Daniel has developed greater control of his attention, finding ways to engage in otherwise uninteresting situations. He has learned to resist temptation and has developed strategies to dampen distracting impulses. He understands that his attention waxes and wanes under influences that he can't always control. He has learned how to monitor shifts in focus without criticizing himself. Best of all, his parents and teachers recognize the shifting, sometimes uncontrollable nature of his attention. They no longer look at his attention issues as a deficit but as a force to channel to engage learning.

Novelty

From young babies to mature teens, the surest way to grab children's attention is novelty. Our minds are naturally drawn to the new, unexpected and out of the ordinary. This primal response has great survival value, shifting attention to the unexpected and different or potential threats and rewards. This innate response is exploited by the Internet, seemingly designed to distract. Web pages constantly flash new and different sights, compelling us to hop and skip endlessly among bits of alluring information and graphics.

The typical classroom can be as distracting as the Web, full of bright images and shiny objects, chatty friends and attractive technology. Repetitive academics and habitual lessons often don't stand a chance.

Introducing novelty into the home or classroom in a meaningful way can be a transformative tool to easily energize and engage children. Mindful learning expert Ellen Langer puts novelty to good use in her approach to mindfulness. From her perspective, mindfulness is the "process of actively noticing new things" which makes us sensitive to present experiences and changing conditions, which naturally creates engagement.[13] Through the simple act of bringing attention to the present, learning experiences transform from heavy-headed thinking tasks into engaging, alert activity.

Langer has developed a number of effective techniques that promote mindful learning, which she calls *sideways learning*. An alternative to "top down" Instructionism and "bottom up" experience and practice methods, sideways learning aims to maintain mindfulness by keeping the observer's attention actively shifting.[14] The key is keeping students alert to changes, or open to trying something new. Children who are open to the new and different are not stuck in their ways, or held back by fixed opinions or reflexive habits.

Sideways learning develops children's sensitivity to differences. It helps them look deeply for distinctions rather than superficial sameness. Children are drawn into material, ideas and activities when they are asked to look for uniqueness, like the special characteristics of a character in a book, a tool or an animal. Examining shifting context, such as settings, characters and event changes, also builds mindfulness. Finally, changing perspectives, from moving to a different seat at the dinner table to taking the viewpoint of an opponent, is a powerful way of using novelty to focus attention and give children a fresh way of investigating and understanding.

In the Flow

Mia, sitting passively in the back of the class, has no diagnosable attention issues. She may spend significant parts of the school day sitting quietly, daydreaming. Yet suddenly, at home and in school, the situation will change. Mia will become so engrossed in an activity or idea that her attention and emotional and cognitive energies will almost fuse with the situation. When she is engaged in dance, reading about any of her interests or just doing simple things with full attention, Mia enters into one of the most wonderful, yet often overlooked, states of mindful learning called *flow*. In this simple state that children slip into with ease, they become completely focused and detached from time and anxiety, more concerned with the immediate experience than self-centered desires.

Flow happens when children engage in their interests and examine novel and self-motivated activities. Children move into flow when they are challenged or motivated to find an answer or overcome a problem. Children are emotionally focused when experiencing flow, so boredom and anxiety negate it. Engaging in "Big L Learning" experiences and creating capabilities often lead to this state of calm, centered attention. Storytelling, deep listening and embodied experiences offer children easy access to flow.

Mihaly Csikszentmihalyi's life's work is the psychology of optimal experience. He has examined the role flow plays in learning, advocating for its place in education. Flow is a condition that makes learning fascinating and nearly effortless, an optimal learning state. With cognitive, emotional and motivational resources fully engaged, learning naturally follows. However, Csikszentmihalyi warns that we shouldn't teach flow or try to make it happen. All parents and teachers can do is remove the barriers that prevent flow from occurring.[15] We can offer children interesting ideas and experiences that challenge them in engaging learning environments. The final element that promotes flow is autonomy; children should feel that they have some control over experience.

Flow is why children love games—board games, card games, physical games, sports games and digital games. Games are highly interactive and engaging, providing problems to solve as well as offering children independence and control of their actions. Games are intrinsically interesting, with clear purposes and goals. They permit children to let go of self-conscious feelings and enter into an almost timeless existence. If this seems exotic, Csikszentmihalyi has researched flow of student experiences in Montessori and traditional school settings. While he found that in both settings learning experiences are quite conducive to flow, not surprisingly, Montessori classrooms provided many more experiences where learning became its own pleasant reward.[16]

. . . .

SMALL MOMENTS THAT CREATE THE FASCINATED LEARNER

There are many ways to spark children's natural desire to learn and to engage the full powers of their minds, or mindfulness. There are three types of mindful learning. The first is Ellen Langer's view that lessons can be structured in a way that heightens children's intrinsic interest, attention and motivation by making distinctions, taking different perspectives and noticing differences.[17] The second way is based on positive psychology by developing learning situations that develop the deep absorption of flow. The third way is mindfulness practices that help children become aware of their bodies, feelings and thinking by practices such as Yoga and meditation.

Adults should let children take the lead in developing interests, uncovering motivations and finding meaning and purpose.

Watch for small interests and what captures your child's attention. Look for activities that promote flow. Encourage your child to pursue these interests.

Expose your child to varied situations and activities. While trips to sporting events and social and cultural activities are productive, so are simple activities such as making and sharing meals, watching traffic, engaging in simple social activities, playing games or just mindfully attending to everyday events.

Autonomy is for children and teens to develop, not something that adults can impose.

Allow your child or your teen to engage in manageable risky activities and behaviors and to seek out novel experiences. Children who are open to exploring new experiences often have an edge in learning and creativity.

Point out differences and distinctions and help your child develop sensitivity to different contexts, circumstances and perspectives that influence motivations and levels of interest.

Help your child find his own meaning and relevance in activities. Avoid rewards and behavioral controls when a child loses interest or rejects activities.

. . . .

Part 3

. . . .

Sense-Making Capabilities

8

The Creative Dreamer

Children live in an imaginary world and so do you. This is not something to lament but something to celebrate. Imagination is both play and one of children's greatest abilities, a critical mind-enhancing skill. Imagination fuels our ability to construct concepts, ideas and mental pictures. It feeds one of our most talked about but misunderstood capabilities, creativity. Imagination and creativity are fundamentally problem-solving processes, powerful ways of melding divergent ideas in new and meaningful ways.

Without imagination, our thoughts, ideas, memories and images would be robotic. Children's emotional and cognitive development depends on it. Imagination helps teens conceive of their present and future selves and adults dream of brighter possibilities. Every worry, hope and plan involves imagination. Every time we remember the past or think about an idea or person, the Creative Dreamer comes alive.

Imagination is also associated with daydreaming, mind-wandering and boredom, abilities that are wrongly frowned upon by our productivity-obsessed academic and corporate culture. Most of all, imagination helps children and teens create the largely fabricated "real world" that gives their life meaning.

Imagination is a key ingredient in one of the most complex "Big L Learning" pathways. The path to a Capable Creative Dreamer begins with sensory and bodily awareness, which is transformed into perception and makes sense of sensory input. Perception is the raw material for concepts such as images, words, ideas and stories, the primary way that we make the direct world of sensory perception abstract. Concepts are an imaginative layer we superimpose on reality—the translation of sensation into words, images and ideas. The end result of this learning pathway is creativity, which arises from divergent ideas, novel concepts and vivid imagination.

The Creative Dreamer goes from sensation to imagination automatically. The speed at which children's minds turn sights, sounds, touch or feelings into concepts is amazing. Some children develop advanced imaginative, conceptual and creative abilities, thus gaining long-term academic and personal benefits. However, we largely leave this capability to the whims of the assumed curriculum or ignore it: we falsely believe that there is little adults can do to develop the full capabilities of the Creative Dreamer. Kids love to dream, imagine and create and, given the opportunity and a guiding hand, go deeper into this capability.

The creative capability is so strong that we rarely just linger with the sensations, almost always translating our impressions into concepts and imaginative creations. Take a moment and pay attention to your current surroundings. Are you able to just take in the sights and sounds or do you automatically label objects, classify situations and judge conditions? A sight is rarely just a sight, a sound just a sound or a feeling allowed to live on its own. Sensation is almost always immediately followed by perception, the incessant need to find patterns, make connections and elaborate on almost every sight, sound and feeling.

Perception also rarely stands alone, as our minds naturally wander into the world of concepts, which is full of words, ideas, images and symbols. From concepts springs imagination that takes our minds to places our bodies can only dream of going. Creativity arises from concepts and imagination, as well as a head full of daydreams, subconscious intuitions and wandering thoughts. Creativity arises when we discover novel associations, see unusual patterns and discover new relationships.

The path from sensation to creative thinking happens with little effort in everyday situations. The sound of a baby crying makes us search for its cause and meaning. We automatically classify the cry, infer its meaning and search for a cause. We imagine the situation, envision our response and begin to look for alternative solutions should our first idea fail. We give the sound a name—crying—and link it to an emotionally rich concept—hunger. We grab a bottle, hoping it will be the solution.

If the tried-and-true method fails to rectify the problem, we must diverge from the familiar response and look for a creative answer. Should we feed the baby more often, keep her closer or change our sleep cycle? Is it time to call the doctor? The benefit of creativity is that it offers fresh solutions when imagination and ideas fail to solve a problem. Automatic responses work most of the time but when they don't, we must think outside the box.

The ease with which we go from a sight or sound into flexible problem-solving mode appears deceptively simple. Yet developing the Creative Dreamer is so vital to "Big L Learning," problem-solving and meaning-making capabilities that it can, at times, engage half of our cerebral resources. Neglecting to nurture this wonderful capability at home or school deprives our children of one of the richest ways to use their minds.

The Capable Creative Dreamer

The Creative Dreamer has the ability to process sensory information with heightened perceptual capabilities. She is aware of her sensory and imaginary environment and capable of creating rich concepts and mental representations from it. The Creative Dreamer has the opportunity to imagine the imperceptible, reflect on the past and envision future scenarios, plans and goals. She has the freedom to daydream and mind-wander, to use imagination to spark creativity and dream up new concepts, ideas and images. She is open to new experiences and seeks alternative solutions and divergent perspectives. She has access to materials and activities that promote imaginative and creative capabilities, from science fiction, music and visual arts to multicultural activities. The Creative Dreamer is free from social pressures that wish to exploit her conceptual and creative powers.

Creatively Imagining Reality

Imagination, concept formation and creativity allow children to build mental representations of the many worlds they inhabit, creating understandings of the cognitive, emotional, social and physical realms. Imagination helps us explain the unexplainable by building mental pictures and representations of things. Children's minds don't deal directly with the real world, but instead with mental representations of it, which are fundamental to everything we learn. They create meaningful illusions or copies of reality, by turning heads full of words, images, concepts and ideas into working models of the world. These representations serve us quite well, just as maps allow us to navigate through complex terrain. But like maps, they are only rough approximations of reality.

Recreate the mental image of your last vacation or birthday party. This image is as real as a 2-D map. Do you remember the conversations you had or just vague impressions, perhaps a few words or, more likely, emotions and feelings? Most likely you can tell an imaginative story about the event, with general descriptions of characters, locations, dramas and resolutions.

Mental pictures are so sophisticated that they are critical to the scientific process. While we may think of science as cold and rational, a realm of facts and theories, it is heavily dependent on imagined worlds. Dmitri Mendeleev used imagination to turn his knowledge of the elements into the periodic table, a grand representation full of patterns, classifications and categories. Imagination is how Charles Darwin conceived of evolution, pulling together millions of bits of information into a cohesive model of the natural world. This is how Rosalind Franklin, James Watson and Francis Crick visualized the grand model of the double helix of DNA, figuring out how four chemical building blocks could be configured to provide the blueprint for every molecule in every organism on the planet.

We can only know about historical events, far-away places and cellular functions through images and concepts. Our lives are enriched by fictional stories, science fiction, dramas, movies and "reality" shows. Large areas of life are imagined, from social constructs to political opinions and religious beliefs. Do we really know what a president believes, the thoughts of long-dead religious figures or why we follow social conventions? The person we conceive of as our self is largely imagined, as our sense of "self" is mostly based on mental images, selective stories and memories that are simplifications of our complex bodies, minds, emotions and social interactions. How else could we understand complex and distant concepts if we didn't use imagination? How could children understand the lifecycle of a butterfly, the death of a loved one or why their teeth fall out without imagination? It is a wonderful and rich way of understanding the many worlds we inhabit.

The Imaginative Mind of a Child

When Mia was just a newborn baby, she lived in a world of pure aware-ness and unfiltered experience. We can imagine that she simply saw, felt, heard and tasted without added layers of understanding. What was it like for six-week-old Mia to experience a pet, take a bath or look into her parents' faces? Cats didn't have names, dogs weren't classified by shape and objects weren't judged or categorized. Art made no sense and music had no meaning. Mia's world was largely undifferentiated, as her senses ran together. She didn't experience the feeling of a brain separate from the body or a self separated from the world. She lived in a world of movement and sensation, responding only through instinct and reaction.

Slowly Mia's life began to take on extra dimensions. Mia's senses and movements took on a second life as she started to interact with the world rather than just passively observing it. She began to notice patterns, that certain reactions were linked to actions, and she unconsciously made associations between a sight and a sound. Sensations began to be conceptualized as names, ideas and relationships emerged. Objects took on functions and behaviors elicited responses.

By the time Mia reached her first birthday she was able to use one object to represent another, she turned cups and spoons into drum kits, blocks became buildings and peas transformed into projectiles. As Mia developed language, the associations grew stronger; objects acquired names and movements were given verbs—this is the next level of conceptualization. The colorful sphere she called a ball transformed into an object of play or attack. The yellow food she liked was called a banana, but it could also represent a phone, gun or bat.

When she became a toddler, Mia engaged in pretend play, using toys to mimic the actions of others. She mimicked her mother making a cup of tea, gave her doll a bath and pretended to be a doctor. Like many children, Mia had an imaginary friend, which is associated with greater creativity and social awareness. Mia imbued her friend with an astounding array of characteristics and emotions, giving her a complete personality—quite a feat for a toddler. She knew how her friend reacted to different situations and gave her well-defined likes, wants and needs. Like most children with imaginary friends, Mia developed greater social and emotional skills, learning how to relieve stress and anxiety while becoming a more caring friend.

As Mia grew older, the depth of her imagination grew. Like many children, Mia was attracted to the scary and the downright frightening. Monsters lived under her bed, faeries cast evil spells from her closet and a wicked elf haunted her mother's car. By the time she reached elementary school, Mia was fascinated by stories about orphaned child wizards, apocalyptical threats and supernatural menaces. By contemplating unbelievably fearful situations in the comfort of her imagination, she learned to problem-solve and find meaning, which helped her deal with more mundane problems. Once Mia had successfully navigated the pretend end of the world, she was less averse to confronting bullies on the playground or playing at a new friend's apartment.

As children grow more proficient with language and memory, their imaginary world grows more creative. By her third birthday, Mia was recasting the past with *could have's* and *should have's* using counterfactuals. She also conjured up ideas about possible futures with *what if's*. By the age of four, Mia was mind reading by imagining the thoughts, feelings and intentions of others.

Fantastic Imagination in the Middle Years

We tend to think that fantasy dims as children grow older, but the creation of imaginary worlds by children between eight and twelve years of age is common. Jacob G. Levernier, a doctoral student at the University of Oregon, along with his colleagues, has studied elaborate worlds called *paracosms*, which children create in their middle years. Paracosms are often highly complex in structure and function, complete with their own languages, cultures, laws, histories and religions.[1] The settings for these worlds are diverse, from naturalistic islands and supernatural forests to fantastic landscapes on distant planets. Children invest so much time in their creation that they construct complete societies.

Levernier believes that these imaginary worlds help children try out possible solutions to moral problems, playing the same role that imaginary friends play in resolving emotional and interpersonal conflicts. He compares the complexity of some ten-year-olds' paracosms to those found in adult fantasy and science fiction novels.[2] Again, if children are capable of this level of social and moral thinking, then we should focus on something a bit deeper than controlling their immediate behavior.

Magical Thinking

The sophistication of children's minds is also evident in magical thinking, where young minds try to establish causal links between thoughts and behaviors by stretching logic and bending reason. Magical thinking is an early attempt to separate the real from the imagined, to develop cognitive skills and explore cause-and-effect relationships. Children use magical thinking to explain more complex events. Youngsters may believe that a negative thought caused their car to crash or a bad behavior was responsible for a parent's job loss.

Magical thinking is another attempt to create meaning out of life's confusing events. On some level, it makes sense to children that a tooth fairy takes away a lost tooth. Why wouldn't sadness cause it to rain? What other realistic reason could there be for the sudden appearance of holiday presents without invoking Santa or a similar holiday spirit?

Children's magical leaps in logic are often amusing and take on lives of their own. Yet the roots of their confused reasoning are similar to those of adults. They struggle to make sense of situations due to limited background knowledge and experience, an inability to objectively weigh evidence and habitual and biased beliefs. Children often fail to see alternative explanations and perspectives, resorting to magical thinking during events, including separation, conflict and death, that even adults may struggle to understand.

Imagination is a powerful force in children's lives, but like all capabilities it has a negative side. Imagination, especially in the forms of role playing and magical thinking, can elicit strong emotions, including frustration, fear and anger. Adults should be concerned when children wrongfully attribute their actions to negative events, become enraged during imaginary play or socially isolated while living in a pretend world. Parents and teachers should encourage positive imaginative explorations, but should also keep an eye out for situations where children become overwhelmed with worry or confusion. While young children generally have a good sense of the boundary between the real and imagined, the dream world can seem all too real to many kids.

Children of the Senses

Where does all this rich imagination and conceptualization come from? The first place to look is the senses. This is a good place to start if we want to nurture a child's imaginative and creative capabilities. Sharp sensory and perceptual skills are critically important to the development of a child's mind and they provide the fuel for imagination.

An important characteristic of creative and high-IQ students is that they process sensory information with greater depth. Many parents and teachers have inferred from this finding that sensory-stimulating environments will improve creativity and cognitive skills. However, sensory stimulation isn't the same as sensory development. As Daniel Willingham points out, many of the studies on sensory development look at sensory deprivation in animals during critical periods of development, such as vision development in young cats.[3] Total deprivation of sight early in an animal's development leads to life-long sensory issues. Yet, the same deprivation in older cats has little lasting effect. Willingham states, "The fact that deprivation results in a poorly developed sensory system does not mean that extra stimulation beyond what's normal would make the sensory system any better."[4] Why not expose children to music because it enriches their life? Why not expose them to nature or the visual arts because they are enjoyable? Does our focus as adults always have to be on some distant goal or remote benefit?

Sensory awareness, the experience of paying focused attention to sensory or bodily stimuli, is a better place to focus our efforts. Daniel is a good example of a sensory-aware child. While most of his friends are distracted by text messages and flashing web pages, Daniel pours all of his focus into the sensory world around him. He notices the feel of a cup of hot chocolate, its distinct smell and the swirl of cream on top. He observes the tone of your voice and the stress on your face as much as the words you speak. When Daniel walks outside in the morning he senses the temperature, the freshness of the air, the early light and the smell of the plants.

This isn't just a simple pleasure but a process that deepens his mind. Daniel's distractibility and shifting focus in school becomes a benefit during his free time. On the outside, his constantly moving attention allows him to notice every pattern, movement or relationship and discover similarities and differences that might not be apparent to a child lost in thought. A walk in the park or a trip to the supermarket is a constantly refreshing wave of stimulation that draws his focus and engages his mind. During an afternoon in the woods, Daniel will interpret dozens of bird calls, identify four types of mosses and lichen, smell the scents of numerous animals and feel every change in wind direction.

Author Diane Ackerman has examined the sensory world in her books, including *A Natural History of the Senses*. She wonders if the sensory connection to the body and nature is being supplanted by a technical world that distorts our senses and crimps our cognitive and perceptual development. In her article, "Are We Living in Sensory Overload or Sensory Poverty?" Ackerman states, "At first glance, it seems as if we may be living in sensory overload. The new technology, for all its boons, also bedevils us with alluring distracters, cyber-bullies, thought-nabbing, calm-fraying, and a spiky wad of miscellaneous news."[5] When she looks deeper, Ackerman feels that the digital world is impoverishing our senses, as we learn about the world without directly experiencing it, always one step removed from the reality, without direct sensory exploration. This distance leaves us separated from our natural learning capabilities and insensitive to "nature's precarious balance, let alone the balance of our own nature."[6]

Ackerman believes that we shouldn't expect children or adults to give up technology. Rather we must balance our virtual lives with activities that enliven the senses by making time for children to experience themselves and their environment directly: "Strip the brain of too much feedback from the senses and life not only feels poorer, but learning grows less reliable. Subtract the subtle physical sensations, and you lose a wealth of problem-solving and life-saving details."[7]

Ackerman takes sensory awareness one step deeper, suggesting that we cultivate presence, spend a few minutes each day paying close attention to nature and listen to our body and thoughts, aware of our environment and actions.[8] Here again is a type of mindfulness training that doesn't require special lessons or techniques. Paying full attention and being deeply involved in immediate experience while focusing less on transient thoughts and feelings gives children a wonderful break from their self-consumed existence.

Perceiving an Imagined World

Like imagination, perception is a mental fabrication, an attempt to build a sensible picture using a highly selective set of information. The five externally-focused senses are joined by a slew of internal sensations, including the sense of balance, pain, time and temperature, body orientation in space, hunger and thirst. In addition to bodily sensations, children experience feelings, from fear and stress to anxiety and excitement, almost constantly.

This wealth of stimuli plays a large role in children's perceptual reality, constantly flooding their minds with millions of bits of information per second. The brain could be easily overwhelmed by this influx, so it filters this information riot heavily, in part by selective attention. This filtering transforms perception into an illusion, not unreal but not as it seems. Just like classic visual illusions, such as the picture that can look like both a candleholder and a facial profile, the way we recognize sensory impressions is not fixed. Perception is altered by our personal experience, sensory awareness and social and emotional influences, which creates a personalized version of reality.

Perception is also altered by the way sensory information is parsed by our nervous system. We may think that vision is distinct from hearing and taste is separate from smell, but this, too, is an illusion. The senses aren't neatly segregated; seeing isn't just visual and hearing is more than auditory. For example, at the moment you are taking in the visual impression of this text with your eyes. But the visual impression is immediately channeled into the auditory system, which turns sound into meaningful speech. The input may be visual but the brain processes it as spoken words. Reading appears to be a visual process but, in fact, is substantially auditory.

Another example of perceptual sense shifting occurs during face-to-face conversation. Since light travels much faster than sound, our eyes input the visual impression of a person talking a fraction of a second before we hear their words. Our brains mesh the two sensory strands together so that we perceive speech without a delay.

Synesthesia, where one sense impression is processed by other senses, is an extreme example of our intertwined senses. People with this condition mix sensory stimuli, tasting colors or experiencing sounds as physical shapes. Synesthesia is believed to be common in newborns, as their senses are not completely compartmentalized, occupying overlapping areas of the brain. Children and teens may experience this magic when they are totally engaged in an experience.

Perceptual Learning

Extracting information from sensory experience is an essential component of learning, whether it involves an infant's perceptual-action learning or the stimulating experiences of teens. Perception is the process by which we make sense of sensory information. Perceptual learning plays a critical role in everything from picking tasty fruit to discriminating between twenty types of sneakers to identifying a face we haven't seen in decades. Our amazing perceptual skills allow us to interpret a graph, identify a song by listening to the first stanza, envision the characters and setting of a story or play complex digital games.

Whether they are aware of it or not, children continuously learn from perceptual experience. Young minds are constantly looking for patterns, taking in information and interpreting it into meaningful forms. They instinctually compare similarities and contrast differences in objects, images, tastes and sounds. From this information they build a database of background information that will help them make sense of future situations or solve novel problems.

Children's minds even detect patterns where none exist, connecting unrelated dots with imaginary lines. Science historian Michael Shermer calls this *patternicity*, the innate attempt to find meaningful patterns in random data.[9] Patternicity is evident when children see faces in clouds or when they make up stories about events about which they don't have much knowledge. These tales may appear to be lies but are really honest attempts to give meaning where little exists.

Perceptual learning doesn't require a lot of heavy thinking or forced memorization. It happens subconsciously as well as when we are paying full attention. It is developed when children are asked to look for special features and fine details or to note relationships. Perceptual learning arises when children are shown how to ignore irrelevant or trivial features and focus on the informative and special. Over time, children develop sensitivity to certain types of stimuli; they become aware of the nuances of jazz or rap, the style of certain types of artwork or the behavioral patterns of their friends. With focused attention over extended periods of time, children's perceptual skills become faster and more accurate. They learn to read a clock effortlessly, identify a character accurately, guess quantities and quickly discern shapes.

Perceptual learning also involves sensing part-whole relationships, which are evident in almost every world that they occupy. Children learn to focus on parts, looking at the details in insects' wings or the shape of a building block. Yet they learn to step back and see how a whole system works. Part-whole relationships enable children to classify and categorize objects, events and ideas.

This is particularly important with reading and math. Spoken language and its partner, reading, are largely a part-whole perceptual learning experience. Speech is composed of parts such as phonemes, syllables, words, phrases and sentences, with reading layering on more parts such as letter shapes and punctuation.

Mathematics is fundamentally about combining and separating objects, numbers and other representations of quantity into elaborate groups and categories. Addition, subtraction, multiplication and division are primarily grouping and separating operations. Many of the best predictors of mathematical ability are perceptual in nature, including *subtilizing* (the ability to quickly identify small quantities), mental or physical number line placement and general visual-spatial abilities. Tests of these abilities in the primary grades are strong predictors of mathematical capabilities years and even decades in the future.

Reading and math are rarely taught perceptually, as parents and educators focus on "higher level" skills and strategies, like letter and number symbols instead of the auditory (in the case of reading) and visual sense of quantity (for math) that are the foundation of these academic skills. Memory-intensive rules are learned for phonics and procedures for math. Little emphasis is placed on exploiting the marvelous auditory and visual pattern recognition capabilities of a child's mind—the exact abilities that allow children to learn with such amazing ease during the first five years of life.

We may marvel at a child who seems to learn to read, write or solve math problems with little effort but never search for the reason. One of the biggest factors separating Zoe's academic ease and Daniel's struggles is their perceptual abilities. Students like Zoe, as well as those who reach her level of expertise, perceive the world differently. They often have heightened perceptual abilities and are able to imagine and conceive with greater ease, accuracy and quickness. The patterns and distinctions are more readily apparent to them. Their heightened perceptual awareness enables them to picture situations and auditorially construct dialogues more clearly.

Despite the gap in their academic performance, the distance between Zoe and Daniel's auditory and visual-spatial ability is surprisingly narrow. Daniel has excellent perceptual abilities, apart from a difficulty processing speech sounds and recognizing symbolic number patterns. He could close this gap with concerted practice in speech awareness and auditory discrimination for reading and number-to-visual quantity skills for math. These activities are as simple as manipulating the sounds in spoken words, visually sorting fractions, placing values on number lines or classifying math word problems by operation. Activities that link symbols with visual, tactile or auditory representations, such as connecting algebraic equations with graphs or written and spoken words, are effective ways of building links between so-called low-level perceptual skills and the abstractions favored by much of education.

If the development of perceptual skills seems difficult, then think of how easily children and teens pick up complex role-playing and strategy games, both digital and card-based, without a word of instruction, a lesson in strategy or hours spent memorizing rules. They seem to readily navigate multi-dimensional worlds, build complex objects and figure out the physics behind all kinds of projectiles with great ease. They even find these challenging perceptual and strategic tasks to be enjoyable and pursue them for endless hours.

Creativity, Attention and Daydreaming

We have examined three vital parts of building the Creative Dreamer—sensation, perception and imagination. The fourth part is creativity. To understand the primal side of this complex ability, we must start with attention and daydreaming, abilities that are always lurking in the background of most capabilities.

Here again, Daniel demonstrates how a deficit in school can be a benefit during his free-time imaginative and creative pursuits. Daniel's attentional style lends itself not only to greater sensory awareness and enhanced perceptual skills, but also to creativity. Daniel's school may demand unwavering attention but, when his focus is allowed free range, he pursues divergent thoughts, tangential ideas and unusual associations—the fuel for creativity. If a *what if* or *why not* crosses his mind, he will impulsively pursue it. His energetic attention style propels him to search out novel or unusual ideas, a trait found in many creative people. He will channel his mental energy to develop the idea with full force. This process may look chaotic in a highly-controlled classroom or home, but Daniel finds it exciting and engaging to expand his interests.

Daniel's attention isn't the only ability that lends itself to creativity. He likes to daydream, allowing his mind to wander in new and different directions. Neuroscientists call this the "default mode," the mind's apparent resting state that is critical to many capabilities. Children may spend half their waking hours dreaming, imagining and mind wandering. In the "default mode" they time travel, review the past and plan for the future.[10]

While the "default mode" can be a jumble of random thoughts and mental chatter, it is also the source of new ideas, inspirations and creativity. Jerome L. Singer, an early investigator of the "default mode," called this state "positive-constructive daydreaming."[11] Not only is this type of daydreaming associated with positive dreams, plans and ideas, but it provides a window for children to observe their minds. One of the founders of American psychology, William James, found daydreaming to be a way to observe one's thoughts, images and ideas.[12] All that is required is for children to have copious amounts of unscheduled down time that is free from worry.

Adults should gently monitor children for signs that their daydreaming is turning gloomy, as Singer and others have recognized the possible negative aspects of the "default mode" on children's emotional health. This state requires a certain inner focus and becomes unproductive when children's thoughts constantly jump around, become obsessive or center on dark ruminations.

Constructive Reflection

Scott Barry Kaufman, the author of *Ungifted: Intelligence Redefined*, is an expert on the subject of the positive benefits of daydreaming. For Kaufman, the struggle between a wandering, creative mind and a learning disability is quite personal, as he spent much of his K-12 years in a special room for children with learning disabilities. A teacher recognized that Kaufman had abilities beyond those valued in academic settings and gave him the opportunity to join a gifted program. He went on to be an accomplished cellist, thanks to the tutelage of his grandfather, and is a respected cognitive scientist.[13]

From this varied experience and education, Kaufman developed an interest in how children learn, with a special interest in the relationship between the "default mode" and creativity. Kaufman says that the "default mode" is not only linked to imagination, but helps children reflect on the meaning of events, develop self-awareness, take perspectives and engage in moral reasoning and compassion. It helps them plan for the future, reflect on the past and make sense of immediate concerns. In short, the "default mode" helps them process abstract information in ways that make sense from a psychological, emotional and subjective perspective. Just like imagination, the "default mode" seems like child's play but is involved with roughly half of what goes on in a child's mind.[14]

The "default mode" is more reflective than productive, requiring free time to reflect. Kaufman states that many researchers in the field feel that "imposing high attention demands on children may rob them of the chance for important reflection that can allow them to make personal meaning out of [instruction] and reflect on the social and emotional implications of that knowledge."[15] Children need time for "constructive reflection," so that they can engage two apparently opposite networks of the mind—the daydreaming default network and the attentive reasoning of the executive system.[16]

This wondrous state of mind is wandering yet focused and open to experience yet thinking analytically. During constructive reflection, a child's inner state is also engaged with the flow of perceptual information, creating what Kaufman calls "a deeply absorbed...brilliant inner stream of consciousness."[17] When parents or teachers demand that children pay external attention for extended periods of time, they deprive them of possibly the mind's most vaunted capability: "If we want to facilitate compassion, future planning, self-regulation, and divergent thinking, we should set up conditions that allow for mind wandering" in a positive, constructive manner, Kaufman says.[18]

Creativity arises out of minds wandering, because children's minds need downtime to freely imagine and generate multiple ideas, images or concepts. Their minds need time to reflect on all the possibilities and weigh the benefits of each idea. When a concept is chosen, they need more time to shape, modify and improve on the initial burst of imagination. Here is where children have the upper hand over adults, as they are less likely to cling to fixed ideas or fall into well-worn patterns of thinking. They have been repeatedly shown to be more creative than business majors precisely because their cognitive abilities are still developing. They respond to ideas and images more fluidly and are open to divergent ideas. While adults are more capable of implementing creative ideas, they still benefit from taking on a childlike mindset. Kaufman reports that when adults are told to act like their imagined seven-year-old selves, they generated more original responses on tests that measure creativity through assessing *divergent thinking*.[19]

Divergent thinking is the source of much creative problem-solving and insightful solutions. It involves expanding one's thinking by coming up with multiple solutions or different ideas—thinking outside of the box. It often takes time and an open mind. Divergent thinking is quite different from the forced brainstorming sessions used in schools and businesses to spur creativity. Creative problem-solving is hampered by the intense analytical thought and outward focus of a scheduled meeting. It takes a child-like mind, which is inwardly focused during periods of reflection and introversion and is open to multiple solutions and novel concepts. Many artists and scientists have reported that moments of creativity arise from unforced moments of insight where new visions suddenly and effortlessly present themselves—not scheduled meetings.

Everyday Creativity

We have looked at the primal side of creativity as part of a "Big L Learning" experience connected to sensory processing, imagination and conceptualization. We have seen how abilities such as daydreaming, mind wandering, constructive reflecting and divergent thinking are critical to developing the Creative Dreamer. We have stressed that children have strong creative tendencies that require free time, encouragement and constructive reflection. What else should parents and teachers do to develop the Creative Dreamer, especially in older children and teens?

First, adults should understand that creativity has become what Joshua Rothman calls a "central virtue," taking on the status of academic success or cognitive abilities. Once, he writes, imagination itself was cherished, but in the 1800s creative imagination became the ideal.[20] The poet and philosopher Samuel Coleridge believed that there were two types of creativity—the workaday imagination used to recall memories and solve daily problems and a nobler imagination that is a "watchful, inner kind of creativity that is not about making things but about experiencing life in a creative way." Currently, Rothman believes, "our current sense of creativity is almost entirely bound up with the making of stuff."[21]

Often the "stuff" is tied to new products or innovative processes that fuel commerce, not the enhancement of the mind of a child. Creativity has become another external mark of possible future success, rather than a way of inwardly enriching a child or teenager's life. Any future achievement derived from creativity will most likely be a byproduct of a mind that richly imagines and conceives, that thinks divergently and pursues unusual associations. Creativity isn't just an inner state but an other-focused event. Despite individual masterpieces and singular creations, most people are creative when they collaborate with other people who also possess fluid ideas and rich imaginations.

Creativity researchers James C. Kaufman and Jerome L. Singer have classified many different forms of creativity as they apply to learning. They have divided creativity into everyday or "little c" creativity and exceptional "Big C" creativity. "Little c" creativity is simple originality, small bursts of insight or uncommon problem-solving. It is creating a work of art, a special project or "getting" the relationship between addition and multiplication. "Little c" is the creative capability available to every child, given the opportunity.[22] Parents may dream of their child someday becoming a legendary innovator, but this is probably more imagined than real. Adults should value the small, everyday moments of imagination and creativity that can infuse a child's life with magic.

· ·

SMALL MOMENTS THAT CREATE THE CREATIVE DREAMER

Children have diverse ways of learning, from sensory awareness and mindful learning to imagination and mind wandering. Parents and teachers should not emphasize one capability at the expense of another. Children's mental and physical states change constantly, as do their interests. There isn't one ideal form of childhood. Sometimes a child's mind will wander and then be highly focused.

Sometimes a child will be imaginative and creative and other times more occupied with a long-term interest. Try not to favor the Creative Dreamer over other capabilities, despite the current social and educational trends.

These Small Moments not only promote imagination and creativity but a wide range of capabilities. Small Moments should create a gentler relationship between child and adult. Try some of these moments yourself—it's never too late to find your own Creative Dreamer:

+ Cherish a child's imagined world.
+ Give children undistracted time to reflect, daydream and mind wander.
+ Free time to play, either alone or with others, is vital.
+ Promote simple observations and descriptions.
+ Have children attentively observe objects, artworks or situations.
+ Time outside improves sensory perception.
+ Encourage fantasy play, imaginary friends and made-up worlds.
+ Involvement in art, music and movement enhances the Creative Dreamer's creative abilities.
+ Explore alternative solutions to problems and small challenges.
+ Promote rich conceptual skills and imagination, especially in older students.
+ Encourage reading of fiction, science fiction, fantasy and graphic novels.
+ Explore constructive/reflective, where imagination and reasoning come together.
+ Be present—spend a few minutes each day paying attention, being aware of your body and sensing experiences and environment.
+ Expose a child to different cultures, people, languages, food, music and art.
+ Promote improvised comedy, poetry, art and music.

9

The Storyteller

One day in school, Mia was learning the craft of storytelling from Martha and Mitch, of Beauty and the Beast Storytellers, who have enriched the lives of thousands of children by showing them the power of the narrative. Mia's level of engagement was through the roof as she practiced delivering a classic fable, *The Crow and the Pitcher*. Mia's classmates were even more entranced. Mia's teacher could sense the heightened memory, listening and reasoning skills and could imagine the visualizations appearing in their minds. Shy, quiet Mia was transformed into an animated character who had every student and adult in the room totally transfixed. She was fully engaged in a special conversation with her classmates that extended beyond words to include emotions, facial expressions, body movements and intonations. The shared communication included empathy, a shared motivation and a common purpose—all these cognitive, emotional and social benefits from a five-minute fable and a little mentoring from a few adults.

If we could travel back in time we would witness the same scene generations ago when an earlier version of Mia sat by the stove and listened with equal intensity to her grandfather, a freed slave, tell the story of his life. Grandfather would have told a transfixed Mia that his culture transmitted wisdom across generations by using this most important of human learning capabilities. He would have started the day's narrative by telling of the time he was abducted from his clan in West Africa and forced into the slave trade. Tears fell down our ancestral Mia's face as this wonderful old man told how he had gone from being a respected elder in charge of keeping the generational wisdom of his people to becoming an economic commodity. He shared with Mia many of the legends, myths and stories that explained our collective knowledge of humans, nature and gods as well as the routine events of daily life—and how that knowledge was stripped from him one fateful day.

The fascination that Mia's class and ancestors found in stories is part of children's nature, a listening and speaking ability full of action and experience that can be nurtured into a powerful capability. Children's minds are finely developed and incessant storytellers. Our minds create stories almost as a second language. Narratives pervade our thoughts, dreams, imagination and conversations. Stories are a primary way that we construct knowledge and meaning about ourselves and the world. They form the framework for much of our inner conversations.

Almost as soon as children can comprehend spoken language they are drawn to stories as if by a magnetic force. Not only are stories universal across cultures but we craft them almost constantly as part of our internal dialogue. Our lives are described in stories to the point that day-to-day reality and hard evidence can be drowned out by the fabricated tales we tell ourselves. We devise stories to explain the simplest events, such as why we left our wallets home. We also use stories to explain the most complex events, such as who we are and how the world works.

Long before the first holy book was scribed, values, parables, morals, fables, allegories, creation myths and tales of wonder and sorrow were transmitted in story form. In fact, the teachings of Jesus and Buddha were only infrequently written down for hundreds of years after their deaths, sustained solely by oral retelling for generations.

Stories are so powerful, because their framework is built from the three critical capabilities of continuous learning, constructing meaning and fluid problem-solving. Deep in the structure of a story is a problem that needs to be contemplated and solved, a learning adventure that leads to the problem's resolution and finally a message that gives the story meaning. From fairy tales and fables to news accounts, stories capture our imagination, because they reside on this very old framework that is fundamental to being human.

Cognitive psychologist Daniel Willingham believes that "the human mind seems exquisitely tuned to understand and remember stories."[1] He says that stories are "psychologically privileged," or able to command attention and memory in a very special manner. Paradoxically, stories get children to think deeply, because they are easy to understand. If we dig deeper into the structure of a story we can see why narratives grip on our minds so deeply, yet also effortlessly. Willingham, as do many psychologists, believes that this is due to "the four Cs," each of which taps into a fundamental cognitive process that we readily use to make sense of life.[2]

The first C is *causality*, which, as we saw, is integral to the Curious Explorer's experimental mindset. Stories aren't just long lists of events but events that are linked through causal relationships. If events happen randomly, the story would not attract us nor help us solve problems. Willingham illustrates the difference using two sentences: "I saw Jane and I left the house" is event recording, whereas "I saw Jane, my hopeless old love; I left the house," shows the cause. Knowing why the person left the house gives the event meaning and emotion.[3]

The second C is *conflict*. Stories are more than just problems looking for solutions; they are conflicts wherein a character is prevented from reaching a goal. Overcoming obstacles that test the character's strength or challenge his values creates a natural tension in stories of all sorts.

Complications, the third C, are sub-problems that heighten the tension. Children subconsciously struggle with personal, internal and environmental conflicts and with the complications that arise as they try to resolve problems. They are easily drawn to fairy tales, because conflicts and complications live large and seem insurmountable. They give children hope when the *character*, the fourth C, is able to overcome problems and life-threatening complications far larger than they will, hopefully, experience. Characters make stories. Their struggles, traits, skills and actions magnetically attract children and teach lessons in powerful ways.[4]

Evolution strongly selected for humans who could both tell and absorb stories. It is universal across the planet and time.[5] Simply stated, if you have something to say, put it in narrative form. The evolutionary pull of the narrative is evident today in the faces of Mia's classmates or the endless stories that teens weave about their relationships, adventures, successes and struggles. It is felt in the pleasure adults derive from studying history, reading fiction, watching TV dramas or exploring their ancestry.

In his wonderfully revealing book, *The Storytelling Animal: How Stories Make Us Human*, Jonathan Gottschall imagines a scenario possibly one hundred thousand years ago. There lived two tribes that resembled modern humans in most ways. The way the tribes lived, worked and survived were basically identical. But one tribe, which Gottschall calls Homo fictus (fictional man), had a gift for storytelling. They could transfer information, skills and knowledge much more effectively from person to person and generation to generation than their story-less neighbors. While the storytelling tribe spent much of their free time engaged in learning, the other tribe merely worked and slept. In Gottschall's telling, over a few generations the competitive advantage of storytelling allowed one tribe to prosper while the other went extinct.[6]

The Capable Storyteller

The Storyteller is able to take the innate abilities to listen and tell stories and transforms these skills into the mature capability to think, speak and write meaningful narratives. The Storyteller weaves words, ideas, concepts, songs, dances and pictures into meaningful narratives that fuel the stories of his life. The mature Storyteller constructs engaging stories as a major way of understanding himself and his relationships to the social, psychological and physical worlds. The Storyteller is able to blend imagination with concrete reality, understanding that stories constantly change and often contain rationalizations and fabrications.

Children have multiple ways of learning, a feature that gives their minds much resilience. Anything that is worth learning can be learned by multiple abilities. Nature has selected for some redundancy in our bodies, giving us two kidneys, lungs, ovaries or testes, arms, legs, ears and eyes. Learning offers us such a huge survival benefit that we evolved many ways of doing it. Children would be unique among animals if they had just one way of learning skills, knowledge or abilities, but having redundant paths to understanding is truly amazing. Daniel's academic struggles, Mia's listlessness in class and Zoe's dropout request have prompted their parents and teachers to exploit this wonderful aspect of children's nature by shifting between learning capabilities. No longer do these adults assume that the children will learn just by modifying the way that content is presented.

We have seen that experience, experimentation, embodied action, motivated attention and interests all provide strong paths for Daniel's learning. With all his struggles in school he has found that a reliable way to learn academic skills and content is by constructing a narrative. Daniel has been able to develop the ability to combine immediate experience and information with past experiences and background knowledge, which is a simple definition of learning. Yet Daniel does it in a way that is discouraged in schools, by creating stories that arise out of daydreams. When his mind drifts into story mode, his thinking deepens. Ideas and images appear, leading him to a deeper level of cognition. The stories come easily to him, engaging his attention and memory. Daniel didn't have to learn this as a separate skill or strategy, nor did he take a class or listen to endless lessons on strategies to deploy this profound learning capability. It is built into the structure of the way children's minds intertwine with stories.

The stories that Daniel constructs are often quite imaginative, far more advanced than the series of sequenced events that pass for stories in elementary school. For example, his class was studying the way that birds evolved from flying dinosaurs. This prompted Daniel to think about larger problems: why does life exist on this planet and why do living creatures change over time? While his teacher was thinking that Daniel wasn't paying attention, he was actively creating a daydream story about meeting aliens who had been scouring the skies for life forms. They had found three planets within a hundred light years that contained life, but only simple bacteria-like organisms. The aliens are astonished by the life forms on Earth, possibly a reflection of Daniel's love of biological life. The aliens ask how the diversity of life arose. Daniel tells them about today's class discussion on how birds evolved from dinosaurs. The aliens tell him that they left their home world because they couldn't do what the flying dinosaurs did tens of millions of years ago—adapt to changing conditions on their planet.

While many of the students in Daniel's class will only remember the simple fact that birds evolved from something like pteranodons, he will remember how they fit into the evolutionary scheme of life. Daniel was naturally using a number of learning strategies, including retelling and explaining information as well as reframing the context.

Social and Self Stories

Zoe uses storytelling in a very personal way, by creating narratives to deal with some of the most frequent problems that children must deal with— understanding emotions and relationships. She uses stories that parallel cognitive therapy to create strategies to deal with future concerns, potential conflicts and perceived anxieties. When she begins to worry about upcoming interactions and situations, she creates stories from multiple perspectives to explore different possible outcomes. The stories help her work out problems and rehearse scenarios from within the safety of internal narratives. The power of stories to solve real and imagined problems is like magic for Zoe. Zoe knows that stories contain a large dose of fiction, that real events rarely follow the plot lines she creates, but they offer her a way of solving problems beforehand.

Zoe is concerned at this point about going on an overnight trip with sometimes-best-friend Molly and her problematic parents. Zoe, like most people who read voraciously, has a deeper understanding of peoples' actions and motivations, as well as a greater ability to navigate difficult social situations, than the average ten-year-old. When Molly invited Zoe over to talk with her parents about the trip, Zoe read the situation like a good novel. Zoe could tell that Molly's parents were frustrated by their daughter's behavior and Molly was tired of their heavy-handed behavioral controls. She surmised that Molly's parents wanted her to join them on the trip, because she was tolerant of their daughter's emotional fluctuations. Zoe was sure that Molly wanted her there to buffer her parents' incessant attempts at behavior modification.

When Zoe got home she began to run scenarios in her head about different ways the trip's plotline might play out. She thought about how a variety of problems might be resolved and how Molly's and her parents' character traits might unfold under different scripts of the trip. From these diverse storylines, Zoe decided to go on the trip and try to dampen both Molly's moods and her parents' concerns about her behavior. Zoe learned from the different narratives that she probably had little control over either situation. Finally, Zoe added a scene to the story where she finds small moments of fun throughout the day.

Blending Imagination and Experience, Memory and Understanding

The stories we just told about Mia, Daniel and Zoe illustrate a larger point about narratives. Tomorrow, when you think about this chapter, see if Mia's grandfather's slavery story, Zoe's trip conflicts and Daniel's tale about evolving pteranodons aren't among the first things you remember.

Daniel's sci-fi evolution story, present-day Mia's love of listening to and telling stories and Zoe's social-emotional tales have one thing in common—they create mental simulations in children's minds. Stories push us to think deeply, not only because they spark causal thinking but also because they don't overwhelm children with information. The children themselves have to paint in the details, purpose and meaning, read between the lines, spark the Creative Dreamer's mental pictures and the Curious Explorer's inferential sense. We rarely see this type of "Big L Learning" happen when teachers lecture, parents preach or children peruse the Internet for fascinating tidbits of information.

Storytelling isn't only child's play, as it becomes especially important during the pre-teen and teenage years. During this period, adolescents develop into capable Storytellers, performing some of the most difficult learning tasks, from constructing meaning to organizing thoughts, simply by spinning a tale, engaging in a dance or creating a song.

The interest in stories, including song and dance, among pre-teens and teens is seen in most cultures in different periods. Evolutionary psychologists believe that the teenage propensity for song, dance, acting and exaggerated tales may be the result of tens of thousands of years of selection pressures. The pre-teen and teen years have traditionally been the time when learning, problem-solving and knowledge and skill development are amplified as they change from dependent children into autonomous individuals.

Studies of hunter-gatherer societies show that the days of pre-teens and teens were increasingly spent in adult activities. Few nights passed without instruction from elders, song, dance or a story. Youth who excelled at these essential cultural learning capabilities had a distinct survival advantage. This advantage may also explain a teen's natural shift to a more nocturnal lifestyle as it provides more time for evening cultural exchanges and increased nighttime adult responsibilities.

Imagine the seismic shift in secondary schools if they tapped into this deeply interesting and motivating way of learning? What if schools emphasized storytelling and related creative endeavors including acting, dancing, singing or short story and novel writing as seriously as they do algebra? There is much concern about motivation and the use of technology to engage children at home and at school. Wouldn't these creative forms of storytelling capture children's attention more than another lecture or teacher-delivered lesson?

The opportunities that create capable Storytellers should be made available to all children. Wouldn't it be easier if these narrative endeavors were part of the school day rather than being afterschool privileges for a select few? School plays, concerts, recitals as well as storytelling and comedy events should be integral to the curriculum and not occasionally provided enrichment.

An Imagined Life

Regardless of the format, storytelling aids in the transmission of knowledge but, more importantly, it helps children create representations of who they are and the worlds in which they live. One of the clearest lessons of brain research is that we enrich the world we experience, rarely satisfied with raw perception. The Storyteller is involved in most of what we sense and think. Stories combine our cognitive powers such as reasoning and memory with our perceptual powers and then add a large dose of imagination. From the fictional stories that young children crave to the great pleasure teens derive from music and melodramatic stories, children's minds translate the raw words into an imaginative reconstruction.

Jonathan Gottschall's *The Storytelling Animal* creatively blends the ancient power of the narrative with the modern power of neuroscience. He talks about how our minds have been shaped into their current storytelling and meaning-deriving form that combines real and imagined images.[7] Gottschall believes that children, teens and adults all live in a world that he calls Neverland. This imaginary world is created by the hundreds of little stories we tell ourselves each day. Neverland becomes more real every time a child fabricates an excuse or an explanation, watches a television commercial or daydreams about supersized sports or celebrity characters. It exists "in the happy mayhem of children's make-believe and what they reveal about stories' prehistoric origins. It's about how fiction subtly shapes our beliefs, behaviors, ethics—how it powerfully modifies culture and history."[8] The inner lives of children are rich and meaningful fictional worlds built from shreds of reality mixed with large doses of imagination.

Children's inner dialogues are largely never-ending stories, too. Like adults, they tell fabricated stories to explain minor events, like why they "like" someone they really hate. Children also try to make sense of their confusing and changing lives by constructing a cohesive narrative out of a hodgepodge of disconnected events and memories. The story changes every time they shift what they are doing and who they are with.

Children tend to inflate stories about themselves and create "depression narratives" that batter their self-stories. Parents may wonder why one day children sound like overconfident little narcissists and the next day they're unsure of who they are. Psychologists believe that many depressed children create oversimplified and negative stories about their lives. There are effective therapies for depression that help them construct more detailed and positive stories about their lives.

In his book, *Daydreaming: Using Waking Fantasy and Imagery for Self-knowledge and Creativity*, Eric Klinger examines our inner storytelling. Klinger cites research that shows that our minds wander into storyland up to two thousand times a day, spending about half of our waking hours in daydreams. Each daydream lasts only about fourteen seconds and most of the time we are not even really aware of them.[9] Even when we sleep, our minds are engaged in storytelling, including the vivid dreams that tinge children's nighttimes, with fears and fantasies creeping into most children's dreams. Researchers used to believe that we only dreamed during REM sleep—about two hours a night—but actually we have story-like dreams for much of the time that we are asleep. Lacking the reality of embodied experience, few of these fantastic tales are retained in the morning's memory.[10]

When our brains are not actively engaged, they wander from immediate experience into the "default mode." Earlier we saw with the Creative Dreamer, daydreaming has many positive aspects, including problem-solving, and helps them plan for the future and process past events. One of the healthiest things that children can do is to daydream, to have downtime where they can read stories and create their own. Capable Storytellers rely heavily on the "default mode" to actively daydream their way into storytelling mode.

Speak Only in Stories

It makes sense since we dream, think, imagine, sing, dance, act, converse and talk to ourselves in stories, to teach using stories. Children pay more attention, devote greater memory resources and are more cognitively, emotionally and socially engaged when they listen to and create stories. Hardly a single bit of information, chunk of curricula or message is better expressed than through a narrative. Parents can frame everything from instructions for cleaning a bedroom to rules and guidelines as stories, preferably with the child as the main character, the problem-solver and the hero.

Replacing educational content with stories may be the simplest yet most powerful way to dramatically improve learning. History inherently lends itself to narratives; wouldn't students remember and recall more about the past if they spent a school year deeply involved in the stories of half a dozen diverse and representative lives who had different perspectives on the same historical event?

With a little creative effort, subjects like physics and algebra can be easily livened up through stories. Daniel Willingham suggests that even the coldest abstract material can be transformed into a meaningful story by framing the lesson with the critical elements of narratives, known as the four Cs—causality, conflict, complications and characters. The history of physics is filled with deeply curious humans, often with character flaws, who overcame endless problems and complications. Individuals and groups who made significant scientific breakthroughs often spent their lives in deep conflict with other scientists, previous research, religious dogma and social forces. Many great female scientists not only faced this type of conflict but also complications that most males avoided. Marie

Curie's discovery of radioactivity, Rosalind Franklin's insights into the structure of DNA and Barbara McClintock's role in creating the groundwork for modern molecular genetics were amazing finds. Yet their discoverers were denied access to academic programs and degrees and were ignored due to their gender. However, by overcoming conflict and complications while exhibiting some of the finest human characteristics, they added to our understanding of nature and human inquiry.

What if parents and teachers discussed the biographies of scientists with students as easily as they discuss celebrities? The stories behind the building of the Hubble Space Telescope and the Large Hadron Collider should cover every topic in physics through the first year of college. Children are naturally drawn to physics when it is presented as science fiction. If neutron stars, black holes, time travel, wormholes, hyperspace and warp drives can be freely discussed by children and teens during lunch breaks, then there are few topics in physics that should be unexplainable to fifth graders.

From Subjects to Stories

Roger Schank, whose twelve cognitive abilities we discussed when presenting our twelve capabilities, has created the *story-centered curriculum*, or SCC. It is based on the idea that a good curriculum should tell a story with students playing central roles. Schank believes that "people live stories. The stories they live become part of them in a deep way. While we may easily forget everything about a traditional course we took in high school, we can hardly forget the roles we have played in real-life experiences."[11] The roles should parallel those that students might perform in real life, confronting the problems and using knowledge in a realistic way.

Schank would ground each year of high school in a role-playing story. In his ideal school, students would have dozens of SCCs to choose from; they would graduate after completing four curricula. Schank has created a story-centered curriculum for a year course in the health sciences. The students play diagnosticians, patients, organ transplant recipients, nutritionists, sports medics, drug designers and infectious disease specialists trying to deal with epidemics, unexpected deaths, sports injuries, drug resistance, organ transplants and much more.[12] In addition to learning vital content and career skills, the SCCs develop Schank's twelve cognitive processes within the context of a real-life simulation. Rather than taking courses in conceptual, analytic and social processes, students would live and learn them in the context of a story.

Three Act Math

As with physics, there are innovative and interest-grabbing ways of teaching math using stories. Educator Dan Meyers has devised a way of teaching math reasoning, called *Three Act Math Problems*, that follow a narrative structure. Meyers's method brings all the cognitive, social and motivational powers to math lessons without having to force children into heavy thinking tasks. His approach dispenses with the superficial appeal of "real world" or practical math problems, which often bore children. He also avoids typical word problems, which put children into the unnatural position of having so much information that must be filtered to find the relevant facts.[13]

Instead, Meyers creates a Three Act Math Problem. First, the problem is introduced as part of a mystery story, often a short clip from a movie, which children have to solve. The mystery can be as spectacular as blowing up a space ship or mundane as sinking a fifty-foot basketball shot. Next, the student protagonists must overcome obstacles such as the lack of data and look for problem-solving resources and strategies. Finally, they must resolve the problem both as a story and with numbers. Students work in groups and take many days to solve and create the answer story. They're free to use slide presentations, create videos or write short plays. Meyers has assembled a series of sample projects and internet videos that should engage any student.[14] Parents appreciate this approach as it replaces nightly math homework drudgery with a creative and "Big L Learning" endeavor.

Mysteries

Mysteries are stories that require the reader or storyteller to figure out a solution based on limited information. Not only are mysteries popular in fictional whodunits, but they also form the backbone of most famous scientific discoveries. Scientists often piece together limited sets of information, by inference, to arrive at unifying concepts that require years or decades of research to really find out if the mystery has been solved.

Approaching questions as mysteries to be solved rather than just providing answers deepens children's curiosity and sets off the strong motivation to complete a story or resolve a problem. When children go missing, airplanes disappear or unexpected things happen, we need the story to be completed, the problem to be solved. How much more engaging would science or history lessons be if they were taught as mystery stories that need resolution? During free time, many questions and problems can be approached as mysteries. Why did the sink leak, why did the dog stop eating food or why did a supposed friend suddenly stop visiting?

Oral Language Before Written Expression

Another area where students show slow progress even after extended effort is writing. Here, too, stories offer a powerful alternative. Mia benefited from Martha and Mitch's skilled development of storytelling in many ways, but perhaps the largest was in her ability to express herself orally and translate these expressions into writing. Mia's mom, Melissa, understands the importance and excitement of putting thoughts on paper, so she provides occasional Small Moments of writing time for Mia. Melissa first looks for situations that interest Mia and then engages her in a conversation or encourages her to draw. The writing that follows flows easily from Mia's mind.

Many students struggle with putting words to paper, because they lack the ability to organize their thoughts and express themselves orally. While children find stories naturally attractive, they may find the construction of complex stories challenging. For many children, their story sense must be developed to an advanced level before it easily supports written narratives.

The craft of writing challenges children on many levels, from the development of motor skills to guide the pen and the taxing and artificial tasks of spelling, grammar and punctuation to connecting one's inner voice with written expression. Children with gaps in social and emotional learning may have limited insight into character development and conflict resolution. Writing also requires access to a range of subconscious processes, including memory for events, working memory and the meta-cognitive task of "thinking-about-thinking." In short, writing requires capable Storytellers, who are finely attuned to both the inner and outer worlds.

Since few parents or teachers approach writing in this comprehensive manner, writing difficulties linger into high school and college for many students and not just for those with learning difficulties. Only about one third of American eighth-graders and one-fourth of high school seniors are proficient writers. Even proficient writers show little growth as they move through high school and the first two years of college.

It would be better for parents and educators to make elementary school children masters of storytelling and oral expression. What if, as an early step toward writing, children told stories to older children and adults who helped them organize their thoughts and scribed for them? It would be more enjoyable and motivating for students to work intensively on developing the Storyteller and our next capability, the Careful Communicator, before having to write anything more challenging than descriptive writing. Wouldn't parenting and teaching be more enjoyable if much of their time with children was spent doing two things that they naturally love—telling stories and having discussions?

Certainly there are students who embrace written expression at an early age; we should not hold them back by restricting their free expression. But writing is a craft, so even the most capable third grade Storyteller benefits from clarified and organized thoughts and ideas and enriched language expression. Even the construction of sentences is a skill that children should practice well into college. James H. Billington, the librarian of Congress, calls the sentence the basic unit of human thought and believes that inability to craft solid sentences is a major reason that students of all ages too often talk and write in disjointed phrases.[15]

Real, Fabricated Stories

Like much of children's lives, narratives contain a large element of fiction. The stories we construct and reconstruct from memory are heavily influenced by our imaginative minds. Stories, even ones that describe events we have just experienced, are fabrications at best, summaries and interpretations of reality, just sketches of our experiences. Even with children, who are prone to exaggeration and hyperbole, the fabrications aren't wholly intentional. The memory that is devoted to recording the events of our lives, autobiographical memory, is fragile and prone to misleading perspectives and biases. We only recall select bits of the past, distorted fragments of information. The recollection is piecemeal, containing only emotionally-charged tidbits, broad overviews and occasionally the gist of the situation. Every time the memory is pulled up it is rewritten in a newly distorted form back to memory.

The perspective often changes, rarely seen through our eyes but often shot from outside of our bodies or shifted to please or anger the parent or teacher. Two children can witness the same event, say a dispute over a kickball rule, and give two completely different accounts. One proven method that parents and teachers can use to resolve disputes is to have the culprits explain conflicts from the other child's perspective.

While it is powerful to use stories as a way of explaining events, interactions and ideas, they are also used to rationalize and justify. Children love to fantasize and live in the realm of mystery and monsters, superheroes and legends. While many young children are very good at separating their fictional worlds from their experiential lives, they do fall prey to fabrications and myths. Their truths may seem like fibs, excuses and lies to adults. We should expect a species that lives largely in the imaginary world of ideas, images, concepts, beliefs and intuitions to blend the made-up with the real. One person's truth is another's fantasy. This is all very normal as even teens and adults are prone to explain, justify and rationalize events and beliefs using real-to-them but untrue-to-others stories.

Stories are a way of looking back, of pulling from memory information and processing it anew. Children have a great need to interpret events and information, often using their imaginative, causal and inferential powers to create understanding where little exists. We try to make sense of every situation, even when the situation is random. Even capable Storytellers will create fabrications that feel real to them but are false by any objective standard. Ask a child, "Why did you do that?" and you will get an answer, even if the child hasn't a clue why the behavior occurred.

Neuroscientist Michael Gazzaniga lays the blame for our fabrications on the inner narrator that springs from our language ability in our left hemisphere. It is constantly interpreting almost anything that catches our attention. This interpreter will try to explain mood shifts, random actions, passing feelings, causal encounters and even its own stray thoughts. All day long our internal narrator "takes input from other areas of our brain and from the environment and synthesizes into a story. FAQs are great but not necessary. The left brain ad-libs the rest."[16]

Children and teens make up stories about past events but also create alternative stories about how things could have or should have been, known as *counterfactuals*. Counter to the facts, ignoring evidence, children engage in what-if's and if-only-I-had's. Unable to change the past, children weave imaginary tales about how things might have been. If only they had studied harder, made the winning goal or weren't afraid to start a conversation.

Probably the place where maturing children and teens learn to decipher the truthfulness of stories, to be aware of the blinding allure of narratives, is in tales political parties and their supporting media tell. Political psychologist Drew Westen believes that the stories that politicians tell us have almost the same impact as those that parents weave. Political stories and commentaries mostly live in the imaginary world of counterfactuals, what could be and what should be. They fit the narrative structure by always having a good guy and a bad guy and a change or a solution to our problems.[17]

While it is vital for children to have meaningful stories about their lives and who they are, they should understand that their self-stories are part fiction and wholly subject to change. A story that is relevant one day may have to be re-scripted the next day as cognitive, emotional and social conditions change.

. . . .

SMALL MOMENTS THAT CREATE THE STORYTELLER

Help children understand the narrative structure of thoughts and conversations.

Use stories to explain and instruct, especially when it is critical that the child retain the information.

Help children create self-stories about daily events and long-term histories.

Show children how stories are prone to fabrication, that the stories they weave about themselves, events and behaviors may be biased by fabrication and imagination.

. . . .

10

....
The Careful Communicator

Language offers human beings survival and learning advantages that benefit almost every aspect of our lives. Conversation is clearly one of children's most robust paths to learning, problem-solving and developing meaning. It provides a unique way of experiencing life. For millennia, listening, reasoning and speaking have been the primary ways that children have learned about themselves and the world. What parent hasn't watched in wonder as a child learns to speak?

Conversation helps children ease tensions, resolve conflicts, reflect on the past and plan for the future. Speaking and listening are primary ways that children build relationships, develop cognitive skills and understand themselves. As a social species, we engage in conversation almost continuously. When we aren't talking to real, live human beings, we are involved in communication through television, radio, phone, podcasts, blogs and texts. Reading and writing are also tools to talk, where authors speak to readers and provoke an internal dialogue. Children continue the non-stop conversation with dolls, toy dinosaurs and friends imaginary and real, present or absent, often in discussions and arguments that exist solely in their minds. The non-stop talking extends to debates and persuasive discussions with different versions of themselves.

Psychologists and philosophers are often perplexed by our incessantly chatty minds. Speech clearly gives humans massive survival, problem-solving and learning advantages, but does it have to invade every other learning capability? Children learn wordlessly in so many ways, from embodied activities to engaging experiences. They are creative and reflective in times of silence and daydreaming, but still there is the near-constant narration and storytelling, the describing, judging and evaluating inner dialogue interpreting almost every situation. Our guess is that inner dialogues and outer conversations bring to light so many forces of mind into one capability, informing us of the many worlds we inhabit. There is always something for our conversational mind to interpret, explain or investigate. The constant conversation serves as an ongoing monitor, keeping us aware of threats and opportunities in our constantly changing physical, emotional, social, cognitive and environmental states.

Despite the dominant role conversation plays in children's lives and the intertwined cognitive, emotional and social processes, language is perhaps children's most underappreciated and neglected capability. Researchers have found that most adults mistakenly believe that speaking and listening are fixed processes, rather than developmental skills that readily respond to instruction and practice.

While most adults understand the importance of talking and reading with children, many falsely believe that there is little we can do to alter the course of language development. Parents and teachers alike fail to appreciate that spoken language is a multifaceted capability and that even the simple act of listening requires active practice over decades to develop into a mature capability.

There are many parts that go into creating capable Careful Communicators. They have well-developed listening, attention and auditory-processing abilities. Careful Communicators have strong social capabilities and are able to listen to another person with full attention and empathy. They are not diverted by inner chatter, are able to listen deeply and non-judgmentally and are undistracted by random or self-centered thoughts. Their listening comprehension is strong and built on a foundation of fluid reasoning and active memory. Yet the Careful Communicator is more than the sum of these individual abilities; by developing this special capability, children strengthen the other eleven learning capabilities and gain insight into themselves and the world.

In a digital age, it is critical that we understand the importance of conversation and the central role that listening plays in a child's development. Listening is an ability that has been cheapened by the toxic political and popular culture, becoming almost a commodity in the age of twenty-four-hour news and advertising invading every message. Researchers who just a few decades ago were concerned with the effects of too much television now must keep up with the influx of technology, from game consoles and cell phones to podcasts and instructional videos. Today's children rely on chatting on cell phones, sending text messages and having rambling conversations on social media. It remains to be seen whether the virtual digital environment can substitute for the type of capability development that face-to-face communications have traditionally provided.

Probably the greatest threat from the digital invasion is to listening as a social ability. The world has grown noisy under the incessant drone of technology, which compromises listening skills with constant, low-quality chatter, sound bites and blaring media messages that garner only the barest of a child's attention. Parents and teachers should be concerned when children are uncomfortable with silence, unaware of environmental sounds like birds chirping or sirens blaring or if they struggle with listening skills such as reading. We should be alarmed when children struggle to engage in discussions, listen openly and respectfully or filter their own incessant chatter. Superficial, distracted listening rarely leads to understanding. Creating capable Careful Communicators, children who are active and empathetic listeners who can engage in reasoned and open-minded dialogues, should be one of our greatest goals.

The Capable and Careful Communicator

Careful Communicators have the opportunity and the freedom to speak their minds and engage in meaningful discussions, with solid listening, reasoning and responding skills. Peers and adults listen to Careful Communicators with empathy and open minds and hear their opinions, ideas and intentions in a supportive manner that promotes cognitive, social and emotional growth. Careful Communicators have the ability to use auditory processes to learn about themselves and others, resolve tensions and develop social competencies. They are able to take different perspectives and explain complex information while developing an awareness of the most important conversation, the internal dialogue.

The Wonders of Speech

Even before Mia was born, she was learning to listen. Language is so important and complex that children need a prenatal head start. During her last five months in the womb, Mia was picking up the muffled sounds and rhythms of Melissa's voice. This unconscious listening allowed Mia to recognize Melissa's special voice at birth, creating one of the first deep connections with her mother. Mia's cries reflected the accent patterns of her mother's speech, complete with Southern, urban and racial flavors. Mia even paid greater attention to passages from books that her mother read out loud while she was in the womb.

Lise Eliot, in her book, *What's Going On in There? How the Brain and Mind Develop in the First Five Years of Life*, details many of these wonderful findings. Newborn babies even recognize the theme songs to their pregnant mothers' favorite soap operas. Fathers and other significant others in a child's life must be patient, as Eliot warns that it will take time before children bond to more distant voices.[1] But after a few weeks their voices will hold greater attention than those of random visitors. This attention to voices is critically important to newborns as they are born with astonishingly poor eyesight. Babies must rely on speech as their primary link to others. Still, a newborn's hearing is underdeveloped and he or she is unable to hear quiet conversations or distant voices.

Melissa naturally spoke loudly and slowly to newborn Mia, exhibiting one of the first of many innate responses adults have that aid the development of hearing, listening and speech. Almost from birth, Melissa began speaking in Motherese, the instinctual, simplified speech common to most cultures and languages. Motherese is slower, higher-pitched speech with exaggerated intonations and simplified word usage and phrasing. As children mature, adults instinctually increase the complexity of words and sentences to match their developing speech patterns.

Eliot believes that Motherese is perfectly suited to develop babies' listening as well as speech. It helps babies pick out syllables and phonemes (individual speech sounds) and establish the sound patterns that form words. Babies like Mia use a sophisticated, if wholly innate and subconscious, statistical analysis to build a neural database of known words, derived from the frequency and pattern of phonemes in words. When a baby utters its first words, they will be composed of combinations of the phonemes that they most frequently hear. By six months of age, Mia's sensitivity to phonemes enabled her to identify the forty-four phonemes of English, discriminating them from the Spanish sounds that Melissa speaks with some of her friends.[2]

From this listening storehouse arises the great experiment children deploy to master spoken language. First, babies start babbling and cooing, producing happy, repetitive sing-songs of simple sounds. Around twelve months they will attempt their first approximations of words, often "dada" or "baba," as "d's" and "b's" are simpler sounds than the "m" in "mama." Mothers shouldn't take this personally as the first words are more experiments in vocalizations than meaningful words. While these early trial and error attempts at speech start slowly, by the age of two most children learn the pronunciation and meaning of words like bagel and stomach after just one hearing.[3]

The innate capabilities in children's genes are of little value unless they are nurtured in a thoughtful way. For example, children who have been deprived of early language experiences may never fully acquire speech. Children from "limited language" homes, where they may hear only a third of the spoken words that the average child hears, may struggle with language and academics once they reach school age. This outcome also awaits children who live in noisy homes where conversations are muffled.

It's not just the quantity of words that matters but also the quality of the language interaction. Having fluid conversations around shared activities like bathing, playing or feeding is as critical to language development as the raw number of words.

Creating a Listener

Speech is expressive, outward and obvious, while listening is receptive, quiet and inward. It is easy to favor speech over listening, forgetting the role that auditory processes play in creating the Careful Communicator. It's simple to understand the power of Motherese in developing speech while failing to grasp the role that adults play in the development of listening capabilities. Adults influence listening as much as they do a child's speech. Parents and teachers shape listening skills through the language environment they provide as well as how they listen and respond to their conversations. Adults' listening behaviors send powerful messages to children and greatly influence their listening and speaking abilities. They can promote children's listening abilities by keeping an open ear, free of judgments and interruptions. Children may become reluctant, distracted speakers when adults use dialogues to control behavior or dominate discussions, verbally or emotionally.

Madelyn Burley-Allen is a pioneer in understanding the importance of listening skills. In her book, *Listening: The Forgotten Skill*, she emphasizes that when children engage in conversation, "a request for listening is usually not a request for giving advice. It is a request to be listened to nonjudgmentally, from the heart."[4] When talking with children, adults often feel that they must take an instructional stance. We control the conversation, lecture and solve problems rather than listening with both our heads and hearts. We tend to offer rational, wordy answers when children are really looking for emotional support. When we offer children a friendly, caring ear—by really *listening*—they receive an emotional release and a chance to talk through experiences. Parents and teachers who listen openly and with empathy allow children to work through their thoughts and feelings and solve their own problems. They also present children with a healthy model for listening.

Many of the behavioral commands children hear from adults send negative messages about conversation. Children may withdraw from conversations with adults when they are told not to argue or interrupt, to be quiet or to shut up and listen. We should think about the message children hear when they are told to be seen and not heard. Adults who ask children, "Are you listening to me?" should ask themselves if they are listening to their children.

Teachers can create students who are fearful of and withdraw from conversation when they are told that it is disrespectful to talk out in class, to speak when a teacher is talking or to talk to friends. Children may be too emotionally upset or consumed with negative thoughts to enter into a meaningful conversation with adults. We shouldn't be surprised when children rebel or withdraw when they feel that no one is listening to them. Conversation and dialogue aren't strengthened when children are rewarded for how little they talk. Rather than disciplining children for talking in class or hindering their ability to talk to friends, we should harness the power of conversation to promote learning.

Empathetic Listening

Negative listening and speaking behaviors can severely restrict children's receptive and expressive abilities. Burley-Allen states that we are only about 25 percent efficient as listeners.[5] To create capable Careful Communicators, we should help children discover that listening is an active process, based on the capability to listen to oneself and others while remaining non-judgmental, objective and empathetic.

Burley-Allen divides listening into three overlapping levels that change depending on who we are with, what we are talking about and the purpose of the conversation. The highest level is *Empathetic Listening*, the open, caring type of listening we value. At this level, the child's attention is focused on the speaker's words, emotions and body language and he or she is receptive to "between the lines" messages. The Empathetic Listener shows this level of openness by both his or her verbal and nonverbal responses in an unselfconscious manner. When all participants are operating on this level, the discussion will be meaningful and rewarding.[6]

The second level is *Hearing Words*, exemplified by the superficial conversations that permeate half-attentive, mostly distracted and barely interested interactions. The communication at this level is superficial, holding little meaning or memory. Children may hear the words coming out of a friend or adult's mouth, appearing to be paying attention but unmotivated to understand or remember.[7] Classrooms and living rooms are inhabited largely by children and adults Hearing Words. Think of Mia sitting in the back of the room or Daniel engaged in one of his imaginative daydreams as his parents remind him to do some routine chore and you will understand Hearing Words.

Burley-Allen's lowest level is *Listening in Spurts*. Stereotypical teens are experts at this level of listening. They fluctuate between being tuned in and out, focused on themselves one minute and the speaker for a few seconds. They may follow a discussion only to watch for openings to interject their thoughts and emotions or purely to interrupt. When children are Listening in Spurts, their minds are consumed with unrelated matters, emotionally-laden judgments or the preparation of talking points and rebuttals. They may be swayed by the speaker's personality, appearance or status more than the content and meaning of his or her words. Superficial judgments such as biases, opposing beliefs or simple lack of respect for the speaker may also cause Listening in Spurts.

Children often listen with preconceived ideas, emotional postures and selfish goals that can turn a simple discussion into a manipulative action. By listening deeply and staying open emotionally and cognitively, children can discover some of life's greatest pleasures, building friendships and belonging to a group. To carry on a conversation requires the listener to respond by moving the speaker's ideas forward.

Inverted Curriculum

Listening with attention and empathy requires high levels of self-control and awareness, capabilities that only develop with practice, coaching and time. Parents and schools too often relegate speaking and listening to the whims of the assumed curriculum. Little effort is given to developing these capabilities despite what should be their prominent role in academics and cognitive, social and emotional well-being. Listening is perhaps the most critical ability in schools, with up to 70 percent of classroom time spent with teachers talking. Students acquire up to 85 percent of their knowledge by listening. Despite efforts by teachers to limit lectures, this auditorially-demanding method is still widely used, forming the default teaching mode. There is a cliché that says lectures are the best way to get information from a teacher's notebook to a student's notebook without touching the student's mind.

Reflecting on this state in 1984, Charles H. Swanson coined the term *inverted curriculum* in a presentation called "Their success is your success: teach them to listen."[8] He noted that the more a language task is used in school and life, the less instructional time it receives. His research showed that students received twelve years of instruction in writing, six to eight years learning to read, a year or two developing speaking skills and nearly no time learning to listen.

The inverted curriculum does a poor job of preparing children for life as adults, who spend about 40 percent of their time listening, 35 percent talking, 16 percent reading and 9 percent writing.[9] There is no question that reading and writing are important, but why should schools and, as a result, parents, spend virtually no time on listening and conversation skills?

It's hardly surprising that most teachers and parents fail to see the value of teaching conversational skills in general and listening in particular as few have experienced effective instruction in these areas. If the adults' schooling had emphasized auditory skills, then they would expect it in their children's education. Education and parenting rely on tradition and habit. If conversation and dialogue received even a fraction of the attention given to reading and math, then the curriculum would be far less inverted.

Auditory Processing

Daniel's academic challenges have many facets but they center on his listening. His attention is least steady when he is subjected to verbal onslaughts lacking relevance or connections. His memory fluctuates most during lectures and forced discussions. His difficulties with memorizing math facts and procedures are largely due to auditory memory issues. Daniel's reasoning ability is sharp when he is engaged in most free-time activities, but fails him when he is suddenly called on in class. His most common requests in class and at home are for statements and directions to be repeated. His difficulties with reading are caused by listening, which is why he has responded so weakly to print-based interventions such as phonics and level books. Difficulties with written expression often have auditory factors, including auditory reasoning and organization. Despite these issues, Daniel is smart and capable in so many ways.

The key concern in most evaluations that Daniel has been subjected to is auditory processing that includes auditory attention, memory, reasoning and discrimination. Auditory issues are often subtle, not "all or nothing" processes, that are easily missed by most parents and teachers. They don't stick out as prominently as reading and writing difficulties but hinder students in most academic endeavors. Even though they cause such pervasive learning difficulties, few parents or teachers, apart from speech therapists, are sensitive to them. They see that Daniel listens to music, follows conversations among his peers and speaks in complete sentences. Daniel's issues only become apparent when he is subjected to hours of auditory processes in school.

Auditory issues are often mistaken for attention or daydreaming issues, which is easy to do with a student like Daniel. When his parents ask him to make his bed or take the trash out two or three times, it's easier to blame his inattention or mind wandering than an auditory issue. He may be listening, but if even one word in the request is garbled, he may miss its meaning or get confused before the message reaches his memory or his impulse to act. If Daniel struggles with simple statements, we can imagine how difficult it is to follow ten or twenty minutes of a lesson his teacher is giving on writing.

Reading as Listening and a Special Conversation

Daniel's struggles with reading and writing are quite typical of students in higher elementary grades and secondary school. Almost all such students have some measure of auditory processing issues. Very few are accurately diagnosed and fewer still receive interventions that address the root problem—difficulty processing spoken words with high accuracy. Phonics, reading practice and English language courses are not clinical therapy for reading difficulties. The failure to address reading difficulties as auditory processing difficulties is a major reason national reading scores have changed little over the last three decades.[10]

If we focus on reading from an advanced primal perspective, we discover three facts, all related to listening and spoken words. First, reading is artificial, as our brains lack neural circuits devoted to literacy. Reading is a mental trick that is wholly dependent on spoken language, from the auditory system that decodes spoken words, to the receptive language areas that give spoken words and phrases meaning, to the expressive areas that give voice to the words. We have the ability to turn all kinds of images into concepts, especially objects into words. Look around the area where you are and name the objects you see. This same naming ability drives reading. Look at the words, composed of little more than alphabetic squiggles and name them. Now you are reading using the naming functions of speech.

Second, reading is a receptive language ability, fundamentally tied to listening. Young children who struggle to understand stories that are read to them most often will have difficulties learning to read to themselves. The assessments that most predict reading ability also measure listening ability:

- Phonemic awareness—the ability to separate and manipulate sounds in spoken words
- Auditory discrimination—the ability to differentiate between two similar-sounding words or phonemes
- Auditory memory—the ability to remember and recall spoken words, numbers and sounds

While these assessments are routine in many elementary schools, they are all but non-existent at the secondary level. This is regrettable, since the levels of listening and phonemic ability it takes to read words that older students confront, such as *strengthen* and *mitochondria*, are far higher than what is demanded by words such as *rat* and *slap*.

Third, from an advanced primal perspective, reading is a special type of conversation between the reader and the text. Proficient readers use the same listening, reasoning and speaking skills, including empathy and attention, when they read. For them, reading is like an author talking to them, effortless and with deep meaning. This conversation is anything but easy for students with subtle auditory issues, as they are magnified when confronted with print, which has no voice. The reading conversation also suffers, as books don't provide feedback and nonverbal information and lack the give-and-take questioning available in face-to-face conversations.

Because we don't address reading as a listening ability, parents and teachers accept diagnoses of reading difficulties that lack clinical or neurological grounding. Thus, millions of students needlessly struggle through phonics and reading-to-read instruction that does little to address the auditory and phonemic issues that limit reading ability and interest. Parents and teachers who have read extensively to children with auditory issues find out that this level of listening, even if provided for many years, promotes listening but isn't effective therapy for auditory-based reading difficulties. Daniel's bedroom is lined with books that his parents read to him and which he enjoyed. However, the phonemic connections between spoken and written words eluded him, even after years of learning about phonics.

Talking with Kids and Teens

Adrián and Lea, Daniel's parents, are well aware of his many strengths and subtle weaknesses in the abilities we lump together as conversation. Adrián and Lea know how hard it is for two adults to communicate, even after two decades of practice. They take extra time to make sure that the conversation is gentle and clear. They rarely talk "at" Daniel but rather aim to talk with him. They engage him in conversation, slowly drawing in his listening and attention. As the discussion progresses, they activate his conversational reasoning by occasionally asking him for his opinion or an expansive question. Finally, they engage his listening comprehension by checking for understanding.

A number of good strategies for talking to children come from research into forensic interviews and delicate conversations with children and teens who have been victims of or witnesses to crimes. These interviews are artificial, as the adults have goals far more compelling than the average discussion. Forensic interviews start from the position that the adult's behavior and attitudes tend to dominate conversations, introducing biases and emotions that heavily influence the child's response. To get children to talk at all is a challenge, but to also get unbiased facts and an honest assessment of events can be quite difficult.

The first principle of forensic interviews is to have the child do most of the talking. Conversations don't go well when adults start with a series of open-ended questions to which the child responds in short phrases. If you ask a child how her day was or who he ate lunch with, then you should expect one-to-three-word replies. Instead, start by building rapport or with a narrative. "You looked tired [or excited] when you got off the bus. You must have experienced problems [or something positive]. How did you handle the problem [or situation]?"

Invitations to talk often elicit a positive response. "Tell me about the bus ride home. Did you have any interactions with children you like or did anyone cause problems for you?" Once the conversation begins to roll, listen more than talk, as the focus should be on the child. Keep the conversation going by asking the child to elaborate, "Tell me more about…" or by using reflective listening, "You said X. What did that mean to you [or how did it make you feel]?"

Inner and Other Conversations

While auditory issues are at the basis of Daniel's struggles in school, they account for a good proportion of Zoe's academic success. Her listening attention is effortless and auditory messages are clearly processed, automatically activating memory and action. When she reads, it's as comfortable an experience as listening to her father reading a story. Since she doesn't expend mental effort turning print into meaningful speech, all her energy can be applied to mental imagery, comprehension and enjoyment.

This easy state of understanding extends to lectures and discussions. Almost every word a teacher or her fellow students utter, she processes, categorizes and finds it a proper place in her systems of understanding.

In addition to experiencing auditory ease while reading or listening in class, there is another area where Zoe excels—with her inner listening and discussions. Zoe maintains both an "other" focus and an "inner" awareness, listening to her inner dialogue while fully attending to her friends' and adults' words. Zoe has an internal discussion, almost a debate with herself, where her inner dialogue forms a powerful way of working out emotional, social and other problems. She doesn't let these conversations get out of hand. She doesn't chase thoughts, talk to the exclusion of others or dominate conversations.

Jan and Jeff promote their daughter Zoe's inner focus by giving her quiet times that don't drown out her internal dialogues. During conversations, they repeat back parts of her thoughts, asking her to listen carefully to what she says. Jan and Jeff also point out to Zoe when she is listening openly, while at other times they ask her if she is making an unreasonable judgment. When Zoe is being hard on herself or a speaker, they suggest that she reevaluate the situation. This gives her a greater understanding of how she thinks and expresses emotions but also how words can make or break relationships. She listens to statements she makes about herself, searching for patterns and beliefs that may hold her back. Zoe's parents point out negative ideas that creep into her thoughts and speech, helping her develop sensitivity to statements that start with "I can't..." or "I should..." or "I'm not good at..." as well as boasting, bragging or bullying.

Burley-Allen believes that "Listening to others gives us the information needed to make the most of our communications. Listening to *ourselves* gives us the information to act in our own best interests."[11] As Zoe listens and reflects on her thoughts and words, she develops greater self-awareness. With this inner insight, she is less susceptible to conditioned, repetitive and biased thoughts and emotions.

Deep Listening

Deep listening engages attention, memory and reasoning and encourages question-and-response discussions. It is the remedy for self-absorbed, passive and superficially-engaged listening that children easily fall into in the age of digital technology. Deep listening builds on attentive, empathetic listening by adding the elements of reflection and evaluation, an open-minded critique. Another pioneer in listening and learning, Sam Duker, believed that the intertwined abilities of listening and reading require deep, critical listening. Duker used the word *critical* to mean analytical, not judgmental. A critical listener considers the speaker's point of view but also his biases, background knowledge and the logic of his evidence. Critical listeners look for the speaker's purpose and consider his expertise. They also try to grasp the take-home message, or the gist, of the conversation, sometimes using questions such as, "So I think what you are saying is..." or "Do you mean that...?"[12]

Critical listeners and readers sense when a speaker or author is trying to persuade them for personal motives. Duker worried that children without critical listening abilities could easily be persuaded by individuals and groups more interested in manipulating than communicating. Long before twenty-four-hour cable news, opinionated talk shows and non-stop political campaigns, Duker warned, "It hardly seems necessary to point out how very greatly the public's lack of skills in (critical listening) have aided glib politicians to wield power over us and our destinies."[13]

While some children develop these skills through their life experiences, most will benefit from deliberate practice. Duker felt that this practice should include identifying common propaganda devices, including social persuasions, such as "Everybody is doing it" or "If well-liked or famous person X is doing it, then so should you" and glittering generalities such as "It will really help the school" or "It's the right thing to do."[14]

Explaining Learning

Educator John Jensen believes that one change that can significantly increase children's learning abilities is to have them explain their understanding of material or ideas. It isn't enough for children to give correct answers or show a basic understanding; they must be able to put their understanding in their own words and then expand the explanation over time. Jensen calls this *Explaining Learning*.[15]

In his book, *Teaching Students to Work Harder and Enjoy It*, Jensen emphasizes that learning to explain information in your own words requires practice, preferably over many sessions. This well-established practice, called *distributed learning*, reflects the needs of memorization memory—it is hard to memorize information in just one shot. Memory absorbs information over time, preferably in small doses spread out over many weeks or months. This is the opposite of the common approach—teaching intensive units for a week or two.

Jensen's method takes distributed learning a few steps further by making the information readily available. Students often get hard copies of basic information in a lecture or discussion, which remain in their hands while they give their explanations. They are not forced to recall information while they are trying to learn it deeply, which removes another memory barrier. The real genius in Jensen's method is the emphasis on the students' oral explanations and understanding, rather than the teacher or parent doing most of the thinking and talking.[16] Critical listening and explaining learning are strong antidotes to Instructionism. They ask children to take the lead in discussions and reasoning, honoring and honing their learning abilities.

Reviving Speaking and Listening

Conversation is an important aspect of childhood and the teen years. We should do everything possible to nurture the capable Careful Communicator. Talking and listening build social bonds, enhance learning experiences and let us know what is on a child's mind. We have witnessed endless situations in public and Montessori schools where children are free to converse while achieving these goals.

Listening, reasoning and speaking promote both an "inner" and "other" perspective. These three main aspects of the Careful Communicator also promote autonomy. Students who learn in groups with focused listening and gentle adult guidance will learn independent problem-solving and learning skills naturally.

Creating the Capable Careful Communicator

Conversational capabilities are easily enhanced by setting aside time and activities that promote deep listening and meaningful discussions.

Small moments that promote conversation can include children consuming a few meals a week with all screens turned off. Conversely, everyone in the home or school could read the same thought-provoking article and discuss it. Remember, how you listen and speak, as well as your behavioral attitudes about children's words, play a large role in your children's conversational abilities. Non-judgmental, empathetic listening is a powerful force in creating the Careful Communicator.

Parents and teachers should actively promote deep listening and open discussions in schools. All children should be tested for auditory processing problems, as they are a factor in almost every learning difficulty. Reading should be approached as a receptive language ability and as a special type of conversation.

. . . .

SMALL MOMENTS THAT CREATE THE CAREFUL COMMUNICATOR

Promote reflective and critical listening and perspective-taking for children a few times a day, at home and in school.

Adults should understand how to talk with young children and teens by practicing the Small Moments with an open mind.

Use Explaining Learning by having a child explain information or situations in their own words. If the material is important enough to learn, then it is important enough to practice by repeated and extended explanation.

Practice Three Step Listening—Attention, Reasoning, Comprehension— checking for attention by asking their thoughts and opinions and looking for listening comprehension.

Adults should remember and utilize forensic science methods like invitations to talk, avoiding open-ended questions and leading with a narrative.

Avoid giving advice, dominating discussions or solving problems with children by listening to them. Understand that children are looking for safe ways to express emotions, not to hear adults' opinions.

. . . .

Part 4

. . . .

Meaning-Making Capabilities

11

....
The Backstage Director

Much of children's ability to learn is hidden from view in their subconscious minds. Just as imagination, feelings and intuitions largely live below the surface, so do most learning capabilities. This is the world of the Backstage Director, who helps children learn with the greatest of ease and turns dreams into reality. This inner capability lacks the overt form of the Curious Explorer or the Action Character and its workings are not readily apparent even to trained observers.

Learning in babies and children has long been a mystery. While children's innate learning abilities based on emotion, perception and interaction are slowly being exposed by research, language development still seems like a miracle to most parents. It is not clear how children learn through play, social interaction and experience or assemble large bodies of knowledge, immense vocabularies and conceptual understanding.

Seasoned educators often resort to generalities, like explicit instruction, repetition and extended practice, when asked to explain how children learn. Even highly-skilled observers have drawn wild conclusions about how learning happens. The revered developmental psychologist Jean Piaget, who systematically observed his children and grandchildren's development for decades, held wonderful ideas, such as children are born with cognitive structures that hold pre-existing ideas about the world; however, he also believed inaccurately that babies were blank slates.[1]

The nature of learning has been such a great mystery, because it largely occurs below the level of awareness. Only a small fraction of our thoughts, emotions, bodily sensations, memories and perceptions reach our active awareness. Parents and researchers alike have grabbed onto the few outward signs of learning and largely overlooked the vast activity just under the surface. Explicit and effort-filled instruction that focuses on words and actions is easier to see than the 95 percent or so of learning that is subconscious in nature.[2]

Since so much of the learning process happens below the level of conscious thought, our conscious minds are free for selective important tasks. The subconscious acts as a filter, allowing only the information requiring special attention or novel solutions to enter our conscious minds. It keeps track of the hundreds of cognitive, perceptual, emotional and social processes and prevents our minds from becoming overwhelmed by sensations, emotions, thoughts and memories. Without these filters, everyday experiences would become psychological nightmares. Even our most cherished cognitive abilities, such as reasoning, decision-making, creativity, judgments and problem-solving, arise from the back stages of our minds.

Quite often our conscious mind is unaware of what we are thinking. Complex thinking is reserved for solving unique problems, examining exceptional situations and improvising when habits suddenly fail us. When our habits and instincts are not up to the task or the situation seems to call for a unique solution, divergent thinking or an uncommon response from our conscious mind come into play.

The subconscious plays an especially important role in children, as they have very limited ability to consciously reason and willfully attend. As cognitive scientist Daniel Willingham asserts in his book, *Why Don't Students Like School?* children's minds aren't designed for heavy thinking, nor to pay attention for anything more than short bursts of time.[3]

While we refer to conscious thinking and subconscious processes as distinct parts of the mind, in reality they are fused into one system. Brain scans don't readily expose the difference between conscious thought and subconscious processes. Conscious activity forms the tip of the mostly subconscious iceberg, with the visible portion vitally connected to and supported by the large mass below the surface. We have fast, automatic reactions and slow, deliberate plans. We can be spontaneous and intuitive one minute and engage in slow, deliberate thought the next. We have cold, rational ideas and wonderful flights of imagination. These activities of the mind happen along a continuum, often using overlapping and intertwined networks of the brain.

Subconscious processes come to the surface in the form of sudden ideas, feelings, images and associations, as well as memories and intuitions. Often they present as a vague impression or a dull awareness, but with a little extra attention we can experience them clearly. All it takes is a little quiet, limited distractions and an inward focus. We also experience subconscious thoughts as tip-of-the-tongue experiences, when a name is suddenly remembered or the answer to a vexing problem comes in a flash. Background thinking shows itself when, in the middle of a conversation, you suddenly say something that seems brilliant.

The subconscious has long been viewed in the West as the Freudian dark side of the mind, inhabited by sexual urges, irrational thoughts, primitive instincts and unwelcomed emotions; our rational side has been conceived as a counterforce—better behaved, clearer thinking and more sensible. If only reason could triumph over emotions, the thinking goes, then a new age of reason will arise, allowing individuals and society to flourish. However, these beliefs are as outdated as those of the blank slate or the disembodied mind. Our conscious side is far from rational, as it is plagued with biases, mental shortcuts and delusions (we will discuss this in chapter 13). We believe the subconscious is nothing like Sigmund Freud envisioned, performing a range of powerful and positive processes. The Backstage Director is the source of great ideas, meaningful emotions and a good bit of wisdom.

Rather than being the mind's dark recess, our subconscious—or technically "pre-conscious"—mind is the site of most learning and cognition, guiding almost all of our thoughts and actions. Researchers have conducted countless experiments that show how the subconscious mind perceives and processes information that goes largely unnoticed by our everyday attention. After attending a lecture called "Better than Conscious," science writer Kate Douglas wrote, "Our subconscious is not an unthinking autopilot that needs to be subjugated by rationality, but a purposeful, active and independent guide to behavior."[4]

The Capable Backstage Director

Backstage Directors are aware of the subconscious aspects of their minds that influence feelings, thoughts, relationships and behaviors. They are aware of the role these rich processes play in experiences, relationships, judgments, decisions, imagination and learning. They access subconscious processes, including emotions, ideas and impulses, when their conscious minds are quiet and have the opportunity to relax, reflect, daydream and mind wander. Capable Backstage Directors understand that the subconscious's automatic emotional responses, habitual behaviors and conditioned thoughts make routine activities easier but should be examined, periodically, for effectiveness. Backstage Directors understand that their minds will revisit the past and plan and practice future events.

Backstage Learning

Educational philosopher John Dewey, in *Experience and Education*, said, "Perhaps the greatest of all pedagogical fallacies is the notion that a person learns only the particular thing he is studying at the time. Collateral learning in the way of formation of enduring attitudes, of likes and dislikes, may be and often is much more important than the spelling lesson or the lesson in geography or history that has been learned."[5] Education and parenting tend to over-rely on explicit and effortful thinking rather than the subconscious processes. However, most of what children learn isn't from instruction but from richer, more engaging "Big L Learning" situations pulling in multiple modules of the conscious and subconscious mind.

Parenting and teaching is most effective when it engages the implicit learning systems of the mind. These systems are largely effortless, demanding little conscious attention. Their role in learning is easily seen in active, experiential learning but also robust in imaginative and created learning situations. Much of Zoe's academic success can be explained by her ability to learn implicitly, with ease. It also explains why Mia learns effortlessly when she is active and why Daniel gains so much from his walks in the woods.

It's not that Zoe has more issues and ideas in her subconscious than Daniel or Mia during academic times, but that the backstage processes are closer to the surface. Images, ideas, memories and background knowledge and other subconscious work are better organized and orchestrated. Zoe makes associations between immediate classroom instruction and her background knowledge and store of experiences. Ready access to these subconscious processes means that Zoe is ready to answer a question before the teacher has finished asking it. In fact, she has been asked not to cry out, "Oh! I know!" and instead raise her hand—which she does with lightning speed. Zoe actually does less heavy thinking than classmates. While their minds work laboriously on a task, answers just come to her.

The Space to Learn

Not only does Zoe have quick and automatic access to subconscious processes, but she can also integrate them with incoming information from instruction. The subconscious space where we combine our inner learning with new teaching is called *working memory*. This is not a specific place in the brain, but a process where inner and outer flows of information are combined in new ways, which results in reasoning and learning.

Cognitive scientist Daniel Willingham describes working memory as the "fundamental bottleneck of human cognition," because it has a limited capacity to hold thoughts and memories for a restricted period of time.[6] Small differences in working memory capacity may translate into significant gaps in academic and social performance. Zoe's relatively large working memory capacity helps her reflect on more plot elements, character traits and background information while she reads, greatly aiding comprehension. Mia's average working memory capacity compromises her math ability, as she struggles to recall multiplication facts, figure out the shifts in quantity in word problems and picture the problem all at one time. Daniel compensates for his small deficit in auditory working memory by employing his expertise in all things natural.

While our understanding of working memory has grown in recent years, there hasn't been a corresponding increase in methods and techniques to expand it. Working memory has proven largely resistant to interventions, but there are a number of methods and strategies that help children who struggle with this important ability. Working memory is influenced by attention; children who can filter out irrelevant information avoid internal or external distractions and shift attention between tasks ease the load on working memory. These three aspects of attention are largely under subconscious control, as any parent or teacher who has asked a child to pay attention knows.

Attention and working memory abilities fade when children are tired or just overwhelmed by mental work. The pace and intensity of academic work added to homework and digital activities take a significant toll on working memory. Homes and schools that limit physical activity and downtime further tax the ability of children with superior working memory and attention.

When children are unable to listen and pay attention, when little enters or leaves memory, parents and teachers should lighten the cognitive load by talking slowly and breaking down instructions and information into smaller pieces.

Children are more capable when they are engaged, find information meaningful and interesting and have sufficient background knowledge or personal experience before learning new information. An effective strategy to boost working memory and learning is to separate the inner memory-based stream of information from the outer stream of instruction.

Children are easily overwhelmed when they have to recall information or stored experiences while processing new information. History class is taxing for Mia as she is constantly asked to recall historic events while listening to new details. When Mia is called on in the middle of this process, her teacher often asks her why she isn't paying attention. Mia may seem to have learned material one day that disappears the next day, because she struggles to fully combine new instruction with her stored learning. She also struggles with multi-step instructions or when the teacher talks in detail for more than a few minutes.

Melissa understands Mia's moderate memory ability and works hard to separate behavioral slights from cognitive limits. As a mother and a teacher, Melissa is aware that the mandated curriculum largely fails to account for the cognitive limitations of children. She knows that children can only read, write and listen productively for short periods and need frequent mental breaks. She rarely demands that children pay attention for long, as their ability to willfully focus is often measured in seconds.

Melissa has seen the cognitive load dramatically increase in recent years. Her school has gone from thirty minutes of reading instruction to ninety minutes in a misguided and unproductive effort to improve scores. Melissa decided this year to place the reality of children's learning abilities above test scores by reverting to two twenty-minute periods for reading, writing and math spread through the day. In between, she has inserted frequent short breaks for creative endeavors, physical and mindfulness activities and just plain, quiet downtime. She has seen a marked improvement in interest, motivation and achievement after instituting this mind and body-friendly schedule.

During discussions at home, Melissa periodically checks to see if Mia is struggling with attention or memory. Mia's mother often starts conversations with, "Do you remember…" bringing up past events or background information before bringing up a new subject. She limits her monologues to a few minutes and frequently checks for understanding and focus. When Melissa asks Mia to follow multi-step instructions, she writes them down or asks Mia to repeat them. If Melissa must shift from one topic to another, she makes sure Mia is following her by asking a question or explaining the context. Melissa makes sure Mia's thoughts and memories are not someplace else before she changes the subject.

Melissa also allows Mia plenty of quiet time so that her working memory and attention are available for their other important purposes—daydreaming, imagination, mind wandering and time travel. These subconscious activities rely on large chunks of working memory. Working memory is essential to planning, setting goals, setting priorities and just thinking about what to do next.

These quieter moments have traditionally been viewed as a waste of time, that "idle minds are the devil's playground." Researchers now believe that mental downtime is not only vital, but also a time when children's minds are most active—mostly on a subconscious level. Psychologist Mary Helen Immordino-Yang, in her article "Rest is Not Idleness," states that times of inner focus are essential for consolidating memories and solidifying learning. The mind uses the quiet space to solve problems, find meaning in confusing events and organize conflicting information. Mind wandering and reflection aren't so much a lack of focus, but rather a diffused inward attention that leads to mental clarity, boosting outward attention and the ability to learn.[7]

Backstage Behavior Director

Another area that the Backstage Director heavily influences is behavior. Conscious behavioral regulation is mostly under the sway of subconscious processes. Children only have a limited ability to consciously control their behavior. Rules and restrictions work the best when they become ingrained into subconscious thoughts and habits.

Children are influenced by external forces, but mostly in the form of social conformity and imitation. Children have an innate ability to learn by mimicking others, letting context guide their behaviors. Copycatting and fitting in are paths of least resistance, especially for young minds that have not yet learned to monitor their behavior. Imitating the behavior of others is far easier than learning to apply externally imposed rules to a wide range of changing and challenging situations.

Imitating is not only easier than using rules to guide moment-by-moment behavior, but it is also a powerful way of learning. Language, motor and social skills are largely learned by mimicry. Children rely heavily on others to show them how to act, relate, make decisions and form judgments. Their ability to quickly infer people's thoughts, emotions and intentions just by visual cues allows them to sum up situations without heavy thinking or what an out-of-sight adult deems appropriate.

Imitation provides children with mental shortcuts to guide behavior that foster what psychologist John A. Bargh calls a "sophisticated unconscious behavior guidance system...Our genes have provided us not with fixed responses to specific events...but with general tendencies that are adaptive towards changing situations."[8] Imitation provides children with an adoptive response to an endless variety of situations; children can move from subsisting out in the wilderness to urban living and quickly pick up the various norms of behavior. Bargh refers to this flexibility as *contextual priming*, where situations provide subconscious cues to behavioral responses, providing "precise adjustment to events and people in present time."[9]

When Daniel walks into an unpredictable situation, such as the day he decided to sit with a different group of semi-friends for the first time at lunch, he must rapidly figure out this new social and emotional territory and plan his behavioral response. His Backstage Director pulls up the little background knowledge he has on the group, quickly combining it with immediate impressions of their emotions and behaviors. Without much conscious thought, Daniel makes a prediction about how they will react to his presence. He relaxes a bit when one of the boys acknowledges him, but Daniel continues to rely on sensory and emotional perception to guide his behavior.

Daniel factors school rules and parental expectations into this cognitive and emotional mix—not consciously but by force of habit. Feelings, intuitions and gut reactions that proved beneficial in the past will also influence his behavior. In this charged environment, Daniel will be evaluating his behavior based on the immediate responses of these new potential friends. Only later will he reflect and review the event and his actions in light of the expectations his parents and teachers have set.

Daniel's conscious mind can also help resolve inner conflicts that arise from primal behavioral influences. His lunchtime decisions will be shaped by approach-avoidance behaviors—should he sit next to his safe and well-known friend or a more interesting but emotionally unpredictable acquaintance? He will wrestle with conflicting emotions; should he suppress his emotions and listen to his new potential friends or let out his feelings about the video game that he started playing yesterday? Behind the scenes, Daniel is weighing whether to seek immediate gratification from the encounter or hold off for deeper rewards later. He will worry about acknowledgment and acceptance, emotions that play a large role in the social lives of children. All this will require time to think, which will be difficult in the noisy and emotionally-charged lunchroom. Instead, there will be time to reflect on the day's events during his solo walk in the woods and then, during dinner, when he can safely confide and converse with his parents.

Busy Downtime

Not every child has the benefit of routine downtime like Daniel, where he is free to reflect, evaluate, daydream and time travel. His parents leave their ideas about productivity at the office, understanding that downtime isn't just about resting the mind but allowing it to shift into another active mode. The Backstage Director may operate from behind the scenes, but is busy in its own way. Even during sleep the mind is churning through the day's activity, consolidating memories, pulling bits of information together and directing dozens of dreams.

The Backstage Director is even busier while it is awake, providing the conscious mind with subtext, context, memories and emotional tones. When it is free from environmental input and sensory stimulation and from teachers teaching and parents parenting, it shifts its resources inward. Attention is directed toward the mind's internal activity. Attention that is usually focused on outward emotions turns to feelings; focus on physical movement gives way to awareness of the body. When conversations fade, the mind is free to focus on inner dialogues and subtler thoughts. Distant neural networks that are normally consumed with specific external tasks begin to communicate within the mind, making plans, running simulations about the future and re-imagining the past.

Inward focus arises when children are free of external stimuli, academic demands and digital distractions. Many children need a calm body and a quiet mind to engage the Backstage Director while others engage their minds while playing, running, swimming or listening to music. While Daniel turns his attention inward during his walks in the woods, he also uses busier times to reflect and organize his thoughts and feelings. One day after a walk, Daniel reviewed the situation as his mother drove him to a friend's house. He asked himself "what-if" questions—What if he had invited another close friend to join them? What if he had confronted one of the boys who was dominating discussion? What if he had bought a sophisticated iced tea instead of childish chocolate milk? His mind also time traveled forward, imagining future lunchtime social interactions. Next time, what would happen if he bought everybody ice cream, invited a close friend or tried to just sit with the two boys who seemed to like his presence? He ran numerous scenarios of future events from the safety of his mind, transforming anxiety about the future into workable alternative solutions.

This level of reflection and planning would have been very difficult in the heat of the moment but arose naturally late one afternoon in the quiet of his parent's car. By the time they had reached his friend's house, Daniel had sorted through the day's events and was comfortable with the next day's possible lunchtime scenarios. He could now put the day's events aside and enjoy an old friendship and a new adventure.

A Sense of Self

The Backstage Director plays a major role in helping children form an image of themselves. This is another example of the subconscious mind filtering an immense amount of information into a form that is useful for our conscious mind. A child's sense of self is a greatly simplified idea, close to an abstract concept or an imaginary character, constructed from an immense array of sensory, social, emotional and experiential information. It relies on reconstructed memories and selected background knowledge to create the sense of a stable personality. This is a perfect job for the subconscious—preventing children from being overwhelmed not just from the external flow of information but from the hundreds of internal learning networks that the mind uses to survive and thrive.

A sense of self prevents children from experiencing a different personality each time they switch from the Reasonable Judge to the Action Character, before being transformed into the Curious Explorer and back to the Backstage Director. Each personified capability has its own way of interacting and learning, engaging different mental states. A single sense of self, a unified character with a predictable personality and a consistent narrative, is a simple solution to having what is possibly the most complex mind on the planet.

Cognitive psychologist Bruce Hood, author of *The Self Illusion: How the Social Brain Creates Identity*, believes that "the self is an effective way of having experiences and interacting with the world," a simple solution to being a complex social being.[10] Hood theorizes that children develop a sense of self around three or four years of age, when they start to form autobiographic memories of experiences and interactions. While some people have vague and fragmented memories of themselves as young as two, there are no remembered events from the perspective of an isolated self: "It's not that you have forgotten what it was like to be an infant—you simply were not "you" at that age because there was no constructed self, and so you cannot make sense of early experiences in the context of the person to whom these events happened."[11]

Babies do form enduring memories, but they feed learning, not an individual sense of self. According to Hood, self-forming memory is composed of "events that we can recall in which we are the main player."[12] Like most memories of experiences, they are rough and selective recreations of events that in no way resemble photographs or videos. Memories are also fragile, forming a fluid foundation for a fixed sense of self, like a story that changes with every retelling. Memories can also be totally constructed. Psychologists can easily convince people that they participated in events that never occurred.

A sense of self built on selected information, unstable memories and rough interpretation of experiences isn't a firm foundation for identity. There are times when children will defend this sense as if it were the core of their being. However, self-identification waxes and wanes in children. Very selfish children consumed with their own needs can become lost in play and act in the most kind and caring manner. Their sense of self dissolves when they are experiencing flow, which, by definition, involves a loss of self-consciousness.

Children's sense of self is often built on perceived social perspectives—what they think others think about them. Self-image in children and teens is heavily influenced by how they imagine they appear to others, wild guesses about what their friends think of them and emotional responses to social interactions. In the primary grades, children tend to make their subconscious assessments of themselves based on their performance on a single task—how well they draw, build block towers or write their names. Their self-image is also heavily influenced by the strength of their relationships with close friends and immediate family.

In their middle years children continue to shape their self-image around judgments about relationships and skills. They tend to look at broader areas of ability, judging themselves not on specific events, but instead on if they are, in general, good students, skilled athletes or capable friends. Teens expand on this formula, basing their self-evaluations largely on their physical attractiveness, ability to make new or romantic relationships and performance in adult tasks. From these broad and often superficial judgments, they arrive at an abstract sense of who they are.

Children's self-image heavily influences their behavior; if they perceive themselves to be successful students then they act like good students. If they judge themselves to be socially incompetent, then they will shy away from challenging relationships and may disregard group rules. The other influences on self-identity are also subconscious, especially moods and bodily feelings. These moment-to-moment self-perceptions are also influenced by memories, habitual ideas, desires and dreams of a more-perfect existence.

With this fragile foundation, children's sense of self is constantly shifting. Many children and teens live in a constant state of judgment and self-evaluation, trying to grab onto a fixed identity in a sea of continual change. When identities are prone to change, particularly during the teen years, both their self-concept (their assessment of their abilities and characteristics) and self-esteem (how they feel about themselves) will fluctuate in unpredictable ways.

The reasoning children employ to form their self-image is prone to biases and distortions that we will explore in a later chapter when we introduce the subject of the Reasonable Judge. Children fall prey to confirmation biases, taking in information that confirms their preexisting beliefs and rejecting input that challenges their images of themselves. Children tend to view themselves as good or bad, happy or sad, fully capable or incapable. They often think about themselves in black-and-white terms with little sensitivity to the nuances of human character.

A Solid Story

Parents and teachers can help children create a positive self-image by helping them build larger family narratives. In "Family Narrative Interactions and Children's Sense of Self," the Family Narratives Lab at Emery University explored the power of shared narratives on children's self-concept. There are many ways that families can share narratives that cover positive and negative individual and group events, encompassing topics as diverse as family vacations to personal conflicts. Shared conversations that allowed for open dialogues incorporating children's perspectives were related to higher self-esteem, especially in girls. Storytelling that involves family members taking individual turns telling stories from their personal points of view also produced positive results, especially for boys. The Emery group accounted for the gender difference by reasoning that girls tend to be more focused on social relations and boys more moved by individual and autonomous actions.[13]

The Emery group found that there was no benefit to children when a parent dominated the storytelling or used personal narratives to force their singular perspective on children. Children pulled back from dialogues that felt like lectures or contained elements of control.[14]

SMALL MOMENTS THAT CREATE THE BACKSTAGE DIRECTOR

- Understand that your explicit instructions about behavior are limited compared to the implicit manner in which children learn.

- Explore children's emotions, feelings, intuitions, dreams and actions as they arise from the subconscious.

- Help children become aware of memories, ideas and images.

- Provide children with quiet time free from external demands on attention or memory.

- Be aware that children may use activities such as running, swimming, listening to music and making crafts as downtime.

- Lighten the cognitive, emotional and social load on children as they are easily overwhelmed.

- Separate memory tasks from new information for children and provide background knowledge before bringing up new topics.

- Understand that behavior is heavily influenced by social cues.

- Help children balance the use of imitation and social cues with rules to promote flexible, context-dependent, appropriate behaviors.

- Discuss your rules and expectations for children in context and during times of reflection.

- Use inclusive narratives and discussions with children to build identity and self-awareness.

- Point out to children the benefits of a flexible and changing identity rather than one based on superficial appearances, transient performances and passing emotions.

12

The Knowledge Architect

Our eighth capability, personified as the Knowledge Architect, is based on a child's primal ability to learn by taking in and organizing information. Children absorb information quickly, be it about the behavior of animal predators or friends on the playground. Acquiring information, a basic component of learning, comes easily to humans. The great biologist E.O. Wilson believes that our minds are so primed to learn that "only small parts of the brain resemble a [blank slate]...the remainder is more like an exposed negative waiting to be dipped into developer fluid."[1] Children are naturally attracted to facts, ideas and knowledge, whether it is how things work, local gossip or why the sun rises in the east. We have seen how babies derive information on everyday physics, language and emotions. Teens absorb sports statistics and the life histories of celebrities and become experts on their special interests.

We have examined many ways that learning comes to children with great ease when they are engaged in capability-building experiences. Active exploration with a curious mindset, inquisitive experimentation and engaging in personal interests and meaningful pursuits all promote "Big L Learning," including factual understanding. Listening with intent, talking with an open mind and explaining information in one's own words also bring a wealth of knowledge. Storytelling (in mathematics, science and history) is a strong candidate for the most effective way to convey information. We have explored the ingrained learning abilities inherent to daydreaming, imagination, mind wandering, mindfulness, flow states and constructive reflection. We have examined the role of backstage processes such as memory, time travel, interpretation, pre-conscious learning and even sleep, all of which engage massive learning capabilities far more than concerted thinking does.

With all these marvelous ways of learning, gaining knowledge and developing capabilities, why should children need other ways of becoming informed and knowledgeable? The simple answer is that our kids are not hunter-gatherers but citizens of a world that supplies and demands mind-boggling amounts of information to be consumed, memorized and recalled. Blogs, websites, social media and even digital games feed children a constant diet of information. Teens may spend ten or more hours a day talking, listening and consuming written and digital media. While not all of this information is retained, yet alone comprehended, the information load is staggering and growing. From 2008 to 2012, the amount of time spent viewing videos doubled and continued to grow at almost 25 percent a year.[2] At this rate, all of a child's waking days could be occupied by digital media in just a few years.

The need for a distinct Knowledge Architect arises, because unless this information wave is organized, processed and assimilated, it does little to strengthen the three super capabilities; scattered facts, naked ideas and raw data do little to promote continuous learning, fluid problem-solving or meaning-making. Information must be shaped, classified, categorized, connected and related to aid learning. If the bits and pieces of information aren't shaped and formed into bigger structures, like an architect turning pieces of cement, glass and steel into functional buildings, then it is of limited value to the child. Facts must fit into a big picture, theory, theme, model, process, system or cohesive argument before they benefit children.

Children today have minds and bodies that differ little from children of five or fifty thousand years ago. What has changed in the last few generations is the amount of information and the demands it places on their minds. A hundred years ago, less than a handful of generations, few people finished high school and fewer went to college. Most people lived on farms or in small towns and became apprentices in specialized skills.

Children didn't have to digitally "multitask," a word that has only been in use for a few decades. They didn't have to process, think or emotionally deal with a daily bombardment of complex domestic and international problems or try to make sense of opinion-laced talk shows, podcasts and websites.

Today most children in "advanced" nations are asked to think, read, write and discuss material at unprecedented levels. Their academic lives are controlled by complex educational standards that have grown relentlessly over the last fifty years. Activities that naturally lead to learning, such as playing, talking and building relationships, have been pushed aside by lessons that rely on symbol interpretation, abstract thinking and rote memorization.

Parents and teachers add to this burden by placing exceedingly high and narrow expectations for cognitive performance, academic achievement and critical thinking skills on children while depriving them of the very activities, from active embodied experiences to daydreaming, from which these abilities naturally arise. Our children don't need more information or greater cognitive demands; they need help putting all this information in context, to make sense and find meaning among the facts.

Where Knowledge Comes From

Parents and teachers who have spent decades in traditional schooling may hold biased beliefs that knowledge comes mostly from formal education rather than capability-building experiences. Our beliefs about the nature of learning capabilities probably haven't disavowed you of the perception that kids learn more content, facts, information and skills in schools than during free time. This parallels a debate long held by scholars over whether knowledge comes primarily from learning experiences or from formal schooling and heavy rational thinking. The consensus is that both paths are intertwined; the knowledge gained in school settings may have a different flavor than that gained in a Learning Capabilities Framework. Formal and capabilities-based learning shouldn't be segregated.

Exceptional academic learners find ways of integrating even the most detached facts delivered in a disembodied, decontextualized and irrelevant form. Children like Zoe clearly learn from forced learning environments by finding their own sense of relevancy, meaning and connections to existing knowledge. Daniel may struggle in educational settings which are mostly limited to reading, writing and math, but even mandated instruction sticks when it excites his imagination, feeds an interest, expands meaning or connects to background knowledge born of experience.

Our goal shouldn't be to cram more information into kids' minds or to make them narrowly academically successful—objectives often associated with content and information acquisition. Rather, parents and teachers should help children learn ways to filter, evaluate and organize knowledge. Not only will this help them develop super capabilities, but it will also achieve the important goal that every adult who works with children should keep in mind: knowledge with meaning and purpose helps children retain their innate curiosity, fascination and love of learning in adulthood.

The Capable Knowledge Architect

The Knowledge Architect is able to make sense of vast streams of information by filtering, organizing and evaluating information and transforming it into meaningful categories, processes and systems of knowledge. She has the opportunity to develop a functional degree of expertise in self-selected areas of interest. She has the opportunity to apply what she knows to solve problems and learn from challenges, experiences, successes and failures. The capable Knowledge Architect has the freedom to question and reflect on facts, opinions and beliefs and to reject ideologies that use or abuse information for narrow personal, economic or social ends.

Children are fascinated with figures and facts and they enjoy turning them into meaningful wholes. They delight in turning a head full of scattered thoughts into big pictures, take-home messages, themes, morals of stories, theories and the many other ways that knowledge can be organized. With a little help they can learn methods that organize disparate facts into meaningful learning.

There are three simple ways of consolidating knowledge that make sense to children and teens alike. These methods are easily integrated into the many ways their minds learn. The first is *process-based learning*, a shift from teaching content and subjects to developing cognitive, behavioral or other learning processes. Process-based learning covers a broad range of cognitive processes, such as making predictions, experimenting, diagnosing and planning and social and emotional processes, such as how relationships and negotiations work or listening and open-minded discussions. Processes also underlie much of the content children learn, from the scientific process to the process of forming a relationship.

The second way of organizing information into accessible and usable knowledge is through a *systems approach* to learning. Where processes are ways of applying information, systems structure it. There is nothing that children learn about that isn't a part of a system. A systems-based approach explores the relationships and interactions between parts and wholes, helping children discover the big picture and take-home messages. There are myriad biological, social, economic and cognitive systems that even young children can explore. Helping children discover systems is a wonderful way of expanding their minds and opening up new paths to learning.

The third way of transforming information into useful knowledge is by *developing expertise* in a topic or area of interest. Children become experts not by accumulating copious amounts of information on a topic, but by organizing it into functional and meaningful understanding. They may be experts about a card game, a sports team, a series of books or a free-time activity. While it may include systems-and-process-based learning, the expert's magic is that he applies specialized knowledge to a wide range of unrelated fields and problems.

Let's look in depth at each of these ways of processing information into meaningful and useful knowledge.

Process-Based Learning

Life is full of big, small, meaningful and trivial processes. Processes can be as simple as a cake recipe, as eventful as the process for getting a driver's license or as profound as a scientific process. There are cognitive processes, such as those that help us make decisions, plan our futures or diagnose a faulty piece of technology. They include the scientific process, where the emphasis isn't just on learning endless facts and isolated bits of knowledge but how scientists make discoveries, explore the unknown and solve problems. This includes the experimental mindset of the Curious

Explorer as well as the scientific process that delineates how discoveries are made. History is also a process: the movement of history is best taught by examining big themes and movements. It isn't enough to know the three branches of government; you also need to understand the process by which bills are made into laws and how nations resolve conflicts.

Processes, like systems, take small steps, bits of information, isolated skills or raw data and organize them into a connected whole. Processes may be a series of related or linked actions or ideas. A process may be linear, like a recipe, or a web, like a cognitive process that assimilates information, attention, memory, reasoning, decision-making and problem-solving into learning.

Learning as a process links cognitive, emotional, social and many smaller processes into a bigger operation, focusing not just on what children learn but also on how they learn. Like all processes, the learning process is about change rather than static information or isolated facts. As children develop learning capabilities, their understanding is ceaselessly modified, revised and reviewed.

The relationship between the learning process and cognitive processes is a specialty of Roger Schank, whose twelve cognitive processes we discussed previously. Schank contrasts knowledge-based learning with cognitive process-based learning, proposing that "knowledge acquisition is a natural result of engaging in cognitive processes that are being employed to satisfy a truly held goal."[3] We would add that the goals include satisfying one's curiosity or need to explore, telling a story or any other capabilities we have discussed.

Schank's book, *Teaching Minds: How Cognitive Science Can Save Our Schools*, is dedicated to the belief that cognitive processes should be at the center of elementary, secondary and college education: "A properly designed school system needs to be focused on cognitive abilities, not scholarly subjects."[4] The processes are quite practical, despite being classified as cognitive, which includes conceptual processes such as making predictions and learning to experiment. They also cover analytical processes, including problem-solving, planning and social processes including teamwork and negotiation.

Mia's mother, Melissa, has studied Schank's cognitive process-based system of learning and utilizes it as a teacher and parent. Her students are deeply involved in planning lessons and long-term activities. They study the process of planning a peace conference or a political campaign. Mia is equally involved in planning. Her mother has Mia map out the process of having a birthday party, planning a vacation and applying to summer camp.

Another cognitive process that lends itself to simple applications at home and school is description. We often look at this as a simple task but it is complex cognitively, involving selective attention, sensory awareness, rich use of language, perspective-taking and reflection. Melissa has her students describe what they observe during science experiments before they dive into more complex comprehension issues. When Melissa watches a video with Mia, she asks her to describe important scenes before discussing the movie more deeply. When they go to the neighborhood park, Melissa asks Mia to describe the interactions of children as they play, argue and resolve conflicts before discussing their behavior.

Melissa finds that the act of describing opens children's minds to situations, activities and ideas, priming a range of other cognitive, emotional and social processes. Her students grow analytically yet also compassionately, more mindful yet gently judgmental, when they observe and describe first.

The process of description, according to Melissa, is especially powerful as a warm-up activity for written or oral expression activities. Mia's mother spends considerable time with her class and Mia creating written and oral accounts, reports and explanations of events and activities. She finds that the simple act of describing ideas and activities unlocks the abilities of children who often struggle with tasks that begin on a more abstract level.

Another cognitive process Melissa promotes is evaluation, which Schank defines as the ability to determine the value of objects, performance, activities or creations on different levels. Children who are quick to judge become more deliberate when they engage in an evaluative process. Evaluation requires discussions about criteria, personal opinion and how success, failure or progress is measured, as well as determining the relevancy of information.

Melissa also combines evaluations with another cognitive process, predictions. Before they begin an activity, she asks her students what they think the outcome will be. The predictions can be about a science experiment, the ending of a story or how their parents will respond to a report card. The evaluation process helps children learn to review and revise their ideas, which often exposes faulty thinking.

Creating Systems

The second way to develop a capable Knowledge Architect is to cultivate an understanding of systems. A systems approach to learning examines the relationships between parts and whole. Almost everything children learn, all the facts, bits of information, content knowledge and skills, are parts of larger wholes. Nature and science are full of systems; solar systems and almost every area of biology, including cells, genes and evolution make sense when the parts are assembled into comprehensible systems. There are political, economic and social systems as well as number systems.

Most kids enjoy synthesizing facts into coherent systems of understanding. They like finding out how complex things work. With a systems level of understanding, children can develop an advantage when it comes to solving novel problems, making sense of confusing information and finding meaning in bewildering situations.

Education philosopher John Dewey warned about learning experiences that were fragmented or disorderly: "A divided world, a world whose parts and aspects do not hang together, is at once a sign and a cause of a divided personality...A fully integrated personality...exists only when successive experiences are integrated with one another. It can be built up only as a world of related objects is constructed."[5] When students are unable to think in larger structures, their brains may be full of facts but miss the big picture. They may become like sports fans who know reams of statistics but can't tell you why their team wins.

Systems are composed of *elements*, *interconnections* and *purposes*. Elements are the parts—electrons in atoms and molecules in cells—that make up tissue that compose organisms. In systems, elements are defined by what they are and how they operate.

Interconnections are the relationships, links, associations and interactions that hold elements together. These include causal relationships, how the action of one part affects the activity of another, and feedback loops, where events influence their causes. Interconnections in nature are rarely linear; only in exceptional cases does A influence B and then B goes on to influence C. Connections in most systems involve loops and circles. Where processes may be linear, systems are webs of interactions, influences and relationships. This causes unpredictable events, unexpected occurrences and unintended consequences.

The third element of a system is purpose or function. Systems all have a reason for their existence. Economic systems exist to modulate the flow of goods and services. Exhaust systems ensure that combustion products safely exit a vehicle. Sometimes the purpose of a system is complex; if you asked a teacher, parent or school administrator the purpose of an educational system, you probably will get a wide range of responses.

Often the purpose or function of a system is hard to define. Life would be simpler if all systems had such simple purposes as the fuel system in a car or that of a playground. The late Donella Meadows, in her book, *Thinking in Systems*, said that the best way to figure out the purpose of a system is to watch it over time and see how it behaves.[6]

The purpose of a system may change based on the observer's and user's perceptions. Many organizations, including families, schools and corporations, have mission statements or similar affirmations of their purpose. They often have little relevance to the day-to-day behavior of the organization. A more practical approach is to discuss with children the purpose of the information they are learning.

How does something as complex as a system make sense to children? The short answer is that interconnections organize parts and wholes in a way that makes sense to them. A tree is an exceedingly complex organism, but the flow of water, sugar and sunlight is easily shaped into a model that children can readily visualize. In a tree, the roots and leaves are connected by the flow of water and nutrients from the soil to the trunk and through the branches. The leaves use photosynthesis to make sugars which are transported and then transformed into cellulose, the wood that makes up the trunk and branches.

Developing Systems of Understanding

Content-laden instruction, in schools or at home, tends to teach children parts rather than whole concepts. We teach them the parts of a cell rather than how the cell operates as a system. We teach them about the three branches of government rather than how and why a government should operate for the greater good of its citizens, how laws are made or how constitutional amendments become ratified. We teach individual subjects that were developed hundreds of years ago based on reductionism, when science and other studies were enthralled with the idea that the four worlds were best understood by taking them apart and studying the component pieces.

To counteract this educational tendency, Zoe's parents have used a part-whole approach to learning with her. When she was in kindergarten, they took her out in the yard one clear summer night to look at the stars. First, they pointed out that all that she was seeing was a very small part of the universe—the biggest whole that is known. The biggest parts of the universe that we can easily see are galaxies. While there are many billions of galaxies in the universe, we can only see a few of these massive parts, the most visible being the Andromeda Galaxy, near the North Star. Stars have their own systems, such as our solar system, composed of parts called planets, comets, asteroids and meteoroids. Planets may be parts, but they also have their own astronomical systems, composed of different combinations of liquids, gases and solids, including oceans, atmospheres and rings.

To examine a system on a smaller scale, Zoe's mother Jan took her to a local pond and talked about the many parts that go into making it function as a system. She pointed out biological systems involving algae and larger plants, insects, fish and frogs. They explored the physical system of the pond, including how the water flowed in from a stream and the sunlight and rain. They talked about how the changing levels of sunlight affected the temperature of the water and the level of photosynthesis, which in turn increased the amount of algae that the fish could feed on. They discussed how the pond and all its components changed over time, from summer to winter and during the longer course of ecological succession, since the pond will someday become a meadow and then a forest.

That day, without prompting, Zoe realized that her body is a system, too. She made the connection that, as a whole system, her body must also contain smaller systems for digestion, elimination and respiration. Jan helped Zoe think about other, less obvious systems, such as the skeletal, circulatory and immune systems. They also discussed the basic biological part of life in the pond and in her body, the cell. These biological parts are composed of amazing systems themselves, many that parallel those of the body.

Zoe and her parents' journey of discovery continued at a gentle pace for years. It included discussions of transportation systems in cities, school systems and the parts that come together to make a computer work. One day Zoe asked why poor people struggled to live and why people of different races and ethnicities all seemed to live close together, leading to an extended discussion not just about social and economic systems but also the connections that link apparently separate entities.

We believe that every child should learn how to repair small engines. This skill, long a key component of vocational training, is debatably the most useful method of teaching systems. There are three major systems in a lawn mower—the fuel system, electrical/ignition system and the mechanical system. Understanding and diagnosing problems in lawn mowers easily transfers to many other systems. A toilet is another system that provides learning. Water flow, flush regulation, bowl design and septic or municipal waste systems are wonderful and assessable systems to investigate. In fact, houses and apartments are full of systems. There are drainage, fuel, foundation, roofing, heating, electrical and many other close-at-hand systems that adults and children can learn and explore together.

Four Fundamental Elements of Systems

Dr. Laura Colosi Cabrera and Dr. Derek Cabrera designed a way of reducing a system to its core while amplifying its power. In their book, *Thinking at Every Desk*, the Cabreras refer to this as passing the tests of life, not just the school tests. They each have extensive teaching experience at Ivy League universities, where they mentored some of our most academically successful students. Colosi Cabrera and Cabrera found that many of these students were full of information but were not "knowledgeable." These students could spew back endless streams of information and pass any test. But they struggled to think critically and creatively. They had little ability to solve problems or express reasoned opinions. Too often, they only knew what they were taught—perfect examples of Instructionism.[7] The finest products of our educational system lacked essential cognitive skills needed to succeed in the workplace and to flourish personally and socially.

This is a widespread problem in colleges and universities. Not only do these institutions graduate only about half of the students who enroll as freshman, but much of the instruction fails to produce growth in learning capabilities. In a widely-heralded study called "Academically Adrift: Limited Learning on College Campuses," sociologists Richard Arum and Josipa Roksa found that 45 percent of students show no significant improvement in the key measures of learning, including critical thinking, complex reasoning and writing by the end of their sophomore years.[8] The researchers found that "not much is asked of students. Half did not take a single course requiring twenty pages of writing during their prior semesters, and one-third did not take a single course requiring even forty pages of reading per week."[9] Thirty-six percent of students did not demonstrate significant improvement at the end of four years. We are sure this isn't what their parents had in mind when they helped plan their children's college future.

Derek Cabrera's journey toward finding a way to rectify the "more teaching doesn't equal more knowledge" dilemma started at "the place I learned to love the pursuit of knowledge. It's the place where I learned to think," his parents' dinner table.[10] Over the years, the Cabrera family not only discussed everything, but Derek's father in particular helped his sons make sense of what they were hearing and learning. His father liked to demonstrate how ideas worked using every object on the table.[11]

After years of being involved in experiential learning and studying systems, Derek Cabrera arrived at a simple yet powerful method of extracting knowledge from systems that focuses on four patterns of thought, known as *Distinctions, Systems, Relationships and Perspectives* (DSRP.) When students can examine systems using this framework, they not only acquire new knowledge, but integrate it with their existing understanding.[12]

These four elements expose the deep structure of systems, transforming information into meaningful and functional knowledge. DSRP helps children organize information and expose bigger, more meaningful pictures.

The S in DSRP stands for systems, reflecting the understanding that Jeff and Jan offered to Zoe—that a system may be a part of a bigger system as well as a whole unit unto itself. These parts and wholes must be defined by the elements that make them unique, or their distinctions, the D factor. A part or a whole acquires its identity through distinguishing features. This requires that individual elements of a system be compared and contrasted with other elements. Visual systems of mammals contain eyes, which have different characteristics and functions than ear systems and are distinguished by their shape and color. If we compare children's shoes, we see that they have special characteristics, from shape and texture to shoelace color, that give them a specific identity. They can also be grouped together based on similarities and differences.[13]

Distinctions help identify ideas, objects and people, both by identifying special characteristics, which define what something is and, equally as important, what it's not. Your identity is defined by your distinct characteristics, such as female, black and teacher. You are equally defined by the fact that you are not a male, white nurse. An insect has six legs, three body sections and a pair of antennae. Insects aren't birds, rarely live in the water and don't have backbones.

The R in DSRP is for relationships, a deep dive into the interconnections that link parts into systems. Relationships flow out of distinctions, the link formed by comparing and contrasting parts. Parts of a system are related both by their similarities and their differences. What makes us different also unites us. We may be divided by artificial distinctions, such as race, class and gender, but also united by seeing the broader connections between people. Birds all have wings, connecting them as one group, but wing shapes may differ greatly in shape and size.[14]

Relationships also arise from cause-and-effect connections. A cause may obviously cause an effect, but quite often the relationship flows in the opposite direction, too. If you help a child learn to read, the child will influence your life. Husbands and wives are related by marriage, which engages them in all kinds of causal relationships that flow back and forth.

The final element in DSRP is perspectives, the point of view or frame of mind from which we view the system.[15] We have seen the power of perspectives in Ellen Langer's mindful learning and in the storytelling and conversations of the Creative Dreamer. Perspective-taking naturally leads itself to "Big L Learning," as it almost forces children's minds to engage in learning in multiple complex ways.[16]

Thinking about Knowing

The Cabreras and others feel that the most important mental process for systems thinking is *meta-cognition*. This process is sometimes considered to be thinking-about-thinking, but more broadly framed as knowing-about-knowing. Meta-cognition is another type of introspection involving review and evaluation not just of verbal thoughts, but also of images, simulations, thinking habits, emotional influences and memories. Meta-cognition is more judgmental than mindful practices and more rational than day-dreaming. It is more than just reflection as it includes an active regulation of cognition.

Not only does meta-cognition aid the processing of information but, more importantly, it gives children a way of reflecting on and evaluating their internal learning processes. Steven M. Fleming, a neuroscientist specializing in this field, believes that meta-cognition gives children the ability to reflect on and judge their learning strengths and weaknesses, see their limitations and plan compensations: "A student who thinks that she is unprepared for a chemistry exam, for example, can devote an extra evening to brushing up on atomic orbitals. When you set an alarm to remind yourself of something you suspect you will forget or make a to-do list to keep track of the day's activities, meta-cognition has stepped in to save you from your own deficiencies."[17]

While meta-cognition is essential to learning, our experience is that teachers struggled to effectively employ it in the classroom. Meta-cognition is often reduced to self-questioning reading strategies. Many of these cognitive and emotional processes, including mind wandering, daydreaming, constructive reflecting and empathizing, may seem distinct but in fact involve overlapping areas of the brain. Daydreaming and mindful awareness appear to be opposite mental states, yet they share a wide range of overlapping neural networks. This is true of meta-cognition and mindfulness, which produce the same results by very different neurological pathways. Pure meta-cognition resides in a singular area of the brain where mindfulness engages vast networks, giving children two distinct ways of gaining insight and control over cognitive processes.[18]

This is yet another example of the overlapping and often redundant ways we have of learning. Examining systems and processes and looking at activities and ideas using simple but powerful tools such as DSRP will take children far. Worrying about whether your child is developing specific cognitive abilities may blind adults to the wonders of that child's learning capabilities.

Developing Expertise

The creation of the Knowledge Architect also comes from gaining a degree of expertise in an area, giving children the knowledge base to apply to all areas of their life. Children become experts when they are able to use knowledge in a more skilled way than their peers. This allows them to reach a deeper level of meaning or problem-solving by producing concrete results. As John Dewey believed, "Knowledge and skills in one situation becomes an instrument of understanding and dealing effectively with the situations which follow. The process goes on as long as life and learning continue."[19] Children who develop a level of expertise in turn are able to apply and integrate their knowledge in new ways, both behaviorally and cognitively. What expertise does for children is give them a way of pulling facts, strategies and skills together into a functional form.

Expertise requires practice, accumulating background knowledge and critical evaluation. As with creativity and empathy, adults' minds may travel to extremes when they contemplate their child becoming an expert. This is not the type of single-minded practice that produces cello virtuosos by the age of twelve, high school semi-pro athletes or junior professors. Daniel, who has studied a fantasy card game for two years and knows the value, power and strategy of hundreds of cards, has the expertise that benefits children. He readily applies his knowledge, skills and strategies to quickly learn and master other games and some difficult social situations.

If we could transport Zoe back a few generations to when her family lived on a farm in Northern Europe, she would have developed expertise in breeding and raising chickens that she would have easily applied to almost any animal and many plants. Mia has studied improvisational dance games and exercises and is able to learn new dance routines quickly. This has helped her find patterns and relationships in other physical activities, from softball to acting, as well as transferring much of her unspoken knowledge to acting and improvisational rap, jazz, poetry and short story writing.

Experts, in most domains, seem to be made rather than born. Researchers have found no innate characteristic or aspect of intelligence that predestines children for expertise. Often they investigate their area of interest over many months (for young children) or years (for older children). Another sign that expertise is acquired is that it will fade with disuse. Daniel's first trip out in the woods after a long winter devoid of most birding opportunities found him struggling to identify some bird songs and silhouettes.

Daniel's area of expertise shifts as he grows. Unlike adult experts, children rarely maintain a high level of interest and understanding as they grow. Daniel's initial area of expertise was a type of card-based cartoon role-playing game. He absorbed multiple versions of the game, requiring ever greater levels of sophistication. He eventually graduated to the computer versions, going from one type of game or author to another or leaping to a new area completely. For a while, Daniel became fascinated with a battleship game, developing strategies that were often superior to his father's. Then Daniel shifted to an interactive, multiplayer digital strategy game. Finally, he settled on chess.

Again, deliberate practice and extended study are keys to expertise. Deliberate practice involves improving your understanding or skills that you have acquired while extending your expertise into new areas or ideas. Children enjoy doing things they are good at, but expertise requires them to take on challenges, learn from failures and question even their strongest beliefs. While parents often push children to study or practice for long hours, not all practice leads to positive outcomes. Many adult experts devote only a few hours a day and a few days a week to their field of interest. The high quality of the study or practice is more productive than long hours of cramming. Practice that dulls children's motivation or interest is highly counterproductive.

Rather than being time managers, adults should serve children's interests by supporting them. While children may benefit from expert mentors, teachers or coaches, most children benefit more from parents who take an interest in and support their child's special passion. Children need help consolidating knowledge, finding new ways to order information and seeing relationships, connections, distinctions and different perspectives.

The Curse of Knowledge

As with all abilities, acquiring knowledge, either through instruction or experience, has its downside. Like most adults, children are easily misinformed and subjected to thinking biases. They are more likely to take in information that conforms to their beliefs. Children's rich fantasies also cause them to believe the unbelievable and to hold onto facts that reinforce their convictions. We will explore the biases, mental shortcuts and misuses of information in the next chapter.

. . . .

SMALL MOMENTS THAT CREATE THE KNOWLEDGE ARCHITECT

The power of teachers and parents to develop the ability to think in systems is hinted at in cross-cultural studies. Studies of cognition comparing Chinese and Japanese children with American children and adults show a marked difference in how they perceive the world. East Asians tend to see the world in a big picture, holistic way, while Americans focus on parts. When Americans look at a picture, they tend to see one or two essential features. The Chinese allow their eyes to roam around the whole picture, taking in a range of details and relationships.

Richard Nisbett at the University of Michigan has explored how people's cultural backgrounds affect their most basic cognitive processes, including perception, learning, attention and reasoning. Nisbett believes that East Asians live in more group-oriented cultures that promote contextual understanding and thinking in more holistic ways.[20] Chinese people tend to move their eyes and attention broadly, shifting between objects in the foreground and the background, while Americans had their attention usually focused on one single object. East Asians may be more concerned about setting and relationships than those discerned by more individualistic eyes. Americans tend to focus on individual parts and distinct categories. East Asians are inclined to listen quietly and absorb the larger context of a discussion or lecture, whereas Americans tend to respond with quick verbal answers. This seems to be a learned ability rather than a deep, primal aspect of different cultures.

Nisbett found that Asian-Americans who live between the two cultures tend to fall somewhere in the middle.[21]

While cultural forces are more widespread than the actions of a single teacher or parent, children and teens have the ability to take in information in a more meaningful, systematic manner.

Use these Small Moments to help children become Knowledge Architects:

- *Build parts into wholes using processes and systems learning.*
- *Help children understand the big picture, theme, take-home message or purpose.*
- *Help children deepen their interests so they become experts.*
- *Make processes obvious to children.*
- *Engage children in cognitive processes* such as planning, diagnosing, evaluation and description.
- *Look for distinctions and similarities* to identify parts and wholes.
- *Change physical, social, cognitive and emotional perspectives* by having children take the points of view of others.
- *Point out connections, look for relationships and find associations.*
- *Have children evaluate their learning* by engaging in meta-cognition mindful reflection.

· ·

13

....

The Reasonable Judge

The behaviors of infants and toddlers give us a good glimpse of the primal nature of children's learning abilities. This is particularly true of our next capability, the Reasonable Judge, which builds on children's innate sense of fairness and equality to create ethical decision-makers. Like all inborn abilities, the Reasonable Judge requires a good dose of nurturing to fully develop. Nature creates the first draft, a rough outline, and then leaves much to experience and the influence of parents, teachers and other social forces.

Perhaps a child's greatest challenge is to learn how to get along with others. They must learn how to be fair and kind when interacting with others and make decisions that reflect personal needs but also those of their families, friends and community. Children are born not just with an ethical sense, but also with a drive to discover the rules and norms that govern social interactions. Sharing and fairness are prominent on kids' radar well into adulthood.

This requires an inner compass that directs them toward helpful and reasoned judgments, decisions and behaviors. If we build on this primal foundation, then we will not have to expend endless energy on lectures, behavioral directions and mildly-effective rewards and punishments.

One of the highest priorities of parents the world over is to create caring children. We universally value children who have a strong sense of right and wrong, who act in a fair and helpful manner and understand the bounds of acceptable behavior. This requires that children are more than well-behaved. They must learn how to make ethical decisions and act in a fair, reasoned manner. To move past a fixation on behavior, adults need to rethink deeply-held beliefs about how children become ethical, trustworthy, reasonable and respectable.

The Capable Reasonable Judge

The mature Reasonable Judge is able to make informed decisions and sensible judgments that flow from an ethical framework based on sharing, helping and caring in an equable manner. The Reasonable Judge also has the opportunity to live and be treated in a fair and consistent manner, not forced, coerced, shamed or humiliated by the judgments of others. The Reasonable Judge comprehends that reason and emotions are easily swayed, distorting judgments and decisions. The capable Reasonable Judge understands that quick judgments and rash decisions need to be tempered to avoid biased and uncaring actions.

The Young Judge

For centuries babies were considered to be blank slates as well as amoral creatures with no apparent sense of ethics or morality. From this belief came the idea that only by constant instruction and behavior corrections could these wayward creatures, only slightly removed from animals, ever hope to be civilized. The moral sense and ethical tendencies had to be forcefully driven into children in the most rational manner. We now know that this belief and the resulting adult behaviors are untrue and often counterproductive. Children are not only born with innate concerns about fairness, but also with an ethical sense that runs deep. They have a strong tendency to learn rules, norms and standards of behavior. Not only do they have a natural concern for fairness, but also an impulse toward helping and sharing. Children also have a built-in judgment system that seeks to reward good deeds and punish unfair actions.

Paul Bloom and Karen Wynn, at Yale University, are pioneers in the study of moral behavior in young children, including their sense of fairness and judgment system. They have shown that fifteen-month-old babies clearly prefer people and even puppets that act in fair and kind manners. One of their more surprising findings is that children who can barely walk are passing judgments on how others share and act fairly. In experimental settings, they consistently reward helpful behaviors and punish perceived negative actions.[1]

Few adults who work with children will be surprised that fairness and sharing are important to children. Judgment also has a primal side, as this ability is equally critical to their survival. Children make automatic judgments about who is friend or foe, helpful or harmful. They evaluate almost everything in terms of good and bad and likes and dislikes, differentiating the helpful from the unhelpful and weighing rewards and punishments. They are keenly sensitive to what is acceptable and helpful behavior even in abstract situations with puppets and cutouts.

Children's sense of judgment, especially the quick and unfiltered variety, is often more suitable for hunter-gatherer times. Their judgment system stays on alert to dangers even in the safest of situations. They sense threats under beds, in closets, when the dog barks and even during dreams. If you listen closely to older children or teens gossip, argue or just converse, you will hear a startling number of judgments, criticisms, evaluations and pronouncements about every imaginable topic.

What do children do with this ability to judge? Initially, they use it to determine who potentially can care for them and who may cause them harm. As a baby, Mia was making wordless judgments and evaluations of the behavior of those around her: like, *Is this action fair? Is this person sharing or being caring?* While these judgments are critical to the well-being of babies, Mia will engage in almost constant evaluations of her situations, interactions and environment throughout her life, for reasons that go far beyond survival.

As Mia grew, the largely instinctual foundation for her judgments and ethical decisions developed a more learned and reasonable sense of right and wrong and good and bad. She learned to observe how friends treated each other and questioned their behavior. She began to reflect on her own actions, rather than just focusing on others. From these insights, Mia learned to modulate her behavior, to not just act on primal instincts and unspoken rules, but to take actions that consider others. Over time, Mia developed a more mature and expansive sense of what was fair and helpful.

Reasoning Cuts Both Ways

In her middle years, Mia fell prey to judgments that were unreasonable and based on biased and disordered reasoning. Her judgments, like most children her age, ran to extremes, taking on the notoriously black-and-white viewpoints and harsh punishments that typify children her age. She often came to illogical judgments and pronounced excessively harsh discipline for small infractions. Mia struggled to put social norms and school rules into perspective, overwhelmed by their complexity. She felt that, in each successive grade, the rules and norms grew more complicated. Mia could no longer rely on simple kindness and fairness to make judgments and decisions. She found that just being helpful and sharing equally were only the beginning of behaviors that adults considered positive. Mia felt that she was too old to be guided by primal ethical emotions, yet too young to reason her way to better judgments and actions.

Judgments are a form of reasoning; they share similar cognitive and emotional roots and are prone to automatic responses. Reasoning starts before children can really reason. Babies make associations between their actions and adults' emotional responses, one of their earliest experiences of learning from their environment. If baby Mia knocked over her juice cup and her mother responded with a strong "No!" coupled with a stern look, Mia quickly made the connection between the wet mess and her wayward behavior. She didn't have an internal debate about intentions and consequences, but she learned an unspoken rule through the association—food goes in the mouth, not on the floor.

Melissa began asking Mia to engage in basic reasoning starting at around the age of three. Her first attempts were little more than building on action-response associations, such as asking Mia if she understood that pulling a cat's tail could have negative consequences. When Mia impulsively shoved a friend, Melissa simply asked how she thought her friend felt. This wasn't a long, drawn-out discussion, a moral condemnation, a heated negotiation or a test of wills. Mia learned as much from her mother's reaction as she did from her words. Melissa always responded with kindness and empathy—the very characteristics that she wanted Mia to absorb.

Over the next few years, Melissa gently expanded the discussions to include not just Mia's behaviors but those of her friends and even of strangers. Melissa didn't just search out negative behaviors, but also actions that reflected positively on a child's character. As a teacher, Melissa feels that the energy she spends observing and correcting children's behavior produces few long-term changes but instead leaves her drained, mentally and physically. So now, Melissa focuses on the big picture instead to let children develop an internal sense of acceptable behavior that helps them solve interpersonal problems as well as personal emotional upsets.

Making Rules Reasonable

Instead of blindly posting regulations, Melissa began to explain the reasoning behind the rules, so that Mia and her students could see their purpose and meaning. To really understand rules, children need to test them. Children may have a primal rule-learning ability but that doesn't mean that they learn rules like facts. To children, rules are loose guidelines, not firm laws. They are often unclear, especially if the rule or restriction is assumed and remains unspoken, unwritten and unexplained.

As every parent and teacher knows, children freely test rules and restrictions to find the boundaries of acceptable behavior. In most children, this is not a sign of wickedness, but a way of learning how rules change in different contexts. Rules that worked in the crib need adjusting as the toddler explores. The young child will need clearer rules than a middle schooler for playing on a crowded playground. A middle schooler attending a first concert may need stricter restrictions on her movement than a teen who is a seasoned concertgoer. Adults who cling to outdated and restrictive rules as children mature may open themselves up to severe judgments by the very people they wish to control. This doesn't mean all rules should be dropped; rather, adults should ease rules and restrictions so that children and teens can experiment with behaviors as they grow into autonomous beings.

To understand rules and how they can promote learning and problem-solving, let's view Daniel as he joins a kickball game during recess. He may test rules, but he also understands the positive role they play in his life. Daniel understands that rules are part of every game. If you change the rules then you create a different type of game. Games without rules quickly devolve into free-for-alls with emotional upsets and hurt feelings that can linger.

As John Dewey said, "games involve rules, and rules order their conduct. The games do not go on haphazardly or by a succession of improvisations."[2] Games are social in nature, not just because it takes two or more people to play most games but because they often involve intense interpersonal interactions. They are an excellent place for children to learn complex social rules and acceptable behaviors.

Daniel accepts the rules, because he has an innate sense of fairness and equality. Rules lessen the tensions that often accompany picking teams, deciding on kicking order, selecting the captain and the pitcher and what constitutes a run and an out. He dislikes the all-too-common conflicts that arise when individual desires clash with group harmony, setting off abrasive negotiations and conflicts.

Daniel finds it ironic that the very rules that are meant to maintain order and ensure that everyone enjoys the game are a large source of bickering and manipulation. Daniel hates the arguing over rules and perceived infractions. He finds that a well-run game prevents one child from dominating or dictating rules to his individual or his team's advantage. He hates it when games devolve into battles of will—which often causes a few children to fight and many more to flee. He looks to older children and adults to help his playmates not just learn the rules, but also to show them how rules make games fairer and more enjoyable.

As we mentioned when discussing the Curious Explorer, there are many who believe that children should be allowed to play without the constraints of adult rules. There are children who can manage to engage in activities without supervision. They usually have strong social sensibilities, ethical standards and emotional stability. They should be left to manage their own activities. However, many children need a guiding hand to limit hurtful behaviors and help learn the subtleties of the game. Most children will not feel that clear and meaningful rules or adult assistance is a restriction on their freedom. Conflicts that arise during play are the perfect place for children to learn complex social, emotional and cognitive skills, including negotiation, conflict resolution and how to balance personal needs with those of the group.

Raising a Kind Child

Researcher Adam Grant examines the moral development of children in relationship to the goals that parents set in a powerful article, "Raising a Moral Child." The first priority of most parents across the globe is not academic success, but forming kind, compassionate and helpful children. Creating kind children is as much a product of nurturing as it is a primal ability. Grant states that roughly one-quarter to a half of a child's ability to be caring and kind is inherited, leaving ample room for nurturing and learning.[3]

Much of the effort, according to Grant, that parents and teachers expend to promote positive and caring behaviors is misspent. Adult actions such as praising good behavior and condemning negative, or expressing personal values, are of limited effectiveness. Rewards, as we mentioned when describing the Fascinated Learner, as well as punishments, including timeouts, are often counterproductive. Children internalize the idea that good behavior, including kindness, is only valued when a reward is in sight.

Grant warns that positive responses, including praise, should be used with caution. Constantly acknowledging good behavior can be as superficial as offering candy. Grant proposes that praise be used to build character, not just behavioral compliance.[4] He suggests that, instead of praising good behavior, adults should praise positive character attributes. Rather than saying, "That was nice that you helped," it is more effective to praise character, such as, "That action showed that you are a kind and caring friend."[5] This helps children internalize kindness into their identity. They begin to picture themselves not just as behaving well, but also as being a good person. By focusing on the child's character rather than just behavior, we help them develop a better sense of who they are. They subconsciously learn that who they are is more important than any momentary behavior. It shows that we value kindness and consideration for others, helping them internalize these characteristics into their identity.

Grant reinforces this idea by showing the value of using nouns in our praise of children rather than verbs. We should emphasize the child, such as saying, "You are such a good helper," rather than the action, by saying, "Thanks for helping." Grant cites a related experiment where cheating among young children was cut in half when children were encouraged to

"Please don't be a cheater" rather than "Please don't cheat." This shifts children's judgments about themselves from their actions to their character. This method is particularly useful with elementary-age students who have not yet fully formed their identity.[6]

When we criticize children's behavior, adults should judge the action rather than the actor, so that the children can reflect on the bad behavior rather than feel that they are bad people.

Guilt and Shame

The related emotions of guilt and shame also play a dominant role in a child's self-esteem. Guilt and shame are emotional judgments that can be distinguished by their use as noun or verb. Shame is a negative judgment about oneself—that one is a bad person. Guilt is a reflection on behavior, that one has taken a negative action. Grant says that "shame makes children feel small and worthless, and they respond either by lashing out at the target or escaping the situation altogether. In contrast, guilt is a negative judgment about an action, which can be repaired by good behavior."[7] Shame is dangerous because it often arises when a parent or teacher is angry.

Both these judgments are so strong that many parents simply avoid making them when disciplining children. By avoiding these powerful emotions we also avoid powerful problem-solving and learning opportunities. The best response to negative behavior is to show disappointment, a gentle but clear judgment on the action. This expression leaves children open to dialogue about the cause and effect of the behavior as well as alternative ways of behaving. By expressing disappointment, the adult is also showing that he or she cares about the child, which shifts the emotional field to empathy, which, we will see in the next chapter, is critical to creating a caring child.

Here again, the adult's behavior is of major importance in changing the child's thoughts, moods and actions. Our actions speak louder than our words. In fact, words and lectures are largely ineffective in creating caring kids. Children look at us as models that drive their own behavior, criticizing our perceived poor judgments and embracing our fair and helpful behaviors. Small acts of selfishness or insensitivity rarely go unnoticed, often having a profound effect on a child's behavior. Stern lectures and cold enforcement of rules do little to increase caring in kids, as the underlying message contains little caring or empathy. If small changes, like shifting from using a verb to a noun, have profound effects on children, then we can only imagine what a neutral and unfeeling response teaches them.

Grant ends his article by saying, "People often believe that character causes action, but when it comes to producing moral children, we need to remember that action also shapes character."[8]

Learning to Tame Hot Thoughts and Emotions

In the West, there has been an exhausting and prolonged debate about the role of reason in ethical and moral behavior. Reason clearly influences our greatest moral doctrines, producing complex social rules and well-thought-out laws such as the United States Constitution. In children, being a Reasonable Judge is as much about primal emotions and observed actions as it is about the capacity to reason. When a child's innate sense of fairness and equality is disturbed, he or she reacts directly, using reason more to justify his or her emotional response than to inform his or her behavior.

Children live in constant tension between externally imposed rules and internal feelings and automatic judgments. This tension had been gnawing at Zoe for some time. As a kind and caring child, she was upset about the raw and hurtful behaviors that she witnessed with increasing frequency among her classmates. She was also disturbed by the intensity of her reactions and the flurry of thoughts and judgments that she couldn't easily shake.

To help her resolve these conflicts, Zoe decided to have lunch with her teacher, Mrs. Sherman. Her teacher was happy to meet with Zoe as she was planning a special class project around the same issues that were upsetting her valued student.

Zoe started by describing the behaviors of her preteen friends who had suddenly become consumed with negative judgments, uncaring actions and selfish behaviors. A few sharp words, a condescending look or a social slight often spiraled into incessant teasing, hurtful actions and regretted words. Her friends, once such caring and considerate third-graders, had started to criticize each other's hair, shoes, backpacks and, of course, how they dressed and acted toward friends and non-friends alike. Nothing was too small to blow up into an emotional upset. There were arguments over who they'd sit with at lunch and even the color of their cell phones—for the chosen few who were privileged enough to possess one. Should a classmate wear the same clothes two days in a row, require a reduced-price lunch or need extra academic help, he or she would be judged as inferior. Judgments around status and possessions, extremely important survival topics for children tens of thousands of years ago, now filled their lives. They acted in a manner more fitting of a hunter-gatherer on the brink of starvation than children in a safe and supportive school.

Zoe understood that her friends were changing, in their behaviors, personalities and how they related to one another. Still, she was perplexed by the quick judgments and uncaring actions among friends who had been taught and raised to be kind and caring. If only they wouldn't rush to judgments and jump to conclusions.

Her teacher was thrilled that Zoe brought those behaviors to her attention, for the project she wanted to discuss involved exactly those issues. Mrs. Sherman had grown frustrated with a classroom of unsettled children who had rarely presented a behavior problem to their previous teachers. The same children who had started the school year as cooperative and caring were now consumed by social friction and emotional tension.

Mrs. Sherman was afraid that the situation called for a different approach, since her usual methods weren't working. She had instituted a reward program for good behavior and had conferences with non-compliant students and their parents. She had made the rules clear and the expectations high. When these measures produced limited results, Mrs. Sherman decided to talk with Mrs. Summers, the school's social worker. Together, they came up with an innovative plan that would not just address the students' behavior, but also their constant judgments and often unreasoned responses.

When Zoe came to lunch, Mrs. Sherman decided to try out some of the ideas that Mrs. Summers suggested on one of her most receptive students. Mrs. Sherman started by explaining that the problem wasn't that her classmates weren't thinking or were putting emotions before reason. Rather, it was that they were spewing out fast, automatic "hot thoughts" based on habits, beliefs and instincts not unlike those that three-year-olds rely on.

"Children live in a sea of thoughts that are fueled by emotions, sensations, memories and bodily feelings. Most of the thoughts are not reflected on or otherwise filtered, but spring to life as "hot thoughts" full of emotions," Mrs. Sherman said.

Mrs. Sherman went on to explain that the problem wasn't just with her friends' actions, but also with Zoe's reactions. Zoe had reacted with hot thoughts and unreasonable emotions that only made the problem worse. She gave transient statements great meaning, coming up with unreasonable reasons why the words were significant and thus feeding an emotional frenzy. Mrs. Sherman said that many of her students were good academic thinkers but struggled with reasoning. She explained that children and adults were subject to disordered thoughts, mental shortcuts and repetitive ideas that clouded their minds and confused their behavior.

Mrs. Sherman's plan was to invite Mrs. Summers in for twenty minutes a few times a week to discuss hot thoughts, off-track emotions and breakdowns in reasoning. They would present two types of lessons. The first would be a modification of cognitive behavioral therapy, which has a great track record with children. This would address the automatic reactions and hot thoughts that so concerned Zoe and would also lessen the emotional upsets, stress and anxiety the ten-year-olds were increasingly presenting. The second approach would involve discussions about how children and adults misuse reason to distort and delude themselves.

Mrs. Sherman decided to use Zoe's real-life situation to demonstrate the power of cognitive behavioral therapy with children who aren't showing clinically significant behaviors. Mrs. Sherman asked Zoe about her friends' judgments and the thoughts and emotions they sparked in her. Zoe described how she got upset when one boy impulsively called her new haircut stupid, saying it made her look like a boy. Zoe said she feared that everyone probably felt that way and started avoiding many of her friends. Mrs. Sherman explained that the ten-year-olds are highly sensitive to the thoughts and feelings of others—often when there is no real evidence that what her friends said was true. Zoe could offer no evidence to support the boy's comments.

Mrs. Sherman said, "That's a perfect example of making a mountain out of a molehill. You blew up a passing falsehood into a big truth.

"I bet that you can't get that idea out of your head. What did *you* think of the haircut? Did it ever cross your mind that it made you look like a boy? Or do you even care what your uncaring friend said?" Mrs. Sherman probed.

Zoe acknowledged that she was fixated on the one negative comment among the many positive ones she had received. She had never worried about how she acted and enjoyed the freedom of engaging in any activity without considering stereotypes.

Mrs. Sherman showed Zoe a list of the twelve cognitive distortions that form the core of cognitive behavioral therapy. Zoe quickly realized that not only did her friends fall into these mental traps but that she was easily ensnarled by them herself. One that stuck out was Black or White Thinking, that she often felt she had to be perfect and she was a failure if she wasn't. She was reminded of the time when she gave a flawless science presentation and couldn't let go of her mispronunciation of "mitochondria." Mrs. Sherman reminded her that she had fallen into the trap of thinking about how things should have been rather than accepting past events as done and over, another cognitive distortion.

Cognitive behavioral therapy is a highly respected and research-based therapy used extensively for those with emotional and behavioral difficulties. With the rising incidences of emotional problems such as anxiety and depression, cognitive behavioral therapy is now used in many schools not just with high-risk students, but also with the general population. The therapy addresses cognitive distortions and emotional conflicts that all children encounter. It offers children another way to reflect on their thoughts, giving them powerful strategies that often lead to more positive behaviors.

The process includes simple discussions and worksheets that make hot thoughts and emotions readily apparent, even to young children. The children map out automatic thoughts and underlying moods that triggered the negative events as well as planning for more constructive and reasonable responses in the future. Children gain functional insight into their ongoing states of mind, helping them to form better relationships with themselves and others—arguably the most difficult problems that children confront.

As the lunch period neared its end, Mrs. Sherman mentioned some other distortions that Zoe, the classroom wonder, fell into. Zoe was thrilled that someone was finally bringing to the surface basic thoughts and emotions that had clogged her mind and relationships. She asked to meet with Mrs. Summers to talk more about the thoughts, emotions and behavioral upsets that were threatening to tear her diverse and generally healthy group of friends apart. Mrs. Sherman hoped that Mrs. Summers would give Zoe greater insight into the issues that had transformed a harmonious group of nine-year-olds, not unexpectedly, into a friction and conflict-laden group of ten-year-olds.

During her meeting with Zoe, Mrs. Summers pulled out a list of fifteen common thinking misinterpretations that she and Mrs. Sherman would address. Zoe quickly recognized a number of the distortions. Zoe clearly saw that she used "filtering," or amplifying negative details and downplaying the positives, in the mitochondria incident. The haircut criticism caused "catastrophizing," turning a small event into an emotional disaster. She was prone to "generalizing," making a broad negative judgment that no one would like her hair style—despite evidence to the contrary. She fell into the trap of "labeling" by allowing the boy's criticism to morph into defining herself as an outsider.[9]

Zoe felt a weight lift from her mind. Now she had the tools to deal with all-to-common thought distortions and emotional upheavals that were a constant drag on her relationships. This made Zoe think—why were her teachers relying on outdated behavior modification methods when a few minutes exploring hot thoughts and wayward reactions had improved her outlook on life? Why had reducing behavior problems taken priority over reducing her emotional and cognitive difficulties? Why was learning to reduce fractions more important than learning how to reduce interpersonal friction? Why did the school curriculum largely ignore the constant thoughts, emotions and behaviors that are critical to children's well-being?

During the lesson, Zoe's classmates went through the same process of recognizing automatic and disordered thoughts and the emotional reactions they cause. Mrs. Sherman handed out a simple worksheet that walked the class through the process of identifying hot thoughts, placing them in a realistic context and learning to respond in a more positive manner. Zoe filled out the worksheet for the haircut blowup, identifying the situation, the hot thoughts and her mood at the moment. She identified "catastrophizing" as the relevant thinking distortion. She then evaluated the evidence for the hot thought, which was slim. Zoe finished the worksheet by discussing the evidence that countered the hot thought, finally coming up with a more reasonable and healthier response to the boy's passing, yet explosive, comment.

Smart Doesn't Equal Reasonable

One of the most shocking truths about a child's mind is that intelligence and reasoning are not naturally linked. Children can be academically smart or score well on intelligence tests, but still struggle to make rational decisions. This is true of adults as well. Ivy League-educated presidents believe unreasonable ideas that are not grounded in evidence or historical experience. Corporate and educational leaders repeatedly make self-serving and shortsighted decisions that negatively impact their employees, customers and the nation. While children rarely spend their time denying reality, science or history, they do live in a fantasy world that often places reasoning to the side. Their limited background knowledge and experience, no matter how intelligently they have consolidated it, offers them a flimsy cognitive foundation that leaves them prone to unreasonable beliefs.

David McRaney's work in cognitive psychology examines just how poorly we reason. McRaney's basic tenet is that children and adults alike think they know how they think, have well-thought-out opinions and understand why they do the things they do. In reality, much of this is a sophisticated form of self-deception: "There is a growing body of work coming out of psychology and cognitive science that says you have no clue why you act the way you do, choose the things you choose, or think the thoughts you think."[10] This is particularly true of children, who easily fall prey to impulsive reactions, logical leaps, imaginative reasoning and disjointed beliefs. Hot thoughts are just the beginning. Our thoughts and actions are guided by cognitive biases, mental shortcuts and logical fallacies as much as they are by reason.

McRaney's book, *You Are Not So Smart*, is an excellent resource for exploring reasoning with children, putting in perspective the drive to produce smarter children with enhanced thinking skills. The book contains short chapters with realistic examples for each of the ways that our thinking can go wrong.[11]

After seeing Zoe's positive response to the whole-class exploration of hot thoughts, her parents decided to meet with Mrs. Summers to find out what they could do to create a Reasonable Judge. Mrs. Summers went over the list of cognitive distortions, giving Jan and Jeff a simple work-sheet for home use. She then explained the benefits of supplementing cognitive behavioral methods with McRaney's approach, starting with a quote from his book: "From the greatest scientist to the most humble artisan, every brain within every body is infested with preconceived notions and patterns of thought that lead it astray without the brain knowing it."[12]

"We start by having the children accept rather than judge their dis-torted thinking," Mrs. Summers explained. "They learn that even the smart-est adults fall prey to these biases. They readily accept this after filling out a dozen cognitive behavioral worksheets. When we get to McRaney's work, they are deeply interested, feeling they have gained access to a hidden world within them. One student said that investigating thoughts and emotions was like playing a strategy game in his head."

They then went over the three types of thinking that cause reasoning and reactions to go astray. The class started with cognitive biases, the repetitive patterns of thoughts and behaviors that help manage mundane tasks but obstruct our reasoning, judgments and decision-making. The students first looked at confirmation biases, the strong tendency to use new information to confirm what we already believe rather than expand our thinking. Maybe Zoe used the situation with the boy to confirm that he is a bully. Possibly the boy took Zoe's reaction to reinforce his belief that she was smart but easily upset.

The class also looked at hindsight bias, the tendency to reflect on new learning and believe that we knew it all along—to think that we are smarter than we really are. Zoe shared with the class that she gets infuriated when something new and negative happens and her friends say with great confidence that they knew it all along. Mrs. Summers had them experience hindsight bias firsthand by having them agree that love is greater than fear. The next day she had the students unanimously agree that fear is greater than love. Most said that they knew it all along.

Mrs. Summers told Jan and Jeff that Zoe was fascinated by men-tal shortcuts, the lazy and habitual responses we use instead of freshly examining ideas or actions. These shortcuts simplify routine thoughts at the expense of reflecting, questioning and reexamining ineffective and irrelevant habits. Surely, children would drown in a sea of mental fatigue if they had to examine every action, from brushing their teeth to choosing where to sit at lunch. However, mental shortcuts lead to lazy thinking and biased opinions.

McRaney's third type of irrational thinking is logical fallacies, or the "arguments in your mind where you reach a conclusion without all the facts, because you don't care to hear them or have no idea how limited your information is." [13]

Many of the fallacies were familiar to Jan and Jeff, having heard politicians use them endlessly. The "Strawman Fallacy," misrepresenting a person's viewpoint to make it easier to criticize, seems like a natural line of attack when a person has little to say. They saw children, and those reasoning like children, resort to the "Ad Hominem" fallacy commonly, leveling personal attacks rather than listening and responding reasonably. It takes less mental resources to make harsh judgments about a person's character than to reasonably argue in a fair and balanced manner. [14]

After talking to Mrs. Summers, Jan and Jeff decided to let Zoe take the lead in exploring distortions and delusions. They made a list of distortions both from *You Are Not So Smart* and a directory of cognitive distortions that is available on the Internet. A few times a week, when they sensed Zoe was motivated to talk about Mrs. Sherman and Mrs. Summers's project, they engaged her in discussions. They listened with an open mind, avoided giving advice and supported Zoe's interest in the subject. On occasion, Jan and Jeff pointed out one of her cognitive distortions, not to focus on bad thinking behavior but to see if she could reflect a little more deeply on the hot thought and the associated mood. On other occasions, Zoe pointed out biases, distortions and fallacies that she observed in her parents—leading to many lively discussions and learning experiences for child and adult.

. . . .

SMALL MOMENTS THAT CREATE THE REASONABLE JUDGE

Nurture fair and equitable reasoning and actions. A sense of fairness and a desire to share are basic emotions but are also powerful forces in a child's life.

Examine judgments, including simple like-dislike and good-bad judgments. Help children understand that they are often automatic and unreasonable. Kindness (the subject of the next chapter) toward oneself and others moderates harsh judgments.

Help children make fair and reasonable decisions by slowing down quick judgments and balancing needs.

Praise the actor, not just the action. Nouns speak louder than verbs and build character, not just compliance.

Fault actions rather than actors so children feel that they just did something bad and are not bad people.

Become familiar with common logical fallacies and use them not to criticize children, but to create Reasonable Judges. Check out *yourlogicalfallacyis.com* to find teaching materials suited for home and the classroom.

Talk with a social worker or psychologist about using cognitive behavioral worksheets with children. Their use has been shown to improve results.

Avoid the role of therapist. Your child or student needs help in learning about the wayward habits of their developing mind.

Become familiar with common cognitive distortions. Here are some that children easily understand:

1. Catastrophizing—making mountains out of molehills. "I think the world just ended."

2. Minimization—the opposite of above. "That's not important."

3. All-or-nothing thinking—thinking in absolutes. "I never do a good job on my work."

4. Emotional Reasoning— "I felt bad, so I must be a bad person."

5. Magical thinking—"I can influence things out of my control." "I am a good person so bad things shouldn't happen to me."

6. Jumping to conclusions with no evidence—including mind reading: "I know what she is thinking" and fortune telling: "I know that things will turn out bad."

Part 5

. . . .

Emotional, Social and Self-Awareness Capabilities

14

. . . .

The Caring Mind Reader

Emotions provide an important stream of information, an essential learning capability, keeping us informed of the inner workings of our bodies and minds. Emotions are also the primary way we connect socially, helping us manage our personal interactions. From the first smile on a newborn's face to the weariness of a dying person, human beings use emotions to connect to and understand others. Empathy, kindness and caring pull us together, while emotions such as anger, fear and disgust push us away from others in times of danger.

The sense of fairness and equality that is inherent to the Reasonable Judge is closely related to empathy and kindness, which forms the core of the Caring Mind Reader. Both capabilities are based on primal emotions and smooth friction between people and social groups. These four related emotional responses not only help children act in positive and pro-social manners, but are also essential for forming friendships and building relationships. They reduce the friction inherent in human interactions, counteracting the negative aspects of our individual drives for survival. They help us understand the complex nature of human relationships as well as our own tangled emotions—the two greatest challenges most children face. Learning to solve social and emotional problems in kind and caring manners offers children an unrivaled source of satisfaction and meaning.

Kindness and caring arise from our ability to judge people's feelings, desires and intentions. Through them, we respond in a manner that strengthens social connections and emotional well-being. Very early in life, Mia could look into her mother's face and infer her feelings and possible actions. She quickly learned to discern when Melissa was happy, playful, serious or concerned. Mia began to learn not only acceptable behavior but also which of her emotional communications resulted in positive responses from her mother. Melissa always responded in a kind and caring manner, even when Mia was uncontrollably upset. Melissa wanted Mia to learn that, even in times of great upset, the social bond between them wouldn't fray and they could calmly resolve difficulties together.

As early as Mia's first birthday, she began to express more complex social emotions, more accurately predicting the feelings and behaviors of those around her. As her mind-reading skills grew, she began to create a mental map of other people's minds. Initially, she used these maps purely to learn how people function. Slowly, Mia began using them to map out her reactions. Passive mind-reading skills sprang alive to touch, hug or rub people, animals and dolls that appeared to be in pain; she even attempted to protect them from harm. She would give a cookie or a toy to a caring child and withhold kindnesses from children whom she judged as hurtful. Mia took these small actions without any encouragement or reward.

Empathy is the ability to sense other's emotions and to sympathetically feel what they feel. We react viscerally to the pain of others, whether it is a baby's cry or soldiers wounded in a war. By peering into a person's face we get a sense of what they are thinking and feeling. It is our primal response to the universal condition of human existence, which is full of problems, challenges and conflicts that cause suffering.

Children, at times, almost instantly mirror the emotions of others, feeling what they feel. The person of concern doesn't have to be present or real for empathy to kick in. Children may feel empathy when they talk on the phone, watch cartoons or read a story. Empathy is a complex emotion that triggers reasoning, helping us make predictions and inferences and examine causes and effects. It motivates us to search for causes and to help. We make these evaluations rapidly and automatically, as another way that we maintain vigilance over our environment. Researcher Nalini Ambady found that empathetic judgments happen in as little as six seconds and are surprisingly accurate.

All it takes is viewing "thin slices," or brief observations of behaviors or emotions, for our minds to start assessing the emotional content of a situation.[1]

A child's ability to read feelings is based on exquisite perceptual skills. The human face is capable of many emotional expressions and children learn to read them well. The subtle shifts in the corners of the mouth, slight changes of tension in the cheeks or a minor widening of the eyes are all clearly visible as changes in emotion. Small variations can register fear, friendliness, concern or care to the attentive child. If the facial expression is ambiguous, the child looks for other clues, including the sound of the voice and a shift in body position. Anger is easily distinguished from disgust and fear from sadness.

Beyond creating emotional connections and summing up situations, empathy provides children with a number of benefits. Empathetic children find it easier to establish and maintain friendships, stand up to bullies and collaborate in groups, teams and other collective efforts. They are better, fairer negotiators, sensitive to people's perspectives and opinions. Empathetic children are less likely to argue endlessly, cling to a single viewpoint or respond in anger. In short, empathy provides children with a wide range of emotional and social problem-solving abilities, offering an alternative to selfishness, greed and manipulation that may otherwise permeate our interactions.

The Capable Caring Mind Reader

To develop the capable Caring Mind Reader, children need the ability to understand how their emotions connect them to society. The Caring Mind Reader feels others' emotions and is able to respond empathically and with caring action. He is able to infer mental states, assess intentions and anticipate actions, constructing realistic "Theories of Mind." The Caring Mind Reader tempers self-centered behaviors with acts of caring, kindness and compassion. He is aware that emotions, including empathy, not only bind us together, but also can be used to bully, manipulate and control others.

The Two Faces of Empathy

Empathy is broken down into two different processes. Affective, or emotional, empathy is the feeling side of empathy, an awareness of and reflecting on other people's feelings. Cognitive, or rational, empathy is the thinking and reasoning side, more concerned with identifying and analyzing people's emotional states than with feeling their pain. It is hardly surprising that a primal ability like empathy has both a cognitive and emotional component. The more we know about the mind, the more we study cognition and the brain, the more it becomes apparent that thoughts and feelings rarely act in isolation.

Both affective and cognitive empathy lead to pro-social behaviors; however, the cognitive form has a dark side. Cold, dispassionate analysis and appraisal of thoughts and feelings can create a rational separation between people, blocking emotional connections and kind and caring responses. Children who exploit empathy may end up manipulating, coercing and bullying—the exact opposite behaviors of empathy.

Ungifted author Scott Barry Kaufman has examined the role the two sides of empathy play in psychology's Dark Triad, personality traits that lead to *Machiavellian manipulation*, *narcissistic self-absorption* and *psychopathic deceitfulness*.[2] While no well-adjusted adult would want their child to grow up to embody these traits, they exist in all children to some degree. There are times when they must think only of their own survival or well-being, even if it hinders others. However, the Dark Triad traits are a source of great psychological distress and antisocial behavior for both the perpetrator and those who must interact with him or her.

The common factors linking the Dark Triad traits are that they rely on a little empathy and produce limited agreeableness. Narcissists and psychopaths tend to be skilled at cognitive empathy, sizing up people's emotional weaknesses, but with little or no concern for their condition. In fact, they may feel positive emotions when they see a sad face or a slumped body, taking pleasure in another's pain. They read emotions in a cold and rational way, looking for people who are vulnerable and easily exploited for personal gain. Narcissists often enjoy social interactions for personal validation, but use their strong cognitive empathy as a source of knowledge to manipulate, exploit and coerce others, even if it causes those others harm.

While a little narcissism may help a child gain a sense of identity, there is a class of narcissistic children who are a great source of pain to themselves and others—bullies. They read emotional signals well, but only to identify their targets and to inflate their fragile sense of self-importance and self-esteem at the expense of others. They exploit their social connections to spread rumors, recruit supporters and verbally attack their victims. For bullies, kindness and caring give way to shaming and humiliation. They are only concerned with inflating their own delusional and exaggerated sense of self.

While bullying is not uncommon among elementary-school-age children, it erupts into a nastier form during the teen years. Teens' insecure senses of identity and shifting social alliances are fertile ground for creating bullies and their victims. Before children reach the teenage years they should learn to identify both forms of empathy and caring and kind responses, for their own good and the benefit of those around them. This requires that adults raise children in a kind and caring manner and build secure and nurturing relationships so children develop empathy and a healthy concern for others.

Overwhelmed by Empathy

In an ideal world, all the children would experience pro-social empathy, leading to long-lasting friendships and healthy social relationships. Cognitive empathy would allow children to accurately assess a person's thoughts, emotions, plans and beliefs, giving them insight into their own emotional states. It would help children engage in positive collaborations grounded in mutual understandings of how each party acts, thinks and feels. However, just as empathetic insights can lead to bullying, excessive or overwhelming empathy is detrimental.

Children who are consumed with empathetic feelings may never start wars or be aggravating bosses, but they suffer the accumulated damage of emotionally experiencing every slight feeling or minor disturbance. They feel everyone and everything's pain and thus may end up in "empathetic distress." They may become frozen, even depressed, in the face of perceived pain and suffering. They, too, need guidance to sort out their conflicting emotions.

Deeper Mind Reading

Like many of the primal abilities we have discussed, mind reading and empathy are found in other higher primates. We have avoided discussing animal abilities that parallel those of children, because animals rarely exhibit these complex emotions and behaviors beyond a very basic level. Just as children shouldn't be viewed as brains, we must see them as much more than sophisticated animals. However, empathy and other pro-social and emotional skills exist in many of our closely related evolutionary cousins. Primates express empathy, caring and kindness behaviors, but they do it in a "small L learning" manner.

Bonobos, our closest living chimpanzee "relatives," express empathy and compassion, have a sense of fairness and often display caring and kindness. They sometimes shake their heads to say "no" to control their infant's behavior. They can extend their hands to beg for food, recognize the faces of kin and play fairly. But they do this mostly from instinct that is sometimes enhanced by learning. When they do learn, it is in a highly restrictive manner, rarely learning in the expansive manner that even human two-year-olds do. Bonobos can actually demonstrate mind-reading abilities. They are able to generate simple plans based on other animals' or humans' behavior. But they are trapped in "small L learning;" if primates learn one thing they rarely use it to learn the next related task.[3]

Many children's mind-reading abilities extend far beyond simple emotional resonance. Even at an early age, they expand their basic emotional instinct into many areas. Their sense of empathy is used to infer, project and make judgments about people, animals, dolls, toys and the environment. Children use their perceptual skills to judge facial expressions, bodily movements and the tone and content of language to get a deeper reading of a person's thoughts, feelings and potential behaviors. This complex and innate process, called *Theory of Mind*, goes beyond inferred emotions and thoughts to include bigger, broader pictures of minds. They add details to the pictures by including attitudes, beliefs, desires and intentions, forming the basis for reasoning. Children use these images to predict interests, guess motivations and decide where attention may be paid. They get into the minds of others, developing a cohesive model of how minds work.[4]

Theory of Mind aids survival and learning, because it is impossible to understand every person we come into contact with or someone who suddenly enters our life. We can't interview strangers or investigate the people we know, so we create a model of their minds to guide our interactions. This assumes that people's minds work in a predictable fashion, not unlike those we know well. If we had to deliberately build a knowledge base about our social contacts, our relations would be based on avoidance and caution at the minimum, often rising to suspicion and fear.

Even before she entered kindergarten, Zoe was using her mind-reading abilities to develop a sense of right and wrong, appropriate behavior in different situations and the rules of games. At about the age of four, Zoe began to abandon her childhood innocence of social relationships and began to build mental models of the people in her life. She was growing a bit fearful of each new person in her life, wondering if he or she would be friend or foe, helpful or hurtful, kind or cruel. She used her perceptual skills to quickly appraise each new individual. These appraisals started with an empathetic response but developed greater detail as her social interactions grew in number and intensity. At first they were no more than first impressions, then they grew more complex as she learned more about others' behaviors, developed memories of past encounters and created a more developed image of their minds. Her models benefited from "Big L Learning" experiences, with greater social and emotional insight, clearer attention and reasoning to add to the picture.

Probably the easiest and most revealing way of understanding how Theory of Mind functions is to discuss a favorite cartoon or story character with children. Pay attention to the way they describe the character's personality, emotional state and positive or negative traits. Notice how they predict how the character will act in different situations and what to expect in the next adventure. You will see clearly how they construct internal models of characters and real people, too.

During Zoe's third year of life, her parents read her stories about humanized animals and she felt she understood their minds, inferred their emotional state and grasped how their interactions with other characters would unfold. She understood causality—how the actions of one animal caused the feelings of another to shift. A few years later, mind reading occupied much of Zoe's mental activity. More than older children and adults, five and six-year-olds are deeply immersed in figuring out how people operate—a task that will consume them throughout their lives.

By the time she was six or seven, creating and using these mental models consumed much of Zoe's time in school and during free-time social situations. Zoe's ability to quickly size up people's thoughts and emotions gives her an advantage when making and maintaining friendships. She is good at predicting how the interactions will unfold and how best to respond to minimize conflicts.

Like most children, Zoe disliked people acting in unpredictable ways. She was startled by unexpected reactions, confused by unanticipated emotions. She learned to expect people to act in ways that conformed to her theories about them. When they didn't, she tried to adjust the model, but many of the emotional upsets of childhood are the result of children's expectations not matching reality.

As Zoe grew, this ability took on a deeper role in her life; Theory of Mind gave her greater insight into the workings of her own mind. Empathy and mind reading solve two of the greatest challenges in her life—figuring out other people and solving the mystery of her own mind. To this end, Zoe pieces together an image of who she is and how she acts, forming the core of her identity. Zoe is comfortable with this identity, allowing it to change as she grows. Children who have a fixed impression of who they are experience more turbulence in life than those who constantly revise their theory of themselves.

Zoe does well in school in part because of her mind-reading capabilities. This ability is the foundation of verbal and written communications. To communicate, children need to constantly read the thoughts, emotions, intentions and motivations of others to feel comfortable in the real or imagined relationship. When Zoe reads or talks, she easily builds a mental image of people and their intentions. She draws from this mental picture to understand the story, predict outcomes and read between the lines. This enables her to understand orally-delivered history lessons, conversations and complex plotlines.

Simple, Everyday Compassion

Zoe's abilities to make friends and understand real and imagined relationships go beyond mind reading. Like all capable Caring Mind Readers, Zoe builds on the ability that we saw one-year-old Mia demonstrate—to move from friendly and understanding to actively caring and helping others. Zoe is compassionate, spontaneously helping and caring for others without coaxing or hope of a reward. She serves others who are in need rather than expressing sympathy or adjusting her mental model.

Compassion, according to Yale psychologist Paul Bloom, is "a more distanced love and kindness and concern for others."[5] Bloom believes that empathy and compassion are often confused. Empathy is a reflective feeling where compassion can be a dispassionate act of helping. Compassion is larger than kindness, as it may obtain little in return. It is a selfless act that enriches children's lives by opening them up to possibly the healthiest of social relations.

We tend to think of compassion as a larger-than-life ability, found in saints and social pioneers. However, compassion is visible in many childhood behaviors, including helping, sharing and caring for others. Empathy and compassion work best in tandem, with insight into feelings leading to calm, caring action.

The helping and caring nature of compassion, like so many abilities, has primal roots that respond strongly to experience and learning. Science writer Emma Seppala, in her article "The Compassionate Mind," states that the selfless drive to help has obvious problem-solving and survival benefits. Seppala states that the evolutionary roots of compassion were recognized by Charles Darwin, who wrote extensively about emotions.[6] His work, which is often wrongly summarized as the survival of the fittest (which actually means survival of the most adaptable group) is better expressed as "survival of the kindest." Darwin believed that communities with "the greatest number of the most sympathetic members would flourish."[7]

While Zoe offers compassionate help without the need for acknowledgment, it actually improves her well-being. This has been strikingly demonstrated by Elizabeth Dunn and Lara Aknin, both at the University of British Columbia. Aknin has shown that children as young as two who gave away treats to other children increased their happiness far more than those who selfishly kept the candy all for themselves.[8]

The benefits of helping don't disappear as we age. Dunn, in separate research, ran experiments with adults who could either spend money on others or themselves. She found that those who gave away more of their money were substantially happier than those who spent it freely on themselves. Other research that studies happiness in wealthy individuals shows that those who hold on tightly to their great wealth are far less happy than those who use it to help others. The tight-fisted also tended to score higher on tests of narcissism and greed than the compassionate wealthy.[9]

Being caring and helpful to others expands our field of concern beyond our immediate, self-centered needs and broadens our perspective to encompass others. Engaging in compassionate activities, as simple as listening to the concerns of others, can significantly lessen feelings of loneliness, anxiety and depression.

When Children are Unkind and Unhelpful

It is easy to argue the benefits of empathy and compassion. However, many parents and teachers see acts of pure selfishness and coldhearted narcissism daily. Some children simply seem not to care about others. Children are naturally a bit self-concerned, living under the constant tension between protecting and promoting themselves and engaging others. They receive conflicting messages telling them to go in both directions at the same time. No wonder they are confused by empathy and compassion.

The Making Caring Common Project at Harvard University examined the reasons that children become self-consumed. They asked ten thousand secondary students what they considered their number one priority to be, with choices that included kindness, personal achievement, happiness and caring for others. Almost 80 percent of the students named achievement or personal happiness as a top priority. Only 20 percent of students ranked helping others and being fair as their top priority.[10]

Their self-centered focus wasn't caused by parents downplaying the importance of caring and compassion. In their study, "The Children We Mean to Raise: The Real Messages Adult are Sending About Values," the Harvard group found a gap between what they called "rhetoric and reality"—the messages adults send about values are often in conflict with those for which they actually push.[11] Study author Richard Weissbourd found that almost all parents in their survey said they wanted to raise ethical, caring kids. However, 80 percent of the children reported that their parents valued personal achievement and happiness highly—the same percentage who stated that these were their top priorities.[12]

These conflicting messages have a real cost for children. Weissbourd states, "When you do not prioritize caring or fairness over aspects of personal success...[then children] are at greater risk for many forms of harmful behavior, including being cruel, disrespectful and dishonest."[13] The risks to children are real; about one third of secondary students report being bullied and over half of female teens report at least one episode of sexual harassment.[14]

While achievement and happiness are important values, there is no guarantee that prioritizing these values over empathy and compassion will ensure that children will grow up to be smiling successes. The Harvard study states that, "the focus on happiness and the focus on achievement in affluent communities doesn't appear to increase either children's achievement or happiness."[15] But all is not lost. Weissbourd's book on the topic, *The Parents We Mean to Be*, states that about two-thirds of teens, while valuing achievement and immediate feelings of happiness, still believe that caring and fairness are important.[16]

If our goal is to raise well-rounded, capable kids, then we need to align our values and our messages to children. This will take more than words. Children and teens will need to see that we embrace caring and helpfulness and have opportunities to practice them. Often these abilities are hidden just below the surface and can be resurrected in almost any child. Beyond the mixed messages, adults should consider how often they engage in helping and caring activities in Small Moments throughout the day. Beyond routine chores, children should be encouraged to care for animals, their friends, younger children and their environment, at home and at school. In addition to Small Moments of helping and caring, children should have the opportunity to participate in activities that help in a larger way, such as tutoring, assisting the less fortunate or participating in social and community-service projects.

Self-Compassion

Children who have insight into the feelings, thoughts and intentions of others may not automatically have greater insight into their own emotions. Some children may become so overwhelmed with the emotional experiences of others that they fail to see how their own emotions are affecting them. They may struggle to separate their own feelings from those of others, compromising their ability to be compassionate. They may care extensively for others while neglecting their own well-being.

Extending a caring and compassionate attitude toward oneself requires insights into the inner workings of one's mind. This will require children to have times of quiet self-reflection, activities that alleviate stress and, in more formal ways, mindfulness practices.

Self-compassion starts with being kind and fair to oneself—suspending harsh self-judgments, accepting mistakes as valuable learning situations and letting go of guilt and shame. Few children can do this by themselves. Many need an insightful adult to point out when they are being too hard, unfair or unkind to themselves.

Parents and teachers need to examine their own beliefs, including the common one that harsh judgments and stiff self-criticism help children stay disciplined. Society sends a strong message that being hard on oneself, willfully driving forward, is a proven method for overcoming motivational and character shortcomings. These industrial-age beliefs may produce short-term benefits at the cost of long-term motivation. This leads students to believe that they should put aside their own interests to study hard, ignore boredom and push through tedious work. This is reinforced by adults who have weak emotional attachments to children, as poor self-control is a common outcome of cold, critical and controlling parenting.

The incessant stress and negativity combined with children's limited ability to sustain willpower can lead to anxiety and depression. Being hard on oneself for perceived infractions and lack of perfection is a recipe for negative outcomes. In contrast, understanding one's limits and caring compassionately for oneself and others provides intrinsic motivation and a sense of accomplishment.

As children grow and develop, the ability to regulate their behavior, adjust their moods and filter their thoughts is often left to the whims of the assumed curriculum in school and at home. The ability to regulate one's emotions and behaviors is part genetic, especially the ability to control impulses. There is a large learned component that is not easily isolated from a wide range of social, emotional and cognitive abilities. Self-control is really a byproduct of growth in many areas. What is clear is that children who are empathetic and have insight into the workings of their minds and those of others are more able to regulate the complex system of thoughts, emotions and behaviors. They are less likely to engage in activities that show a lack of concern for themselves and others.

The level of emotional support children receive at home and in school is a key factor in developing their abilities to regulate their behaviors in pro-social ways. This may be as simple as offering identity-building praise and appreciating children's acts of kindness, fairness and sharing in authentic manners.

Creating the Caring Mind Reader

Daniel's parents, Adrián and Lea, are taking the recommendations of the team at Making Caring Common to heart. They are helping Daniel learn how to "zoom in and zoom out." He zooms in by listening attentively to his immediate circle of friends, engaging in open-minded discussions and developing his Careful Communicator's mind. He zooms out by expanding his social range, taking in the bigger picture, assuming multiple perspectives and developing the mind of a Knowledge Architect. To really zoom out, children and teens should be encouraged to understand the perspectives of people far outside of their social circle, including those who are often marginalized and invisible. In an age of political conflict and social stratification, zooming out should include understanding the views of the opposing party.

The Harvard group also recommends that children have role models from whom to learn values and caring behaviors. We have seen that children and teens are more influenced by what they see than by what adults say. They need active, embodied models for appropriate behavior, especially with regard to kind, caring and helpful abilities. The role models don't have to be perfect or even consistent, but they should be able to zoom in and out themselves, cultivating their capacity to care. Children who witness parents or teachers who appear to be motivated heavily by self-interest may become overly concerned with their own little world, too.[17]

Weissbourd, like a wide range of child experts, believes that to heighten positive emotions like empathy, caring and kindness, children need ways of handling their more destructive feelings.[18] Adrián and Lea help Daniel become aware of his negative emotions, which occasionally include anger and guilt. They both have been through cognitive behavioral therapy, in part to accept Daniel's limits and promote his strengths.

They are familiar enough with disordered thinking to point out his hot thoughts and unreasonable emotions. Adrián and Lea have had long discussions about the value of achievement and caring. They have emphasized that Daniel can incorporate kindness and caring into what constitutes personal success. He understands that his well-being is strengthened by smooth relationships with others. His parents have helped Daniel understand that lasting happiness is not just tied to fleeting personal feelings, but also linked to helping and caring for others.

Daniel's parents understand that his feelings are easily hurt when relationships break down. Rather than dwelling on the negative, they encourage him to problem-solve during these difficult times. Learning to get along with others, especially during times of struggle, is one of the greatest abilities a child can develop. Children should learn the joy that comes from actions that benefit friends, family, strangers, animals and their environment.

SMALL MOMENTS THAT CREATE THE CARING MIND READER

- Encourage children to play with and care for younger children.
- Pretend play and role playing help children feel what others feel.
- Monitor levels of empathy so that children don't become emotionally overwhelmed or employ empathy to engage in narcissistic behavior.
- Don't overemphasize academic achievement and immediate feelings of happiness.
- Expand children's "circle of concern."
- Help children zoom in and listen to their immediate social connections.
- Help children zoom out to see the big picture and social concerns.
- Promote children's occasional big acts and daily small acts of kindness and compassion.
- Help children to see multiple perspectives, especially when they are holding fast to one point of view.
- Help children resolve personal upsets in a fair and caring manner.

15

....
The Inclusive Friend

Children's minds are deeply social, thriving on human connections based on kindness, fairness, sharing and compassion. These are critical, but not sufficient, abilities that children need to form positive social interactions, relationships and friendships with diverse individuals and groups. These relationships may provide some of life's most rewarding and meaningful experiences. They will also present children with many of their greatest challenges, including making and maintaining friendships, understanding rules, avoiding conflicts and simply understanding other people. They will face social challenges that include getting along with twenty or more classmates, being a member of all kinds of teams and organizations and working in groups composed of people with different backgrounds, interests, needs and goals.

Complex social relationships of children require extraordinary perceptual, emotional, social and cognitive abilities. Children need exceptional mental powers to read minds and plan reactions, to monitor themselves as they figure out others. They must constantly size up social situations and evaluate people, understanding their emotions and intentions. Children must weigh fairness and determine equality, regulating their behavior in response to changing social situations. No wonder the social nature of home and school life exhausts children and drains their parents and teachers.

The exceptional effort and ability children need to navigate emotionally-laden social situations requires a special type of brain in a unique embodied mind. Researchers theorize that human beings' advanced cognitive, emotional and perceptual abilities developed largely in response to numerous and complex relationships. People's brains are large, twice the size of most apes relative to body size, because we have long lived in large bands of about one hundred and fifty individuals—also twice the size of most primate groups.[1]

The idea that a species' brain size correlates with the average group size is called the social brain hypothesis. A consistent finding of anthropologists is that, the more social interactions a species has, the larger the neocortex, the paper-thin outer layer of the brain that allows for "higher functions." The relationship between brain size and functional group size holds for a wide range of social animals, including primates, dolphins, horses and mice.[2]

Large brains enable humans to live in big groups with many children who require extended care before reaching maturity. The human brain is sized to maintain stable relationships with about a hundred and fifty people, allowing us to live in larger groups with complex social relationships. British anthropologist and evolutionary psychologist Robin Dunbar determined that one hundred fifty people is the average number of relationships we can keep tabs on, having some real idea of who they are and how they function.[3] This number of connections holds for most human groups, whether they are modern city-dwellers, extant Amazon hunter-gatherer bands or African tribes in prehistoric times. Relative brain size also correlates with the time it takes a species to become socialized, usually defined as the end of puberty. As we have noted, no other species shelters its young for nearly as long as human beings. No species has anything that resembles adolescence, as nature favors independence at an age similar to kindergarteners.

Tribalism

As a species that forms many relationships, it is human nature for people to form groups. Our social brains enable us to be a caring and kind species, capable of selfless acts. We have Internet friends whose cats we care deeply about, we worry about individuals in distant lands and are concerned about people who are different from us in every way. Still, we have a strong instinct toward tribalism, the tendency to form strong loyalties to a group, often by arbitrarily excluding others. We root exclusively for a particular sports team while fanatically hating rival teams. Across the world, members of different sects of the same religion engage in conflicts, from doctrinal disputes to wars. Political parties tend to divide into smaller, specialized and selective groups. Tribalism is apparent in associations of five-year-olds as well as in global economic, social and political conflicts.

Our groups are selective and exclusive, giving us a special identity that we protect with little regard for the excluded. Children select exclusive groups of friends which can change as often as the weather. We will cooperate endlessly with those in our immediate circle but put up resistance to those outside. We reserve much of our caring and kindness for our special group, with the selfish hope that we will benefit. Helping and caring are reserved for an in-group and sharing only extends to those who can reciprocate.

Tribalism arises from our primal tendency to care about those closest to us. Three-month-old babies have a strong preference for people whose skin color they most often see. At six months, they are drawn strongly to people who speak their native language, even before they utter their first words. By the age of three, children are drawn to those who share their tastes in toys, clothing and food.

Children aren't natural-born discriminators. Rather, the growth of a child's mind depends on making associations and classifications, noting differences and distinctions and comparing and contrasting objects and actions. Babies have an innate survival instinct to determine who is helpful or a hindrance, kind or mean and sharing or greedy. As they grow into young children, they develop a strong approach-avoidance instinct, causing them to be cautious about who is allowed into their inner circle. This instinct forces them to evaluate everyone with whom they come in contact—the beginning of the Theory of Mind.

Children's natural caution around others forms the roots of tribalism. They are highly selective of who is considered kin, friend or group member. These behaviors have a primal flavor, having served our ancestors well while living in small bands of hunters and gatherers in threatening environments. The great biologist E.O. Wilson, who researches social insects and human societies, feels that it isn't surprising that humans form strong team alliances: "In ancient history and pre-history, tribes gave visceral comfort and pride from familiar fellowship, a way to defend the group enthusiastically against rival groups. It gave people a name in addition to their own and social meaning in a chaotic would."[4]

Wilson and others believe that this social drive propels our most positive outward abilities, including kindness, compassion and altruism. Tribalism promotes selfless acts that benefit groups, as well as offering personal protection due to strength in numbers. This also puts children on an emotional roller coaster as they race between individuals and groups that seem to alternate between acceptance and rejection.

This primal instinct may work well for children, but if it continues into their teen years it can become a source of bias, discrimination and conflict. Tribalism also affects the larger groups children join, from religions, educational and economic groups to political parties and nations. Strong, unquestioned tribalism can lead to inter-religious strife, political extremism, civil wars and gross social and economic inequality.

Creating the Capable Inclusive Friend

An Inclusive Friend has the opportunity to participate positively in groups and learn to balance individual and social needs. The Inclusive Friend understands how to resolve internal and external conflicts, while avoiding exclusive relationships that only benefit their immediate members. He understands that the boundaries between individuals and those that define groups are artificial, separating people who have much in common. The Inclusive Friend understands the demands as well as the rewards of relationships, balancing his need for social connections with a healthy ability to be alone.

Flexible Friendships

As social beings whose emotional well-being is tied to our connections to others, we value friendship almost as much as familial relationships. Friendship is a critical social connection, often the first relationship that moves children outside of their social comfort zone. Once thought of as a learned social convention, researchers have concluded that forming friendships has a deep primal foundation. Friendship bonds are evident in some primates and are universal across cultures. So, too, is the widespread anxiety adult caregivers express when children struggle to bond with peers.

Friendships involve frequent and consistent interactions between a few individuals that provide mutual benefits. Healthy friendships are largely free of self-serving or manipulative behaviors. Generally friendships form between children with similar social status, age, gender, race and interests, leading to overlapping identities. Friends know each other almost as well as parents and have strong insight into each other's minds.

Through mind reading and experience, children gain a substantial store of information about their friends. Friendship is a learning experience, as children grow knowledgeable about social norms and customs from the safety of a solitary relationship. Friends also teach each other about the beliefs and behaviors of people in their social network, an invaluable source of knowledge. They help define acceptable social and emotional behaviors of their associates and underlying motivations, intentions and desires. This expands both friends' perspectives on relationships.

While Zoe's closest friends share many of her characteristics, she also has many casual friendships that spring to life periodically. All of Zoe's friendships are built on a deep personal knowledge of each other and rely heavily on empathy, compassion and mind reading. Zoe is sensitive to her friends' habits, emotions and ways of thinking. She is often aware of slight shifts in their moods, changes in long-held beliefs and long-term desires. Zoe experiences long periods of separation almost as a loss. She gets upset when they argue and sad when her friends drift apart. The emotional connection and the frequent occupation of each other's minds means that Zoe's friends inhabit a special place in her memories; they have become a permanent part of the story of her life.

Group Identity and Me

Children derive a large part of their identity by having friends as well as by joining groups, teams, clubs, cliques and gangs. Friendships and memberships offer children great opportunities for learning as well as great challenges. Friends and relationships help children understand who they are as individuals and as social beings. These sources of identity help children and teens redefine themselves at times of transition, offering a sense of being special and important during times of doubt and uncertainty.

A child's individual identity may be so tightly connected to that of the group's that lack of acknowledgment or rejections can be devastating. The exclusive nature of friendships and group associations may cause a child to feel special or superior, leading to an artificially-inflated sense of self-importance and callousness to others. The tenuous nature of friendships may leave children open to emotional turbulence.

Melissa has seen Mia's emotions soar when she is accepted into a select group, only to crash when individual dynamics pull the members apart. To counteract these tendencies, Melissa has helped Mia see that only part of her identity is defined by her social relationships. They have reviewed past friendships and affiliations and discussed their benefits and drawbacks. Mia understands that social connections are often temporary and artificial, with boundaries as real as lines on a map.

As a woman who has faced discrimination and exclusion, Melissa promotes inclusion to counteract Mia's tendency to pick and choose her friends purely because they are popular. While Mia has a few friends who are similar to her in almost every way, Melissa encourages Mia to embrace others with different identities, interests and associations. She doesn't want Mia to think she is special just because she hangs out with this week's special children. Melissa knows that having a diverse set of friends promotes a broad and flexible personal identity, free from the sharp edges that cause conflict.

Melissa has helped Mia establish relationships with children from different neighborhoods. Mia attends an after-school program at a distant community center and spends time with her fourteen-year-old cousin. Mia also plays with younger children and takes piano lessons from an older boy who lives in her apartment. Melissa feels that this provides her daughter with a practical form of diversity that she supplements with diverse cultural activities as opportunities arise. As a result, Mia is largely free of identity rules; she rarely limits herself by thinking what a ten-year-old biracial girl should do or who she should associate with or what she is capable of accomplishing.

While Mia's school doesn't resemble the remarkably homogeneous schools that many children attend, it is hardly the ideal. She has little opportunity to interact with children of different ages, genders and interests—opportunities that should be available to every child in every school.

Melissa understands that her behavior has a profound impact on Mia's choice of relationships. Adults possess strong, even overwhelming, tribal influences on children, passing down (sometimes forcefully) their values regarding class, race, religion, political affiliations and social biases. Most children choose their parents' complete set of cultural affiliations, practicing the same religion, joining the same political party and aspiring to the same social class as their parents. Melissa is comfortable with her identity and freely discusses the positives and negatives of her racial, economic and political views with Mia. She hopes that her daughter will avoid a narrow personal group identity that might feed biases and prejudices or lack empathy and compassion for those with different identities and orientations.

Mutually-Beneficial Relationships

Children live in a perpetual balancing act between their individual needs and alliances to friends and groups. Their well-being is tied to those of others, but they also wish to be autonomous. Independence and interdependence don't need to be mutually exclusive, as it is possible to benefit personally by serving the greater good. Children and teens who expand their circle of concern receive benefits far beyond those obtainable through self-centered actions.

Branching out from a few select associates broadens children's perspectives, enriching them cognitively and emotionally. Children with wide social boundaries are comfortable interacting with individuals who might otherwise cause them anxiety, frustration, anger or fear. They may gain a flexible and multi-faceted identity that doesn't require the psychological defenses common to individuals with a narrow, fixed sense of self. Children with inclusive, pro-social abilities may avoid excessive self-preoccupation that can lead to anxiety and depression. Those who are more inclusive and cooperative benefit emotionally, just as children who are caring and fair do. They more easily make and maintain positive friendships and are less prone to loneliness and hatred.

The Value of Gossip

Another benefit of friends is that they provide important information about how emotional and social minds operate. A major source of this information is gossip. Gossip is an important form of social learning, an exchange of public opinions, which helps define social status and determines who is acceptable and who should be excluded. It enforces group values and tastes. While gossip is widely seen as idle talk with a mean side, it is universal across cultures—even those without social media, texting and blogs.

Christopher Boehm, of the University of Southern California and the Jane Goodall Research Center, has long studied hunter-gatherer and primate societies. Boehm has concluded that "public opinion, facilitated by gossiping, always guides [a] band's decision process, and fear of gossip all by itself serves as a pre-emptive social deterrent because most people are so sensitive about [their] reputation."[5]

Gossip provides children an outlet to express emotional problems, deal with relationship issues and influence the behavior of others. Studies of gossip have shown that children with greater pro-social abilities tend to gossip the most. Without the drama and emotions of destructive gossip, positive gossip often goes unnoticed by adults. Often rejecting negative and hurtful gossip, socially capable children use gossip to exchange information, only occasionally passing judgments on their connections. They will do this even if it hurts their reputation. They are more concerned with promoting group harmony and cooperation than enhancing their individual status.

Destructive gossip often involves information that degrades a child's reputation. It focuses on hurtful words and negative behaviors designed to exclude or defame others. Negative gossip is used to condemn behaviors, hand out punishments and set restrictions on relationships. It focuses on differences rather than commonalities. Children who engage in destructive gossip still condemn selfish or self-glorifying behaviors. The fastest way for a child to become the target of negative gossip is by showing a lack of concern for group values and infringing on unspoken rules of conduct. Boehm has found that reputations are best enhanced by altruistic behaviors, including caring and helping.[6]

While gossiping may rival storytelling as an important communication channel, it lives in the shadows in most homes and schools. Gossip should be quickly pulled out of the assumed curriculum to expose its constructive and destructive nature. Children should know the value of gossip and how these private discussions can either harm or help individuals and groups. They should see it as another perspective that has the power to both unite and divide.

Children who embody fairness, equality, caring and compassion will easily learn the positive power of gossip and how it promotes healthy relationships. The personal benefits of positive gossip include group respect and a solid reputation. Positive gossipers, not surprisingly, are far less likely to engage in anti-social behavior.

Collective Intelligence

Human beings have always banded together to optimize their survival, working together to solve problems and learn in meaningful ways. Cooperation is a key component of friendships, a way of establishing trust in others. Cooperation requires that children let go of the heavily self-centered nature of early childhood. One of the classic learning theories is that of Lev Vygotsky, a noted Russian psychologist. In the 1920s, Vygotsky proposed that cooperative learning behaviors involving groups of adults and children building meaning together are critical to learning. He believed that children's cognitive abilities are magnified and solidified when a group of children put their heads together and create group intelligence that overwhelms the abilities of the individual.[7]

A common belief is that great leadership, scholarship and creativity stem from the singular efforts of exceptional individuals. Schools are largely set up to award individual achievement. However, Thomas Malone, a researcher in group dynamics, and his colleagues believe that "having a band of smart people in a group doesn't necessarily make the group smart."[8] Research into group intelligence consistently shows that groups that include members who embody pro-social values, emotional awareness and strong mind-reading skills are more successful. Social collaboration consistently outperforms groups that are dominated by exceptional individuals. Groups that value cooperation, kindness and fairness are more successful, satisfying the needs and goals of the individuals and the organization.

A group doesn't have to be large to experience collective benefits. Group intelligence arises from close child-adult relationships built on mutual goals that respect the social and emotional dimension of learning. Many traditional forms of learning, including children learning in domestic, hunting, farming and food-gathering situations, as well as mentorships and apprenticeships, have long records of mutual learning and problem-solving. Adults don't just transmit learning, they also learn. Group members develop socially, emotionally and experientially while gaining greater insight into each other's minds and actions.

One important factor in successful groups is the presence of females. Girls and young women have greater awareness of group dynamics, are better mind readers and possess superior emotional and social sensitivities. They temper alpha males who strive for individual dominance and singular success.[9]

The Social Skills of the Introvert

While children benefit from developing pro-social capabilities, they should be comfortable when they are alone with their thoughts, emotions and interests. Children who have an inner focus may be neglected by societies that favor bold, assertive and outgoing personalities. It is easier to appreciate talkative, socially-engaged and outwardly successful extroverted personalities than children who are quieter and more reserved. However, introverts have much to teach us about relationships and social capabilities. About a third of children can be considered to be introverts; they have a special ability to adapt to social pressures. They are highly skilled in understanding social situations and their own minds.

Parents and teachers often put children under intense pressure to socialize. We want them to have playmates and make friends and behave in socially complex environments—from the classroom to the cubicle. But socializing has its costs, creating all kinds of tensions while taxing our mental capabilities and social brains. Introverts understand the costs and live lives that minimize draining social relationships.

Introverts aren't necessarily shy or loners, but members of a social species who require substantial time alone. They aren't heavily reliant on others to entertain, distract or think for them, as they do a good job of these things by themselves. They possess a Curious Explorer's mind, have many interests and are good daydreamers. Their creative side is often drowned out by noisy and self-interested voices. They make good team members who contribute well-thought-out ideas that boost group intelligence.

While introversion is a personality type, all children can benefit from the strategies introverts apply to socialization and learning. They offer valuable lessons about the nature of children's minds and how they adapt to social challenges. Introverts take a cautious approach to social situations, as they are aware of the benefits and the deficits of relationships. They are selective socializers, easily drained by the mandates of six-hour school days and endless, scheduled afterschool activities. They often enjoy social gatherings of their own choosing, usually on a smaller scale. They may enjoy social media, tweeting and texting on their terms.

Daniel's extroverted friends, parents and teachers may not understand why he doesn't crave endless validation from his relationships or derive a substantial part of his identity from others. He has a few close friends who understand his quiet side and they enjoy playing strategy games, building things and exploring nature with him. Daniel appreciates being with his friends but also his time alone, as he has endless interests and activities that intrigue him. He explores nature, plays games and builds things for endless hours in a state of flow. He listens to music, reads and manages his fantasy sports team without a hint of loneliness or sadness.

Inner-focused and self-entertaining children like Daniel are often selective about their friends. They don't search out friendships just to boost their social status, for emotional stimulation or to gossip. Daniel finds small talk, especially when it includes criticism or backbiting, boring. He would rather talk about big-picture ideas than about the transient behaviors of self-absorbed children. He rarely looks for identity in the loud, proud or bold, as they are often the source of social conflict and emotional confusion. He seeks out quieter, unique associates who may share his interests rather than peers whose biggest interests are with social interactions and conformity. He has friends who are older and younger, female and male, richer and poorer.

Children who are reserved and comfortable with themselves, who don't crave attention or social stimulation, may be perceived as outcasts.

Perhaps instead we should question the behaviors of extroverts and their relationships. Shouldn't we examine those who crave social attention, need constant acknowledgement and often have limited ability to reflect on their thoughts and actions? Shouldn't we be concerned about children who are uncomfortable being alone, who need constant stimulation or interactions to maintain their emotional stability? Why do so many people value assertive individuals who dominate interactions, who are non-stop talkers with poor listening skills? Why don't we appreciate children who are quiet and cautious and who entertain themselves? Why should we desire socially-constructed ideas of how children should be instead of understanding who they are?

Children will spend much of their lives trying to relate to a diverse range of social situations—many not of their choosing. Introversion offers a successful solution to balancing the needs of an individual with those of the group. Not only do they reflectively monitor their social interactions to limit emotionally- or cognitively-draining interactions, but when they do engage in groups they offer many positive attributes. Contrary to social myths, introverts are strong leaders, precisely because they are good mind readers and listeners. Introverts are better at fostering group intelligence, divergent thinking and creative solutions. They rarely bully or emotionally manipulate others. When they are with a small group of friends, their listening and mind-reading skills often make them valued companions.

Resiliency

The cautious and reflective nature of children with an introverted side helps them foster resiliency—the critical social-emotional ability to solve problems rather than being overwhelmed by them. Introverts possess many of the key abilities that create resiliency, allowing them to bounce back or crawl out of life's devastating problems. Their mind-reading skills help them avoid emotionally-charged and socially-manipulative people. Introverts' inner focus helps them reflect, not just ruminate, over disruptive life events. Their ability to take different perspectives and evaluate people and situations more deeply allows introverts to adapt to challenging events.

Al Siebert, the author of *The Resiliency Advantage,* believes that we should "do everything in our power to choose habits that will serve to strengthen our ability to bounce back in difficult times."[10] Siebert recommends choosing our connections carefully and having a few strong relationships, rather than many demanding ones. Resilient individuals are more reflective and spend time to evaluate the emotional nature and social benefits of relationships. This may lead to a mindful presence, where the resilient child learns to value the present moment free of judgment rather than being consumed by past events. He finds that resiliency grows as people spend more time in the "default mode," spending time daydreaming about alternative possibilities.[11]

Siebert concludes that resiliency springs from helping others and small acts of kindness and caring that build new, healthy connections to others. By being kind and caring to others, children who have suffered significant setbacks in life learn to be kinder, less judgmental and caring rather than critical.

Social Learning

We have seen the tremendous role that social interactions, friendships and group memberships have on children's abilities to learn, problem-solve and find meaning. The social and emotional capabilities of children grow best when parents and teachers focus on big abilities, including fairness, caring and a bit of selflessness.

Social learning specialist Michelle Garcia Winner warns that we should maintain a "Big L Learning" focus when it comes to social and emotional abilities: "A more effective pathway towards social learning is to start by teaching our students a process that not only leads to specific skill development, but equips our students with the ability to use this social knowledge to branch out into other social directions."[12]

Winner's concept, called the *Social Learning Tree,* takes a systems approach, using the roots, trunk and leaves as a metaphor for building social-emotional capabilities. In Winner's view, the roots aren't isolated pieces but a mutually-interdependent system that works together to form social and emotional learning. The roots of social learning involve the primal abilities that appear during the first few years of life. These include joint attention—when two individuals' focus is drawn to the same object—emotional sharing and reciprocity and the early stages of mind reading. Early language and cognitive abilities are also social roots.[13]

The trunk of the Social Learning Tree applies the root abilities to daily experiences. Children don't just read but also react to other people's thoughts, emotions and behaviors. At about five years of age, children begin to develop more advanced social capabilities by engaging positively with others. Some children, who Winner defines as those born with "weak intuitive social learning abilities," may need more explicit support to develop social skills.[14] Before children learn to use social language effectively, listen openly, take different perspectives and understand bigger points of view, they will need mentoring in cooperative play, turn taking, being a friend and dealing with change. Winner feels that humor and "human relatedness" are critical elements of the trunk, which involve learning to relate not just to people but to their minds, emotions and needs. Telling and responding to jokes requires a mutual understanding of both of the parties' minds, dependent on a close connection between those minds.[15]

The leafed branches of social learning grow along with more refined capabilities. These include reading comprehension and storytelling and written and oral expression that are sensitive to emotions and social connections, exposing multiple perspectives. Winner strongly believes that many social learning programs start on this top layer but many children struggle with root and trunk abilities. Students who learn skills in isolation, such as perspective-taking during a lecture, may be unable to develop full capability in non-classroom situations.[16]

Four of Roger Schank's twelve cognitive abilities involve social processes with a decidedly "Big L Learning" flavor. They include learning to influence others by understanding how people respond to requests in a manner that is free of manipulation. He believes that students should learn to work in teams to develop group intelligence as well as achieve mutual goals by working in coordinated and collaborative manners. Human interactions often involve negotiation, that process that involves give-and-take, mind reading and conflict resolution.[17]

SMALL MOMENTS THAT CREATE THE INCLUSIVE FRIEND

Some activities that naturally lend themselves to developing the Inclusive Friend include:

- mind-reading activities, including role playing, acting and storytelling
- perspective taking
- pro-social abilities, including expressing empathy, caring, helping and sharing, as well as learning to act fairly
- helping children reflect on and evaluate their relationships
- fostering pro-social gossip
- selectivity in choosing friends and associations
- promoting inclusiveness and diversity, helping children to interact with those from other neighborhoods, social and economic classes, genders, ages and races
- understanding that groups have artificial boundaries designed to give individuals a sense of being unique or special. These boundaries are a major source of identity but also a cause of many of our personal and social problems.
- teamwork that values group intelligence, negotiation and influencing

Conclusion

. . . .

The Balanced Mindful Juggler

Our last capability, the Balanced Mindful Juggler, isn't a new or separate capability, but the one that ties the other capabilities together into a system of learning. The Learning Capabilities Framework offers the exciting possibility of creating more capable children. There are a large number of abilities, states of mind and Small Moments and an array of concepts, including continuous learning, problem-solving and meaning-making abilities and an "Inner, Other and Autonomous" focus.

By focusing on the big picture, we can see larger learning opportunities and the chance to create well-rounded, resilient children and teens. Conversely, when children are encouraged to achieve narrow academic results or singular performances in a specialized skill, be it high levels of creativity, extraordinary curiosity or exceptional math skills, their overall well-being and long-term learning, problem-solving and meaning-making abilities could be compromised.

The Balanced Mindful Juggler offers a solution for this array of concepts by focusing on the big picture, the take-home message and "Big L Learning." This unifying capability is composed of two all-encompassing elements that will help children and adults create capabilities with grace and ease. The first element is balance—using capabilities to balance children's often chaotic lives in a stormy academic, economic, emotional, social and technological world. The second is mindfulness in the broadest form, encompassing focus, interest, attention and awareness.

The Need for Balance

For children and adults, life is a juggling act, with their balance thrown off by confusing activities and experiences, conflicting motivations and desires and upsetting thoughts and emotions. Children with a balanced range of capabilities will maintain equilibrium during the constant challenges and changes inherent in growing from a toddler to a teen in just a few years. Capable children will handle the persistent changes in their bodies, minds and relationships as learning and problem-solving experiences, rather than being thrown about by every passing event.

Restoring balance to children's and adults' lives requires balancing—not throwing out—current parenting and teaching methods with capability-enhancing approaches. Balance comes not from radical change or strict adherence to a rigid schedule of Small Moments, but by gently shifting the relationship between children and adults to be more interactive. This will result in lifelong learners with a curious fascination for all the worlds they inhabit.

Here are some suggested ways to use capabilities to balance typical activities in which children and teens engage.

Using Embodied and Engaged Exploratory and Experimental Capabilities to Create Balance

- Balance instructional time with experiences big and small.
- Balance indoor time and screen time with outdoor time.
- Balance time spent seated with active undertakings.
- Balance forced instruction and homework with activities that hold personal interest.
- Balance times of extrinsic or little reward with activities that are self-motivating.

Using Sense-Making Capabilities to Create Balance

- Balance periods of heavy thinking with quiet time and daydreaming.

- Balance and infuse dry content or activities with imagination and creative activities.
- Balance routines and habits with creativity and divergent thinking.
- Balance passive listening or slanted, opinionated discussions with intentional listening.
- Balance and infuse lectures with critical listening, open-minded discussions and explanation learning.
- Balance lectures at home or school with storytelling and conversations.
- Balance online time with sensory awareness and nature exploration.

Using Meaning-Making Capabilities to Create Balance

- Balance instruction that is fact-heavy with meta-cognitive and mindfulness activities.
- Balance new studies or activities with time spent pursuing areas of expertise.
- Balance home or school factual discussions with processes and systems thinking.
- Balance one-sided instruction or discussions with perspective-taking.
- Balance piecemeal instruction with activities that create the big picture, a take-home message or systems of understanding.

Using Social and Emotional Capabilities to Create Balance

- Balance socialized time with time alone for introspection.
- Balance times of individual achievement with times of group effort.
- Balance times of mindless activities with mindfulness in all its iterations.
- Balance self-absorbed attention by taking different perspectives.
- Balance times of self-indulgence with ethical decision-making.

Broad, Mindful Attention

The second solution that the Balanced Mindful Juggler provides is the focused attention, awareness and mindfulness that figures into the creation of every capability. An attentive, observant, aware, interested and reflective mind is fundamental to learning. Children's minds tend to wander, sometimes in a positive way and other times just by simple distraction. Their minds change states, from curious to contemplative and flowing to daydreaming, depending on thoughts, emotions, social situations and body states. Sometimes they are aware, present in the moment and focused on the activity at hand. Yet too often they are simply pushed and pulled by repetitive thoughts, subtle feelings, selfish desires and social influences.

To counteract these random attentional tendencies, children should learn how to observe and guide their attention and focus their minds. This can be as simple as paying undivided attention to an activity or listening intensively to a discussion. It may be as easy as looking for distinctions, seeing relationships and altering perspectives. It can be creative reflection or observant mind wandering, but attention must be paid.

Creating the Balanced Mindful Juggler in children and adults also requires refocusing attention and awareness toward more primal ways of learning. This capability doesn't require that children dramatically change the way they think or behave, but rather how they focus their minds when they are actively experiencing, pursuing an interest or gossiping with a friend. Children who know what draws their attention and how to be present are capable of learning in different ways. Learning comes naturally to children who are mindful, focused, motivated and interested.

William James, often called the father of American psychology, believed that "the faculty of voluntarily bringing back a wandering attention, over and over again, is the very root of judgment, character, and will...An education which should improve this faculty would be the education par excellence."[1] Children and teens learn little when they are disinterested, unmotivated and forced to pay attention. Each capability engages one or more ways of focusing children's minds. The active, experiential capabilities rely on awareness of the body, senses and the environment. They require understanding motivations and interests. The Flow State arises from being fully involved in activities and interests.

The sense-making capabilities are built upon sensory awareness, daydreaming and an imaginative and creative mind. Listening and conversing with an open-mind requires a high level of attention and sensitivity to the words and actions of others.

The meaning-making capabilities are dependent on meta-cognition, awareness of hot thoughts and emotions and the activities that move between the conscious and the subconscious mind.

Mind-reading abilities engage a different way of looking and perspective-taking. The Reasonable Judge requires a heightened awareness of one's reasoning patterns, judgments and decision-making abilities.

The social and emotional capabilities require self-awareness, sensitivity to emotions and awareness of feelings. They are dependent on flights of mind, including storytelling, perspective-taking and role-playing. Luckily, children don't have to be taught how to engage their minds in a primal manner, as these engagements arise naturally under the right conditions.

While there are methods that enhance daydreaming and imagination or improve empathy in the emotionally challenged, there are also mindfulness practices that will enhance almost any lesson, interaction or experience. Today, many schools are introducing mindfulness programs as a way of reducing stress and improving focus, motivation and behavior. Mindfulness Based Stress Reduction (MBSR), a researched-based practice free of religious overtones, has proven successful in schools nationwide. Students develop body and sensory awareness, avoid distractions and learn to monitor their thoughts and emotions in a non-judgmental manner. Mindfulness practices have a profound effect on students' academic and behavioral performances and may possibly prove more significant than the introduction of technology to student well-being.[2]

The limitation of mindfulness training and other types of meditation is that they are taught as special practices rather than integrated into children's active experiences in school and during their free time. We believe that mindfulness isn't just the specialized practice of sitting quietly and focusing inward. Mindfulness in its broadest sense is heightened by practices such as Ellen Langer's Mindful Learning, activities and lessons that induce the Flow State, meta-cognitive practices and attentive embodied action and sensory awareness during a walk in a park.

Today, in a world full of distraction where attention is at a premium, helping children become more aware and mindful can't be left to the assumed curriculum. It must become part of the regular school day and the mission of parenting.

This might take the addition of a new subject, mind studies or the adoption of a school schedule modeled on the Finnish school day. Blocks of instruction are kept short, based on the belief that children and teens learn best in twenty or thirty-minute sessions. Between each block is a fifteen-minute break, often used for recess. If homes and schools used similar break times to create balance or for mind studies, then children's levels of interest and engagement, focus and awareness would improve. School would be less stressful and more concerned with children's well-being.

It's time for mind study to be part of every child's school day with mind and relationship-building activities supplanting homework. Our proposed psychology course wouldn't resemble a college psychology 101 course but involve:

- body awareness and yoga
- mindfulness and stress reduction practices
- teaching children how they learn
- recognizing common thinking distortions and biases
- classroom-based cognitive behavioral therapy
- learning to pay attention and to direct one's mind
- how to handle hot thoughts and emotions
- managing relationships
- building pro-social abilities, including fairness, caring, empathy and compassion
- understanding motivation, desires and needs
- negotiation, conflict resolution and persuasion

Parents and teachers should be as concerned with developing a child's inner focus as with outward signs of success. Children who are comfortable with their own thoughts and feelings and aren't in need of constant distractions and scheduled activities are better equipped to handle emotional and environmental upsets.

Mutual Benefit

The capable Balanced Mindful Juggler provides benefits to children and adults alike. Both parties benefit when Small Moments are used to build learning relationships between resourceful adults and capable kids. Both have the potential to be more curious and inquisitive, more active, involved and engaged, seeking out common interests. Exchanging and discussing personal stories, listening openly and reflecting on each other's stories strengthen relationships. Adults and children benefit when constant judgment and adult controls give way to more mindful forms of interaction.

Adults who are better problem-solvers and lifelong learners who find purpose and meaning in their lives may find the difficult tasks of parenting and teaching to be rewarding. A relationship built on molding information into meaningful processes and systems, based on kind, considerate and fair interactions, is far healthier than one held together by demands, warnings, unrealistic expectations and sheer force of will.

Childhood and the teenage years are a unique time of growth and learning. A Learning Capabilities Framework will hopefully restore some of the joy and wonder to childhood as well as to parenting and teaching. Capable children have a good sense of their changing identity, how they fit into society and a concern for their environment—physical and biological. These capabilities all involve active, attentive engagement that enriches a child's mind. They will be better equipped to confront life's small and large problems with minds that are prepared with multiple modules or capabilities from which to choose.

More Rewarding Relationships

Creating the Balanced Mindful Juggler will create more rewarding relationships between children and adults, ones that are based on deep appreciation of children's immense primal learning abilities. Adults will be less worried and stressed when they focus on children's immediate experience rather than distant and abstract goals, alleviating as least some of the natural anxiety adults have about children's futures. Adults will feel more satisfied when some of the responsibility for learning, behavior and problem-solving are shifted back to children, creating a more enjoyable learning experience for all. For parents and teachers to focus on realigning their relationships with children, we offer a simple guide to capability creation.

If a child or student is engaged in an activity:

- Nudge it into a learning experience that fosters curiosity, inquisitiveness or an experimental mindset.
- Push it toward a more active, embodied experience—from drawing to building.
- Deepen the interest and heighten the fascination by building on it immediately or in the future.
- Make a mental note of interests, activities and experiences as keys to motivation.

If your child is daydreaming, lost in thought or talking semi-attentively or in narrative form:

- Give them time to be quiet, to daydream and to imagine in order to create the Creative Dreamer.
- Tell them some stories and listen to theirs to create the Storyteller.
- Dance, sing, play and listen with them to create the Action Character.
- Listen with less judgment and offer minimal advice and maximum emotional support to create the Careful Communicator.

If children are rattling off facts, struggling to find meaning, overwhelmed by judgments or lost in scattered thinking:

- Explore their backstage plans, dreams, ideas, images and memories to create the Backstage Director.

- Help them turn parts into wholes by looking for distinctions and relationships to create the Knowledge Architect.
- Uncover hot thoughts, biases and distortions to create the Knowledge Architect.
- Help them make fair and ethical decisions to create the Reasonable Judge.

If children are emotionally overwhelmed, confused by relationships or acting in selfish manners:

- Encourage them to mind read by taking different perspectives, acting, storytelling and role-playing to create the Caring Mind Reader.
- Value empathy, helping and compassion and only occasionally praise their academic and other singular accomplishments to create the Caring Mind Reader.
- Encourage pro-social behaviors to create the Inclusive Friend.
- Help them navigate the pros and cons of friendships, groups and associations using strategies familiar to introverts to create the Inclusive Friend.

Creating capable kids has an added benefit—it creates adults who are more capable learners, too. We hope that utilizing our twelve capabilities helps you create more capable children and that, in turn, you become more capable as well!

Endnotes

Chapter 1

1 U.S. Department of Education, Institute of Education Sciences, National Center for Education Statistics, National Assessment of Educational Progress (NAEP), 2009.

2 Kasey Klepfer and Jim Hull, "High School Rigor and Good Advice: Setting up Students to Succeed," Center for Public Education, October 1, 2012, accessed December 20, 2014, http://www.centerforpubliceducation.org/Main-Menu/Staffingstudents/High-school-rigor-and-good-advice-Setting-up-students-to-succeed/High-school-rigor-and-good-advice-Setting-up-students-to-succeed-Full-Report.pdf.

3 Susan E. Gathercole and Tracy Packiam Alloway, *Working Memory and Learning: A Practical Guide for Teachers* (Los Angeles, CA: SAGE Publications, 2008), 1-6.

4 Daniel T. Willingham, *Why Don't Students like School?: A Cognitive Scientist Answers Questions about How the Mind Works and What It Means for the Classroom* (San Francisco, CA: Jossey-Bass, 2009), Kindle Edition, 333.

5 The Alliance, "Paying Double: Inadequate High Schools and Community College Remediation." Alliance for Excellent Education. October 1, 2006. http://all4ed.org/wp-content/uploads/remediation.pdf.

6 U.S. Department of Education, NAEP, 2009.

7 Scott Barry Kaufman, *Ungifted: Intelligence Redefined* (New York: Basic Books, 2013), 281.

8 Diane Ravitch, *The Death And Life Of The Great American School System: How Testing And Choice Are Undermining Education* (New York: Basic Books, 2010), 1-14.; Barbara Strauch, *The Primal Teen: What the New Discoveries about the Teenage Brain Tell Us about Our Kids* (New York: Doubleday, 2003), 215.

9 Paul Tough, *How Children Succeed: Grit, Curiosity, and the Hidden Power of Character* (New York: Mariner Books, 2013), Kindle Edition, 183.

10 Suniya Luthar, "The Problem With Rich Kids," *Psychology Today* (November 5, 2013), accessed December 30, 2014, http://www.psychologytoday.com/articles/201310/the-problem-rich-kids.

11 Tough, How Children Succeed. 81.

12 David Eagleman, *Incognito: The Secret Lives of the Brain* (New York: Pantheon Books, 2011), 219.

Chapter 2

1 Diane Ravitch, *Left Back: A Century of Battles over School Reform* (New York: Touchstone, 2001), 29-32.; National Education Association of the United States, "Committee of Ten on Secondary School Studies," (1894); Michael Kirst and Michael Usdan, "The Historical Context of the Divide Between K–12 and Higher Education," *The National Center for Public Policy and Higher Education* (2009), accessed September 28, 2014, http://www.highereducation.org/reports/ssc/ssc_Cha_1.pdf.

2 Ibid.

3 Ibid.

4 Claire Gilbert, "The Truman Commission and its Impact on Federal Higher Education Policy From 1947 to 2010," *Association for the Study of Higher Education* (2010).

5 David B. Tyack and Larry Cuban, *Tinkering toward Utopia: A Century of Public School Reform* (Cambridge, Mass.: Harvard University Press, 1995), 33-34.

6 Andrew Rudalevige, "Adequacy, Accountability, and the Impact of 'No Child Left Behind'," *Hks.harvard.edu* (October 1, 2005), accessed December 30, 2014, http://www.hks.harvard.edu/pepg/PDF/events/Adequacy/PEPG-05-27rudalevige.pdf.; David P. Gardner and Others, "A Nation at Risk: The Imperative For Educational Reform. An Open Letter to the American People. A Report to the Nation and the Secretary of Education," Editorial Projects in Education Research Center. Issues A-Z: A Nation at Risk, *Education Week.* (2004, August 3), accessed December 30, 2014, http://www.edweek.org/ew/issues/a-nation-at-risk.

7 "Federal Education Policy and the States, 1945-2009: A Brief Synopsis," New York State Education Department Archives (December 1, 2009), accessed December 30, 2014, http://www.archives.nysed.gov/edpolicy/altformats/ed_background_overview_essay.pdf.

8 Charles Darwin, *The Descent of Man, and Selection in Relation to Sex* (Princeton, N.J.: Princeton University Press, 1981), 69.

9 William James, *The Principles of Psychology* (Mineola, NY: Dover, 1890), 13-16.

10 Ann Hulbert, *Raising America: Experts, Parents, and a Century of Advice about Children* (New York: Alfred A. Knopf, 2003), 9-12.

11 Ken Robinson, *Out of Our Minds: Learning to be Creative* (Wiley: New York, 2011), 8.

12 John Dewey, *Experience and Education* (New York: Touchstone, 1938), Kindle Edition, 117.

13 Paulo Freire, *Pedagogy of the Oppressed*, 30th Anniversary ed. (New York: Continuum, 2000), 73.

14 Stephen P. Hinshaw and Richard M. Scheffler, *The ADHD Explosion: Myths, Medication, Money, and Today's Push for Performance* (Oxford: Oxford University Press, Feb 3, 2014), xxvi.

15 Charles H Swanson, "Their success is your success: teach them to listen," (paper presented at the Annual Conference of the West Virginia Community College Association, Charleston, WV, October 19, 1984).

16 Madelyn Burley-Allen, *Listening: The Forgotten Skill* (Hoboken, NJ: John Wiley & Sons, 1982), Kindle Edition, 107.

17 Robinson, *Out of Our Minds*, 60.

18 David F. Lancy, *The Anthropology of Childhood: Cherubs, Chattel, Changelings* (Cambridge: Cambridge University Press, 2014), 6-8.

19 Willingham, *Why Don't Students Like School?*, Kindle edition, *1493*.

20 Neil DeGrasse Tyson, "I Am Neil DeGrasse Tyson – AMA," Reddit (December 17, 2011), accessed December 30, 2014, http://www.reddit.com/r/IAmA/comments/ngd5e/i_am_neil_degrasse_tyson_ama.

21 Rebecca Mead, "Starman," *The New Yorker* (February 17, 2014), 34.

22 Chip Walter, *Last Ape Standing: The Seven-million Year Story of How and Why We Survived* (New York: Walker & Company, 2013), 32-38.

23 David Geary, "The Primal Brain in the Modern Classroom," *Scientific American Mind*, (October 1, 2011), 24.

24 Leda Cosmides and John Tooby, "Evolutionary Psychology and the Emotions," (Center for Evolutionary Psychology, 2000). http://www.cep.ucsb.edu/emotion.html.

Chapter 3

1 Nicole S. Simon and Gary W. Evans, "Poverty and Child Development: Beyond the Schoolyard Gate," *Underprivileged School Children and the Assault on Dignity*, ed. by Julia Hill (New York: Routledge, 2014), 48-76.

2 Jennifer Senior, *For Parents Happiness is a Very High Bar*. (Ted Talk, March 2014) http://www.ted.com/talks/jennifer_senior_for_parents_happiness_is_a_very_high_bar?language=en.

3 Ibid.

4 Ibid.

5 Jennifer Senior, *All Joy and No Fun: The Paradox of Modern Parenthood* (New York: Ecco, 2014), 172-176.

6 Harry Brighouse, *On Education* (New York; Routledge, May 2, 2006), Kindle edition, 606.

7 Ibid.

8 Ibid.

9   Ibid.

10 Howard Gardner, Interview with Steen Larsen. *Education and humanism* (2002, Spring). Denmark: Padaogiske Universitet. 5-8.

11 Kaufman, *Ungifted*. 302-307.

12 A. Mani, S. Mullainathan, E. Shafir and J. Zhao, "Poverty impedes cognitive function," *Science*, 341 (2013): 976.

13 Alan S Kaufman, *IQ Testing 101* (New York, NY: Springer Pub., 2009), 117.

14 E. Young, *Intelligence Testing: Accurate, or Extremely Biased?* (2013), accessed December 19, 2014, http://www.theneuroethicsblog.com/2013/09/intelligence -testing-accurate-or.htm.

15 Brighouse, *On Education*. Kindle edition, 660-681.

16 Ibid., 219.

17 Eagleman, *Incognito*. 219.

18 Bruce Hood, *The Self Illusion* (London: Constable, 2011), Kindle edition, 229.

19 Eagleman, *Incognito*. 219.

20 Antonio Damasio, *The Feeling of What Happens: Body and Emotion in the Making of Consciousness* (New York: Harcourt Brace, 1999), 279-295.

21 Daniel J. Siegel, *Mindsight: The New Science of Personal Transformation* (New York: Bantam Books, 2010), 51-55.

22 Ibid., 52.

23 Daniel J. Siegel, "TEDxBlue - Daniel J. Siegel, M.D. - 10/18/09," Tedx Talks (October 18, 2009), accessed December 19, 2014, http://tedxtalks.ted.com/ video/TEDxBlue-Daniel-J-Siegel-MD-101.

Chapter 4

1   Ellen Galinsky, *Mind in the Making: The Seven Essential Life Skills Every Child Needs* (New York: William Morrow 2010), 1-3.

2   Ibid.

3   Ibid., 4-11.

4   Ibid., 39-40.

5   Roger C. Schank, *Teaching Minds: How Cognitive Science Can save Our Schools* (New York: Teachers College Press, 2011), Kindle edition, 30.

6   Ibid., 63.

7   Ibid., 20.

8   Martha C. Nussbaum, *Creating Capabilities: The Human Development Approach* (Harvard University Press, April 30, 2011), 17-20.

9   Ibid.

10 Ibid., 33-35.

11 Ibid., 28-29.

12 Ibid., 28-29.

13 Elaine Unterhalter, Rosie Vaughan and Melanie Walker, "The Capability Approach and Education," (http://www.nottingham.ac.uk/educationresearchprojects/doc- uments/developmentdiscourses/rpg2008walkermclean9.pdf).

14 Ibid., 1-3.

15 Sean Reardon, "No Rich Child Left Behind," *New York Times*, April 28, 2013. http://opinionator.blogs.nytimes .com/2013/04/27/no-rich-child-left-behind/?_r=0.

16 Ibid.

17 Ibid.

18 Ibid.

Chapter 5

1 David Dobbs, "Restless Genes," *National Geographic*, January 1, 2013, 57.

2 Ibid.

3 Jerome Groopman, "Birth Pangs" *New York Times*, September 30, 2010, accessed December 19, 2014, http://www.nytimes.com/2010/10/03/books/review/Groopman-t.html?pagewanted=all.

4 John Abbott, "Adolescence; a Critical Evolutionary Adaptation," *The 21st Century Learning Initiative* (2005): 19, accessed December 30, 2014, http://www.21learn .org/wp-content/uploads/adoles_crit_evo_adapt.pdf.

5 Gary F. Marcus, *The Birth of the Mind: How a Tiny Number of Genes Creates the Complexities of Human Thought* (New York: Basic Books, 2004), 167-168.

6 David C. Geary, *The Origin of Mind: Evolution of Brain, Cognition, and General Intelligence* (Washington, DC: American Psychological Association, 2005), 22.

7 Alison Gopnik, *The Philosophical Baby: What Children's Minds Tell Us about Truth, Love, and the Meaning of Life* (New York: Farrar, Straus and Giroux, 2009), 20.

8 Ibid.

9 Alison Gopnik, "How Babies Think," *Scientific American*, July 1, 2010, 76-81.

10 Susan J. Hespos and Kristy vanMarle, "Physics for infants: characterizing the origins of knowledge about objects, substances, and number," *WIREs Cogn Sci* 3 (2012): 19-27, accessed December 30, 2014, doi: 10.1002/wcs.157.

11 Ibid.

12 Ibid., 157.

13 Ibid., 157.

14 Natalie Angier, "Now We Are Six," *New York Times*, December 26, 2011, D1.

15 Ibid.

16 Lancy, *The Anthropology of Childhood*. 14.

17 Ibid., 99-100.

18 Ibid.

19 Scottye J. Cash and Jeffrey A. Bridge, "Epidemiology Of Youth Suicide And Suicidal Behavior," *Current Opinion in Pediatrics* 21, no. 5 (2009): 613-19.

20 Ammie Feijoo, Sue Alford and Deb Alford, "Adolescent Sexual Health in Europe and the US," Advocates for Youth (March 1, 2011), accessed September 29, 2014, http://www.advocatesforyouth.org/publications/419-adolescent-sexual-health -in-europe-and-the-us.

21 Robert Epstein, "The Myth of the Teen Brain," *Scientific American Mind*, April 1, 2007, 57-63.

22 Robert Epstein, "The Adultness Test," How Adult Are You? (2014), accessed December 20, 2014, http://drrobertepstein.com/EDTA-unabridged/.

23 Dewey, *Experience and Education*, Kindle edition, 465.

24 Ibid.

25 Ibid.

26 Ibid., 476.

27 Ibid., 476.

28 Ibid., 243.

29 Ibid., 243.

30 Ibid., 617.

31 Alexander Sutherland Neill, *Summerhill: A New View of Childhood* (New York: St. Martin Press, 1992), 15.

32 Ibid.

33 Peter Gray, *Free to Learn: Why Unleashing the Instinct to Play Will Make Our Children Happier, More Self-reliant, and Better Students for Life* (New York: Basic Books, 2013), 5-9.

34 Ibid.

35 Richard E. Mayer, "Should There Be a Three-Strikes Rule Against Pure Discovery Learning?" *American Psychologist* 59 (2004): 14-19.

36 Paul A. Kirschner, John Sweller, and Richard E. Clark, "Why Minimal Guidance During Instruction Does Not Work: An Analysis of the Failure of Constructivist, Discovery, Problem-Based, Experiential, and Inquiry-Based Teaching," *Educational Psychologist* 41 (2006): 75-86.

37 Gray, *Free to Learn*, 6-12.

38 Richard Louv, *Last Child in the Woods: Saving Our Children from Nature-Deficit Disorder*. (Chapel Hill, NC: Algonquin Books of Chapel Hill, 2005), 32.

Chapter 6

1 Richard J. Davidson and Sharon Begley, *The Emotional Life of Your Brain: How Its Unique Patterns Affect the Way You Think, Feel, and Live—and How You Can Change Them* (New York: Hudson Street Press, 2012), Kindle Edition, 2172.

2 Annie Murphy Paul, "The Body Learns: For Years We've Been Telling Kids to Sit Still and Pay Attention. That's All Wrong," *Slate.com*, June 10, 2014, accessed December 30, 2014, http://www.slate.com/articles/technology/future_tense/2014/07/educational_technology_s_next_move_tools_to_help_kids_learn_with_their_bodies.html.

3 Antonio R. Damasio, *Descartes' Error: Emotion, Reason, and the Human Brain* (New York: Putnam, 1994), 156.

4 U.S. Department of Education, Institute of Education Sciences, National Center for Education Statistics, National Assessment of Educational Progress (NAEP), 2009 Reading Assessment.

5 Arthur Glenberg, "How Reading Comprehension Is Embodied and Why That Matters," *International Electronic Journal of Elementary Education* 2011 (2011), accessed December 30, 2014, http://www.jourlib.org/paper/2558172#.VJX_yF4Bds.

6 Ibid.

7 Ibid.

8 Arthur M. Glenberg, "What Memory Is For: Creating Meaning in the Service of Action," *Behavioral and Brain Sciences* 20, no. 1 (1997): 41-50.

9 Stephen R. Daniels, "Associations between Physical Activity, Fitness, and Academic Achievement," *The Journal of Pediatrics* 155, no. 6 (2009): A1.

10 Alan Fogel, "Psychotherapy, Medication, or Body Sense for Mental Health?" *Psychology Today — Body Sense*, 2011, accessed December 1, 2014, http://www .psychologytoday.com/blog/body-sense/201112/psychotherapy-medication-or -body-sense-mental-health.

11 A. Senghas, "Children Creating Core Properties Of Language: Evidence From An Emerging Sign Language In Nicaragua," *Science* 309, no. 5731 (2005): 1779-1782.

12 Ibid.

13 Ibid.

14 Maria Konnikova, "What's Lost as Handwriting Fades," *New York Times*, June 2, 2014. D1.

15 Anand Giridharadas, "The Kitchen-Table Industrialists," *New York Times*, May 13, 2011, MM 50.

16 Kaufman, *Ungifted*. 158-161.

Chapter 7

1 Alfie Kohn, *Punished by Rewards: The Trouble with Gold Stars, Incentive Plans, A's, Praise, and Other Bribes* (Boston: Houghton Mifflin, 1993), 432.

2 Scott Barry Kaufman, "Interest Fuels Effortless Engagement," *Scientific American Beautiful Minds*, March 5, 2014, accessed December 19, 2014, http://blogs.sci-entificamerican.com/beautiful-minds/2014/03/05/interest-fuels-effortless -engagement/.

3 Daniel H. Pink, *Drive: The Surprising Truth about What Motivates Us* (New York, NY: Riverhead Books, 2009), 85, 165.

4 Ibid.

5 Ibid., 125.

6 Ibid., 131.

7 Ingfei Chen, "How a Bigger Purpose Can Motivate Students to Learn," *MindShift*, August 18, 2014, accessed December 19, 2014, http://blogs.kqed.org/mindshift/ 2014/08/how-a-bigger-purpose-can-motivate-students-to-learn/.

8 Ellen J Langer, *The Power of Mindful Learning*, (Reading, Mass.: Addison-Wesley, 1997), Kindle Edition, 646.

9 Ibid., 656.

10 Ibid., 665.

11 Annie Murphy Paul, "The Brilliant Blog," November 1, 2013, accessed December 30, 2014, http://anniemurphypaul.com/2013/11/the-power-of-interest/.

12 Gopnik, *The Philosophical Baby*, 116.

13 Langer, *The Power of Mindful Learning*, Kindle edition, 236.

14 Ibid., 232.

15 Mihaly Csikszentmihalyi, *Flow: The Psychology of Optimal Experience* (New York: Harper & Row, 1990), 107.

16 Kevin Rathunde and Mihaly Csikszentmihalyi, "Middle School Students' Motivation And Quality Of Experience: A Comparison Of Montessori And

Traditional School Environments," *American Journal of Education* 111, no. 3 (2005): 341-71.

17 Langer, *The Power of Mindful Learning*, Kindle edition, 673.

Chapter 8

1 Jacob Levernier, Candice Mottweiler and Marjorie Taylor, "The Creation of Imaginary Worlds in Middle Childhood," *Probing-the-boundaries*, accessed December 22, 2014. http://www.inter-disciplinary.net/probing-the-boundaries/wp-content/uploads/2013/05/jglvernier-etal-wpaper-play2.pdf.

2 Ibid.

3 Daniel Willingham, "Ask the Cognitive Scientist - Brain Based Learning," American Federation of Teachers, September 1, 2006, Accessed December 21, 2014, http://www.aft.org/periodical/american-educator/fall-2006/ask-cognitive-scientist.

4 Ibid.

5 Diane Ackerman, "Are We Living in Sensory Overload or Sensory Poverty?" *New York Times*, June 10, 2012, A18.

6 Ibid.

7 Ibid.

8 Ibid.

9 Michael Shermer, "Patternicity: Finding Meaningful Patterns in Meaningless Noise," *Scientific American*, November 17, 2008, accessed December 30, 2014, http://www.scientificamerican.com/article/patternicity-finding-meaningful-patterns/.

10 Kaufman, *Ungifted*, 249-254.

11 Scott Barry Kaufman, "The Origins of Positive-Constructive Daydreaming," December 22, 2011, accessed December 19, 2014, http://blogs.scientificamerican.com/guest-blog/2011/12/22/the-origins-of-positive-constructive-daydreaming/.

12 Ibid.

13 Kaufman, *Ungifted*, 3-6.

14 Ibid., 254.

15 Ibid.

16 Ibid.

17 Ibid.

18 Ibid.

19 Ibid.

20 Joshua Rothman, "Creativity Creep," *The New Yorker*, September 2, 2014, 34.

21 Ibid.

22 Kaufman, "The Origins of Positive-Constructive Daydreaming."

Chapter 9

1 Willingham, *Why Don't Students Like School?* Kindle edition, 1167.

2 Ibid., 1173.

3 Ibid.

4   Ibid.

5   Jonathan Gottschall, *The Storytelling Animal: How Stories Make Us Human* (Boston: Houghton Mifflin Harcourt, 2012), Kindle edition, 60.

6   Ibid., 61.

7   Ibid., 115.

8   Ibid.

9   Eric Klinger, *Daydreaming: Using Waking Fantasy and Imagery for Self-knowledge and Creativity* (Los Angeles: Jeremy P. Tarcher, 1990), 27.

10 Gottschall, *The Storytelling Animal,* Kindle edition, 327.

11 Schank, *Teaching Minds,* 106.

12 Ibid., 107.

13 Dan Meyer, "The Three Acts of a Mathematical Story," *The Three Acts Of A Mathematical Story,* May 12, 2011, accessed December 20, 2014, http://blog .mrmeyer.com/2011/the-three-acts-of-a-mathematical-story/.

14 Dan Meyer, "Math Curriculum Makeover," *YouTube,* March 6, 2010, accessed December 30, 2014, http://www.youtube.com/watch?v=BlvKWEvKSi8.

15 Sam Dillion, "In Test, Few Students Are Proficient Writers," *New York Times,* April 3, 2008. E1.

16 Michael S. Gazzaniga, *Who's in Charge?: Free Will and the Science of the Brain* (New York, NY: HarperCollins, 2011), 90.

17 Drew Westen, *The Political Brain: The Role of Emotion in Deciding the Fate of the Nation* (New York: PublicAffairs, 2007) 147.

Chapter 10

1   Lise Eliot, *What's Going on in There?: How the Brain and Mind Develop in the First Five Years of Life* (New York, N.Y.: Bantam Books, 1999), 242.

2   Ibid.

3   Ibid., 253.

4   Burley-Allen, *Listening: The Forgotten Skill,* Kindle edition, 141.

5   Ibid.

6   Ibid.

7   Ibid.

8   Swanson, Charles H. "Their success is your success: teach them to listen." Paper presented at the Annual Conference of the West Virginia Community College Association, 1984. 2, 3.

9   Ibid.

10 A. M. Galaburda, M. T. Menard & G. D. Rosen, "Evidence for aberrant auditory anatomy in developmental dyslexia." *Proceedings of the National Academy of Sciences,* (1994). 91, 8010–8013. J. Paulesu and U. Firth, "Dyslexia: Cultural Diversity and Biological Unity." *Science,* (2001) 291: 2165-2167.

11 Burley-Allen, *Listening: The Forgotten Skill,* 211.

12 Sam Duker, "Basics in Critical Listening," *The English Journal.* 51 (1962), 565-567.

13 Ibid., 565-566.

14 Burley-Allen, *Listening: The Forgotten Skill.*

15 John Jensen, *Teaching Students to Work Harder and Enjoy It: Practice Makes Permanent* (Lanham, Md.: Rowman & Littlefield Education, 2012), 33-42.
16 Ibid.

Chapter 11

1 W. Huitt and J. Hummel, "Piaget's theory of cognitive development," *Educational Psychology Interactive* (2003), accessed July 24, 2014, http://www.edpsycinteractive.org/topics/cognition/piaget.html
2 Eagleman, *Incognito*, 56-59.
3 Willingham, *Why Don't Students Like School?* Kindle edition, 155.
4 Kate Douglas, "The Subconscious Mind: Your Unsung Hero," *New Scientist- Life*, December 1, 2007, accessed December 20, 2014, http://www.newscientist.com/article/mg19626321.400-the-subconscious-mind-your-unsung-hero.html.
5 Dewey, *Experience and Education*, Kindle edition, 460.
6 Willingham, *Why Don't Students Like School?* Kindle edition, 139.
7 MH Immordino-Yang, JA Christodoulou and V Singh, "Rest is not idleness: implications of the brain's default mode for human development and education," *Perspectives on Psychological Science* 7 (4), (2012) 352-364.
8 John A. Bargh and Ezequiel Morsella, "The Unconscious Mind," *Perspectives on Psychological Science* 3.1 (2008): 73–79.
9 Ibid.
10 Jonah Lehrer, "The Self Illusion: An Interview With Bruce Hood." *Wired.com*, May 25, 2012, accessed July 29, 2014, http://www.wired.com/2012/05/the-self-illusion-an-interview-with-bruce-hood/.
11 Hood, *The Self Illusion*, 76.
12 Ibid., 79.
13 Robin Fivush, Marshall Duke, Jennifer Bohanek and Kelly Marin, "Family Narrative Interaction and Children's Sense of Self," *Family Narrative Project*. January 1, 2006, accessed December 20, 2014, http://www.psychology.emory.edu/cognition/fivush/lab/FivushLabWebsite/papers/FamilyNarrativeandInteraction.pdf.
14 Ibid.

Chapter 12

1 Edward O. Wilson, *Sociobiology*, abridged ed. (Cambridge, Mass.: Belknap Press of Harvard University Press, 1980), 79.
2 Viacom Media Networks, "'Story Of Me' Research Study," Viacom Press Release, November 1, 2013, accessed December 30, 2014, http://biz.viacom.com/sites/nickelodeonpress/.
3 Schank, *Teaching Minds*, 96.
4 Ibid.
5 Dewey, *Experience and Education*, Kindle edition, 439.
6 Donella H. Meadows and Diana Wright, *Thinking in Systems: A Primer* (White River Junction, Vt.: Chelsea Green Pub., 2008), Kindle edition, 211.

7 Derek Cabrera and Laura Colosi, *Thinking at Every Desk: How Four Simple Thinking Skills Will Transform Your Teaching, Classroom, School, and District* (New York, N.Y.: W. W. Norton, 2010), 1-3.

8 Richard Arum and Josipa Roksa, *Academically Adrift: Limited Learning on College Campuses*, (Chicago: University of Chicago Press, 2011), 36.

9 Ibid.

10 Cabrera and Colosi, *Thinking at Every Desk*, 9.

11 Ibid.

12 Ibid.

13 Ibid.

14 Ibid.

15 Ibid.

16 Ibid.

17 Steven Fleming, "Metacognition in Mammals—and Machines," *Scientific American Mind*, September 1, 2014, 32-36.

18 Ibid., 36-37.

19 Dewey, *Experience and Education*, Kindle edition, 438.

20 Lea Winerman, "The Culture-cognition Connection," APA.org, February 1, 2006, accessed December 26, 2014, http://www.apa.org/monitor/feb06/connection.aspx.

21 Ibid.

Chapter 13

1 Paul Bloom, "The Moral Life of Babies," *New York Times*, May 5, 2010, sec. 44.

2 Dewey, *Experience and Education*, Kindle edition, 536.

3 Adam Grant, "Raising a Moral Child," *New York Times*, April 11, 2014, SR1.

4 Ibid.

5 Ibid.

6 Ibid.

7 Ibid.

8 Ibid.

9 John Grohol, "15 Common Cognitive Distortions," *Psych Central.com*, January 1, 2009, http://psychcentral.com/lib/15-common-cognitive-distortions/0002153.

10 David McRaney, *You Are Not So Smart: Why You Have Too Many Friends on Facebook, Why Your Memory Is Mostly Fiction, and 46 Other Ways You're Deluding Yourself* (New York: Gotham Books/Penguin Group, 2011), 1-6.

11 Ibid.

12 Ibid.

13 Ibid.

14 Ibid.

Chapter 14

1 Lea Winerman, "'Thin Slices' of Life," *American Psychological Association*, March 1, 2006, accessed December 20, 2014, http://www.apa.org/monitor/mar05/slices.aspx.

2 Scott Barry Kaufman, "The Dark Triad and Impulsivity," *Psychology Today — Beautiful Minds*, July 1, 2011, accessed December 20, 2014, http://www.psychologytoday.com/blog/beautiful-minds/201107/the-dark-triad-and-impulsivity.

3 Rowan Hooper, "Bonobos and Chimps 'speak' with Gestures," *New Scientist- Life*, April 30, 2007, accessed April 30, 2007, http://www.newscientist.com/article/dn11756-bonobos-and-chimps-speak-with-gestures.html#.VJ7QrV4Bds.

4 Martin Doherty, *Theory of Mind: How Children Understand Others' Thoughts and Feelings* (East Sussex: Psychology Press, 2008), 1-23.

5 Paul Bloom, "Against Empathy," *Boston Review*, September 1, 2014, accessed December 20, 2014, http://www.bostonreview.net/forum/paul-bloom-against-empathy.

6 Emma Seppala, "The Compassionate Mind," Association for Psychological Science, May 1, 2013, accessed December 20, 2014, http://www.psychologicalscience.org/index.php/publications/observer/2013/may-june-13/the-compassionate-mind.html.

7 Ibid.

8 L. B. Aknin, M. I. Norton, E. W. Dunn, and J. Quoidbach (2013). "Prosocial bonuses increase employee satisfaction and team performance," *PLoS ONE*, 8(9), e75509.

9 E. W. Dunn, L. B. Aknin and M. I. Norton, "Prosocial spending and happiness: Using money to benefit others pays off," *Current Directions In Psychological Science* (23, 2014), 41-43.

10 Richard Weissbourd and Stephanie Jones, "The Children We Mean To Raise: The Real Messages Adults Are Sending About Values," Making Caring Common Project, January 1, 2014, accessed December 20, 2014, makingcaringcommon.org.; Richard Weissbourd, *The Parents We Mean to Be* (Boston: Houghton Mifflin, 2009), 165.

11 Ibid.

12 Ibid.

13 Ibid.

14 Ibid.

15 Ibid.

16 Ibid.

17 Ibid.

18 Ibid.

Chapter 15

1 Erin Wayman, "Humans Evolved Big Brains to Be Social?," *Smithsonian*, October 31, 2011. 37.

2 Ibid., 39.

3   R.I.M. Dunbar, "Neocortex size as a constraint on group size in primates," *Journal of Human Evolution*, 22 (1992): 469–493.

4   Edward O. Wilson, *Sociobiology*, 79.

5   Eric Johnson, "Groups and Gossip Drove the Evolution of Human Nature," *Slate.com*, October 3, 2012, accessed December 20, 2014, http://www.slate.com/articles/health_and_science/human_evolution/2012/10/groups_and_gossip_drove_the_evolution_of_human_nature.html.

6   Ibid.

7   Saul McLeod, "Lev Vygotsky," *Simply Psychology*, January 1, 2007, accessed December 27, 2014. http://www.simplypsychology.org/vygotsky.html.

8   A. W. Woolley, C. F. Chabris, A. Pentland, N. Hashmi and T. W. Malone, "Evidence For A Collective Intelligence Factor In The Performance Of Human Groups," *Science* 330 (2010): 686-88.

9   Ibid.

10 Al Siebert, *The Resiliency Advantage: Master Change, Thrive under Pressure, and Bounce Back from Setbacks* (San Francisco: Berrett-Koehler Publishers, 2005), 4-7.

11 Ibid.

12 Michelle Garcia Winner, "Social Thinking-Social Learning Tree," *Social Thinking*, January 1, 2012, accessed October 27, 2014, http://www.socialthinking.com/what-is-social-thinking/social-thinking-social-learning-tree.

13 Ibid.

14 Ibid.

15 Ibid.

16 Ibid.

17 Schank, *Teaching Minds*, 150.

Conclusion

1   James, *The Principles of Psychology*, 304.

2   Jason Marsh, "Why Mindfulness Matters," *The Greater Good*, May 17, 2010, accessed December 20, 2014, http://greatergood.berkeley.edu/article/item/why_mindfulness_matters.